Miriam Ali was born in Birmingham, where she still lives with her husband and her youngest son, Mo. She divides her time between her grown-up children, her grand-children, and the many people she comes into contact with through the tragedy of abducted children. She is co-founder and advising counsellor for Lost Children International.

Jana Wain was born in Kent and now lives in Birmingham. She is also a co-founder of LCI, and works there as secretary and counsellor.

Lost Children International is an organisation set up to support those parents left behind when their children are spirited away to foreign countries and cultures.

Without Mercy

A Mother's Struggle Against Modern Slavery

Miriam Ali

with

Jana Wain

WARNER BOOKS

A *Warner* Book

First published in Great Britain by
Little, Brown and Company in 1995

This edition published by Warner Books in 1996
Reprinted 1996 (three times), 1997, 1999

A CIP catalogue record for this book
is available from the British Library.

ISBN 0 7515 1635 X

Typeset by Hewer Text Composition Services, Edinburgh
Printed in England by Clays Ltd, St Ives plc

Warner Books
A Division of
Little, Brown and Company (UK)
Brettenham House
Lancaster Place
London WC2E 7EN

This book is dedicated to all the little children in
'Little Birmingham'. . . and to Nadia.

God keep you safe and speed your return home.

Justice can never be done, but right must be done.

Prologue

In 1965, Miriam Ali, a pregnant Birmingham housewife with a hectic, happy young family of four, experienced a trauma beyond the tolerance of normal people. Her two eldest children were taken to Yemen by their father – and he returned alone.

In 1980, that same housewife, now a mother of seven, experienced further pain which knocked her world right off its axis when the same man, Muthana Muhsen, sold his two under-age British daughters, Zana and Nadia, into illegal marriages in the same desolate and bankrupt Middle Eastern country, forcing them into a life far removed from that of their native England.

Her family shattered and bruised, Miriam Ali embarked on a long trial of endurance that was to embarrass governments and hit the headlines worldwide. Desperately trying to keep her remaining family together, she had to change everything about herself in her long fight for freedom for her children.

Fourteen years after she was sold, Nadia's health deteriorates as she remains imprisoned in Yemen while her captors, still unpunished, are free. Miriam needs to tell her story – a mother's struggle against modern slavery

– for Nadia and the children she has been forced to bear for her owners.

Yet Nadia is not the only British child bride in Mokbana, Yemen, known as 'Little Birmingham'. This true story is being told to bring attention to Nadia's plight, and that of others also held in Yemen, and to caution others at risk.

In 1992, the British government issued a statement from the Foreign Office in London. The figures it contains, calculated on the basis of those whose abductions were *reported* over the *previous year*, show that the number of parentally abducted children taken away from the United Kingdom in 1991 was a staggering 1,100.

Three children a day.

Most are holders of 'dual nationality', enabling them to be taken to Middle Eastern countries. It is a situation that must be exposed, and one that Miriam Ali is determined to see changed. For the sake of all the children.

Chapter One

I had had yet another huge row with my stepfather. He was of the opinion that I should be outcast from the family home.

My mother, a small quiet woman, had previously been married to a Pakistani man and bore him two children of mixed blessings, myself and my brother Henry. After our father's death she had taken up with this white Englishman who had very Victorian values and strict standards of code of conduct. He completely disregarded her previous marriage and us, as young children. I loved my mother passionately and over the years, chose to keep the peace as often as possible. This time, however, I could only do that by moving out. I was now working full-time and felt that I could look after myself.

I found a room in a huge lodging house in Anderton Road in Sparkbrook, in my home town of Birmingham. It was at the very top of the house, in the attic. The wages I earned as a seventeen-year-old were not excessive, but the room was cheap and cheerful and I did not need heating as I moved in the flaming month of June. I busied myself trying to adapt to being young, free and single in the new

3

'swinging sixties', a dramatic change from my way of life with my mother and stepfather.

One day, going into the lodging house and beginning the long ascent to my room, I passed a young man on the stairs. We exchanged greetings. Nothing more than that, really. I wondered why he had taken the time to speak to me. I was very shy and more or less ran up the rest of the stairs to the sanctuary of my room.

A couple of days later we bumped into each other again. We talked for some time and eventually I agreed to go out on a date with him. To my eyes he was very handsome. It was the first time that I had ever gone out with anyone, let alone someone from his kind of background – Muthana Muhsen was an Arab. There were several more dates and I fell more and more deeply in love with him. I was young and impressionable and I was enchanted with his aura and personality. My Arabian knight.

We got along brilliantly, spending all our time together. He had come to England in 1956, when many Arabs had arrived, and had learned English at school here. He spoke it very well, with a soft accent. I was besotted with him and he guarded me possessively and passionately. We spent so much time together, every given moment, that I soon lost my job. Muthana, or Fred, as I affectionately called him, had many friends and I enjoyed going out with someone so popular. It never bothered me when he and his friends spoke in Arabic, knowing that I could not participate in the conversation. I found it all so exciting and watched Fred proudly as he spoke in a seemingly complicated language with confident ease.

We had already decided to make a go of life together. My stepfather, predictably, was furious, and told me the family would have nothing to do with me if I took up with

Fred. My mom, bless her, tried to smooth things over by explaining that my stepfather's hatred of Arabs was due to a bad experience in Egypt in the Second World War.

I could not imagine any man in my life other than Fred; I had no interest in anyone else and he assured me that I was the girl for him. Fred was Maraise, from a farming tribe in the south of Yemen. He told me briefly that he had been married; an arranged marriage which had taken place in Aden. He had been only fifteen years old and his wife was a little younger. The marriage had not been consummated. He could not afford to keep himself and a wife in Yemen so he had come to England to find a niche for himself and earn some money to send back home. He did not love his wife – that kind of emotion is an unknown to the male – and, after he met me and told me that he had fallen in love with me, he sent her a *nakhar*, a complete Islamic divorce. We did not know how long this would take to go through so the question of marriage was swept under the carpet and somehow it was never mentioned again. Some while later a letter from his father in the Yemen arrived with news that Fred's ex-wife had married again and had died in childbirth, along with the child.

Chapter Two

Within a few months Fred announced that he had managed to buy a house not far from our lodgings. It was a nice house but completely empty. We had nothing at all when we moved in, not even a bed. We slept on the bare floorboards. Thankfully he was working very hard and gradually we got things together and made a home for ourselves. He decorated the house and made it cosy. It was hard work, and took a long time, but I was used to far less. I hadn't had a nice home before and not much of a home life, either, so it didn't bother me at all to go without for a while. We let rooms in our house to a family with two children to help make ends meet.

I had implicit faith in Fred. He was proving to be a hard-working partner and good provider, which was important because, the following April, in 1962, I gave birth to Laila in hospital. Fred doted on her. He could not do enough for her and spoiled her rotten. I was happy and content, and I had Sheila, our lodger, for company.

In May the following year I gave Fred his first son, Ahmed, who was to become the apple of my eye, and then Zana was born, at home in the July of 1964. Within fourteen months of her birth I was expecting my fourth child, this time carrying with difficulty.

The house was becoming overcrowded and money was getting even tighter. We had to ask our lodgers to move out to make room for our new baby, and the increasing number of nappies. I was to have their old room. Fred was working hard trying to cope with one baby after another and I was working full-out chasing around after my group of little toddlers as well as carrying another baby.

In October Fred had to rush home after a long day at work and look after the three toddlers while I strained and worked hard to give birth prematurely to Nadia. The labour was hard and long but eventually she arrived and I was left to rest. But not for long – by the next morning I was up and hanging over the edge of the bathtub, washing clothes.

That was so difficult. I crawled on all fours back into bed, the sweat pouring off me. Both Fred and I found this a very trying time. He was still working all hours and I was now ill after Nadia's premature birth. He looked as haggard and ill as I was myself, and Nadia was so tiny, weighing just five pounds at birth and narrowly escaping the need for an incubator. The midwife voiced her concern for me to Fred: it was too much to expect that I should have baby after baby. But he dismissed this as the way of life in his homeland, expressing the view that a man had to sow his seed. And here, in England, things should be far easier with our superior technology.

Fred was angry – not with us having four small children, because he wanted it this way, but because, now that we had lost the income from letting our spare room, our finances were strained to the limit. He became silent and broody, and worked even longer hours. He snapped a lot, and the tension built daily. Suddenly he announced that he was going to sell the house and go back to the Yemen for a holiday to see his dad and stepmother and attend to his interests there.

Fred broached the subject of going to the Yemen very carefully. He said that he would take Laila and Ahmed on this holiday, for a month or two, reasoning that I needed a break, too, from the constant demand on my attention of four small children so soon after such a bad birth with Nadia. Of course, I didn't quite see it this way. I always had time for my kids, even if I felt at death's door. I knew that I wasn't so worn out that I couldn't cope with them. However, I had to admit that since the birth I was very tired. I hadn't had much energy to take the kids to the park, or to go out for walks.

My social life was Fred and the kids. As Laila was only four and Ahmed three, I didn't really feel that they would benefit from such an exotic holiday. I could imagine the journey being awful. But Fred told me about his family there who were all impatient to see the kids. He described in detail the rolling hills his father owned, the green pastures, the animals, the fields of corn, the fruit trees. And Fred would inherit it all one day. It was all too much for someone like me, who had never even seen the sea in my native England, to imagine.

Here we were, living in the heart of England, and my kids were lucky if I had the time to take them to the park. So it was decided. Fred and the two older kids would go to Yemen within the next few months. The plan was sealed when I became pregnant with our fifth child.

Fred managed to sell the house we had lived in for the past five years, and used the money to finance the trip to Yemen, leaving a little for me to get by on. Zana, Nadia and I moved into rented rooms again and Fred, Laila and Ahmed left for the Yemen.

Christmas 1966 was awful. We had no tree, no cards, no decorations, no gifts, but worst of all no money. We had jam sandwiches on Christmas Day, and although the kids were good, I felt terrible. Other people would be tucking into turkey and stuffing and Christmas pudding . . . I wondered if there was anyone else in the world who was as broke and despondent as me right then. Fred was a modern-day Ebenezer Scrooge, thinking more of his bloody property than of his poor kids. I felt a little sorry for myself, too.

My stepfather's words scorched my heart. 'You go with a no-good bloody Arab and you will only ever know grief. And you will be alone, because your family will have nothing to do with the likes of him and nothing to do with you!'

My heart felt heavy as his words echoed in my ears. I could still clearly see the face of my stepfather as he banged the table in my mom's kitchen, spitting out his hate and contempt. My mom's attempts to explain his attitude were no excuse to me, but that was in the days when Fred could do no wrong. When I loved him heart and soul. When he had not taken two of our children thousands of miles away, leaving me broke, pregnant, alone and totally responsible for two more, disregarding my feelings or opinion. Not that I was ever given a real chance to express either. A thousand thoughts invaded my mind. I wondered about the wisdom of letting Fred and the kids go away. I wondered if I would ever see them again. Doubt battled with desire. Of course they would come back. Why wouldn't they?

Chapter Three

I was in the lodging house with the kids, in the late stages of pregnancy, my belly heavy. By now the money had long since run out and I was on Social Security. It had been eight months since Fred left for Yemen. In all that time I had had only one letter from him, and that had been over a month ago, saying that he would be home in the next few weeks with Laila and Ahmed. Every day I waited for the knock on my door, and every night I eventually gave up hope and retired to bed with the kids.

Finally it happened. The knock came.

Fred stood in the doorway looking down at me. He didn't smile, didn't rush to greet me, didn't embrace me. I thought that the sight of my advanced condition had caused his cold reaction. I was very tired and very pregnant. If I had known he was coming I could have made a little effort to make myself a touch more presentable, however difficult and impractical this would have been, what with the kids and everything.

I tried to look past him, peering into the darkness of the night, to see the children behind him. He didn't budge.

'Where are the kids?' I asked, thinking that perhaps he had let them play around in the yard.

'I've left them in Yemen.' Cool as anything.

I laughed. Obviously I didn't believe him. 'Don't, Fred, you're joking! Where are they?' I scanned the area that I could see behind Fred.

'I said, I've left them. In Yemen.'

My heart started to thud in my chest. I looked up into his face. His voice was so cold it turned my spine to ice and he had an awful look on his face. I knew then that he meant it. I was stunned. I froze, clamping up immediately. I could not take it in. He was so cold and hard.

He pushed past me and went into our one rented room to where Zana and Nadia were sleeping in the only bed, huddled together. I turned and reluctantly closed the door, realising that doing so would indicate acceptance of the fact. I could not move from the door. My feet were weighed down as if with lead. It was as if I was watching a film. The distance from the door to the centre of the room seemed like three miles. I watched Fred lightly kiss the sleeping bundles and thought what a hypocrite he was. If he had felt any love for me or the kids, he would have brought Laila and Ahmed back here to me and their sisters. He didn't look at me as he moved to the fireside chair. He sat down heavily, huffing as he did so, sniffed and settled back into the depths of the chair.

Within minutes he was asleep. I might have stood there all night if it had not been for the baby moving inside me. I felt my unborn child kicking, and my stomach tightened as it shifted. I rubbed my swollen flesh, wondering what sort of life this child would have, and the tears began to course down my face. Everything became a blur. Somehow I managed to get into the bed close to the girls and cuddled up to them, trying not to cry out loud, trying not to wake them. I

11

cried all night. Sleep just would not come to relieve the turmoil.

Fred didn't come to me, not that I would have wanted him to just then. I was totally confused and it hurt so much. I waited until he woke the next day, then I badgered him constantly. 'Why did you leave them, Fred? Please, get them back!'

He coolly looked me up and down and sighed. 'Look, they wanted to stop with my parents, just for a short while. Look at us, Miriam. We live in one room, we have four children and another on the way. I have made sure our interests in the Yemen are safe. While I was there, I helped my father with his house. We built an extension. He is doing very well with his land and business investments and it will all be ours one day. I will inherit it all and we can either sell it or live there. That is a long way off yet. The kids are very happy there and get on very well with my family. It will give us a little more scope and they will be having a great time.'

Fred went to his case and opened it. I was curious, thinking that maybe he had brought gifts from the Yemen for Zana and Nadia. Instead, he produced a large buff envelope and took out its contents. He handed me half a dozen photographs and he started to speak again, but I had lost interest in his excuses. I was engrossed in the colour prints before me.

Captured in full Kodak colour were glossy images of Ahmed and Laila, seemingly running in a field of corn. Then up on the stone steps of a large white building, sitting close together, eating some kind of fruit, grinning and filthy. Another showed women carrying water in jugs on their heads and Laila copying them with an empty basket.

It all looked very entertaining for the children. I felt guilty for wanting them with me, depriving them of the adventure, but I missed them so much! As I flicked through the photographs yet again, Fred's voice filtered through to my brain. 'I want to get a job as soon as possible and build our lives again, Miriam. Bigger and better this time!'

'But what about the kids, Fred? I can't just forget them!'

'They are OK. Don't worry about them, Miriam. Look, you can see the photographs, they are happy and well. My parents love them and the rest of the family just dote on them.'

'But I want them back!' I was becoming distraught and I felt that Fred wasn't really listening.

'You will have them back, soon! Now they are fine. Let's just get ourselves settled. I want to get a job and find us another house. Then we can have them back. Maybe if I work hard enough and make enough money we can all go out there and bring them back with us. Let them have fun while they can.' He turned his back and went out, grabbing my cigarettes on the way.

In a daze, I got the girls dressed and tidied myself up. I took my purse from the drawer to go to the corner shop for bread, milk – and cigarettes.

It was cold for early April in 1967. I held the two girls firmly by the hand as we hurried to the corner shop. The bell on the door clanged as we went inside. I turned to pick up the milk in the crate on the left, cradling a loaf of bread in the crook of my arm.

'Miriam?' A deep voice called my name. I turned to face a woman. After a few seconds I recognised the face.

13

'Ann! Hello!' It was Ann Sufi. We had gone to school together and had been good friends once.

'These yours?' She smiled and ruffled Nadia's hair.

'Yeah!' I thought of Laila and Ahmed and swallowed at the lump in my throat.

'Are you OK, Miriam?' Ann touched my arm, concern in her voice.

All I could do was nod, but already the tears were fighting to escape.

'Why don't you come with me to my house? I can make you some tea and we can have a chat – that's if you want to.'

I stared at the floor of the shop and felt hot tears scalding my cheeks. I sniffed them back and coughed. I dug the money out of my purse for my shopping and handed it to the man behind the counter.

'Thanks, love. Where are your other two kiddies? I haven't seen them for ages.'

My breath came in ragged gasps as I closed my eyes and fought a losing battle with my emotions. I dropped the few coppers of change and spun on my heel to get out of the shop as quickly as I could. I barked an order to the kids and flew out of the door.

'*Miriam!* Wait!'

Ann chased after me, catching me easily as I lumbered along. I stopped in the street, feeling totally defeated. Ann prised the bread out of my arm. It was squashed into an hourglass shape.

'Never mind, it will still taste the same. Come on, Miriam. I'll make you that cup of tea.'

She took me by the arm and led me to her house, which was not that far from mine. Looking back, it is amazing that we had not bumped into each other long before.

Now, as I sat in her house, my hands cupped around a steaming mug of tea, I poured out my woes. It felt so strange telling someone how I felt and what had happened. I had been so very alone.

Ann listened and comforted me. Zana and Nadia were playing round the apple tree in her garden, and I could hear their giggles from the back garden as I sat in Ann's kitchen. It made me think of the photograph of Ahmed and Laila in the cornfield.

Ann's husband came home from work and was introduced to me. He was a very tall man, softly spoken and gentle. Ann told him what had happened and he promised to help.

'But what can you do?' I asked.

'Maybe it would be productive to write to the Foreign Office and ask them for their advice and assistance.'

He smiled and I was in awe of his intelligence and manner. I would never have thought of that.

He left the room and Ann smiled proudly.

'I wish Fred was like that,' I said. 'You are very lucky Ann. He is a very nice man.'

Chapter Four

On 21 April 1967, a few weeks after Fred's return from Yemen, I gave birth to Ashia. It was a comparatively easy birth and both Ashia and I were healthy. Fred had managed to find a job quickly and we had just moved into a new house in Small Heath.

A letter had come from the Foreign Office, to Ann Sufi's house, to express their regret that as the two children were 'dual nationals' there was little or nothing that could be done. I saw that my only hope was badgering Fred and keeping up the letters to his father in Yemen. He was writing about once a month, telling me how happy the two kids were, how well they were doing. Occasionally, I would get a photograph and I would cherish the images of my children, still laughing, happy and contented. I would persistently ask Fred when they would be home, and he would always answer, 'Soon. They will be home soon.'

The house in Golden Hillock Road was beautiful. It was large and the garden went down well with the girls after the confines of the single room in the lodging house. I was so happy that we had a bathroom and toilet to ourselves. Now that we had a comfortable home, surely it was the right time for the children to come home.

The relationship between Fred and me had suffered since he had taken Laila and Ahmed. I had tried to console myself that they were better off in green, rolling hills than they were with me and three other kids in a single room and on Social Security.

Around June I asked Fred again if the children could come home now, but Fred was more interested in the Six-Day War between the Arabs and the Jews. He said that the Jews were gaining territory in the Sinai, had taken the Gaza Strip and the Egyptian fortress of Sharm el Sheik. When Egypt admitted defeat, he went crazy.

Aden had seen fighting, too, and a British woman had recently been killed at an official dinner party. I became worried for the kids, but Fred said that they were safe in the countryside, out of the main city, and could not be moved for their own safety. So once again it was all put on hold.

At the end of November 1967, 128 years of colonial rule in Aden came to an end and the Arabs were celebrating the formation of the new People's Republic of South Yemen. Fred was fairly jubilant about all this until I asked him if this would be a good time for the children to come home.

'Don't you know that the pound has fallen again? Have you not heard of the credit squeeze? Times are bad now, Miriam. There are good times to come in Aden now that the British have been ousted. The south has always been better than the north. In the north they are pigs, stupid pigs. You watch, now. All the work that the British have done will benefit us in the south and again we will be even stronger than the stupid religious idiots in the north. They can keep their Islam, we will take the money!'

He turned from me and stuck his nose in the newspaper

17

again, audibly sucking air through his teeth. There was a knock at the door and he crumpled the paper into a heap on the table and rushed off to answer it. A group of Arab men came into the house. I watched them walk upstairs with Fred, chatting in Arabic all the while.

An hour or so later, after they had gone, Fred announced that he was renting out the whole of the upper house to these Arab friends of his. We, that is, Fred, myself and the three girls, were to live in two rooms on the lower floor and share the kitchen, bathroom and breakfast room. I turned and went into the front room. I sat in the hard chair by the fire and lit a cigarette. Will it ever end? I asked myself. I felt totally fed up and my world was getting smaller all the time. I was far more protective now. I was engrossed in my children – they were the essence of my life and I guarded them with all my might.

Later that night, Fred came home after being out with friends. I could hear him breathing as he came closer to me in the darkness of the bedroom. I jumped up and clicked on the light, shielding my eyes from the stark glare of the bulb dangling from the ceiling. I squinted around the room and grabbed a dressing-gown from the back of a chair. Pulling it around me, I opened the door and shot down into the kitchen to make myself some tea.

Fred sauntered in after me. 'What are you doing?'

I tutted and turned to face him. He stood before me, leaning against the kitchen wall, his hands inside his pockets and one leg crossed over the other.

'Tea. I want tea.' I turned back to the cup and heaped sugar into it.

'Why now? You were sleeping.'

I heard him shift his weight slightly and the hairs on the back of my neck prickled.

'When are they moving in?'

I tried to control my emotions, but the strain showed. I hated the idea of losing my home to a bunch of Fred's friends but I knew I hadn't much choice. Fred had made it abundantly clear that he ruled the roost, and that all the major decisions were to be made by him, but after he had been away for so long and I had rekindled my friendship with Ann Sufi, I felt slightly independent for the first time in my life. I was beginning to grow away from him. I had had eight months to realise that I could indeed make my own decisions and I had managed to support us after the money that Fred had left had run out. There had been no Fred to scold me for smoking more than my daily ration of five cigarettes; I could sleep at night without thinking that at any time now Fred would want his desires satisfied. But the most important wedge between us was the fact that he was still reluctant to return Laila and Ahmed to my care, continually telling me that they were happy and having a better life than I could offer them with his support.

As far as I was concerned, I wanted to live my own life with the kids. I could feel this decision forming in the well of my soul. If only I had the courage, the confidence . . .

As I stirred my tea, Fred continued to watch me. I knew what he wanted. I knew what he was waiting for. I shuddered within. Now I knew what I wanted, too. I wanted to leave. I wanted to live my own life, with my children. But could I actually do it? I had always been fiercely dependent on Fred, ever since I had known him and, although I felt brave now, the thought of putting my independence into action was still frightening.

I sipped at my tea, burning my tongue, but rather that than let Fred think that I was willing to go into the bedroom. Fred must have known that I was stalling so he went alone to the bedroom to wait for me, knowing that sooner or later I would have to go in too. He grinned smugly as he turned and sauntered out of the kitchen. The least I could do was make him wait a while knowing that the longer he waited the quicker it would all be over and done with.

Chapter Five

Within a matter of weeks they had moved into my house. There were three of them, single young Arab men making a mess all over the house. When Fred had first managed to get this house, the previous owners had left a virtually brand-new electric cooker. Our lodgers managed to destroy it within their first fortnight. I could do nothing about it. Any complaints fell on deaf ears because, in addition to being lodgers, they were Fred's friends too, and I knew who took first priority in his esteem. I kept to my two rooms and only ventured to the shared breakfast room and kitchen when necessary. Even this luxury was taken from me when Fred suddenly started to build an 'extension' to the kitchen.

It was, I remember, the spring of 1968. Fred was being industrious in the garden, banging and sawing. By the time I gave in to my curiosity and peered out of the kitchen window to see what was going on, he had already constructed what looked like a timber frame, which he attached to the exterior wall of the kitchen. It only took a weekend. By the following Tuesday afternoon, Fred announced that he had rented out the front room too, and the girls and I were to evacuate to this new 'room' of his.

The ceiling was very low – not that this would affect the girls, who were small, or me, for that matter, being all of five foot one tall – but it made the 'room' claustrophobic. There was just one tiny window for ventilation. This was to be our new living quarters, with the only remaining room we had inside the house acting as a bedroom for me, Fred and the three kids.

I was so angry at being shoved out into the garden while the prime areas of the interior of the house were being let to a bunch of lazy and messy men. To add further insult to injury, just a couple of weeks later, Fred came home with an Arabic couple who had just come over from the States. It was the first time he had met them.

He had been out for most of the day, and just arrived with this 'American' couple and then went out again without a word to me, leaving them in the house. He returned a couple of hours later with the carcass of a recently slaughtered sheep and fifty friends or so, to cook a meal in honour of their visit.

We had no money. Fred had been shouting at me, just hours before, because I had spent money on a quick visit to Ann Sufi the previous day. Lo and behold, here he was lugging this smelly dead sheep, with a gaping hole in its neck, all over the house. The acrid stench was filling the lungs of all the people inside as he mistakenly cooked the animal complete, with the intestines intact, without cleaning it first.

I could not bring myself to eat something that smelled so bad. Everyone else tucked in to this gastronomical delight, gorging themselves until there was nothing left but bone and fat. They stayed for hours and hours, ending the evening with a major card-playing session. Two of them went to sleep in our bed, and I had to try to settle the kids down on the floor of the extension, now steeped in the lingering stench of the sheep.

I asked Fred what the hell was going on. He said it was his duty to honour his guests, 'out of great respect'.

I tried to work out how you could bestow such great respect on a total stranger in front of your family, who had gone without even the most basic of necessities for as long as they could remember.

I think I felt most resentful because he had invited all these 'friends' of his, whereas I, it seemed, was not allowed friends. I had had to lie and tell him that Ann was my cousin just so that I could keep up my friendship with her, otherwise Fred would not have permitted the association at all. He had said as much. It was another factor in the idea that I should leave Fred. But how could I do this, when I knew I was pregnant yet again?

Fred's extension was condemned by the Environmental Health people after complaints by neighbours and he was ordered to pull it down immediately. This meant that the lodgers had to move out and we could have the lounge back. I was fairly pleased until I realised that the money that we had coming in would be affected and we would be struggling even more. I was about four or five months pregnant and very depressed.

Most of my time was spent looking after my brood, which I enjoyed. I was even more possessive and protective with them, refusing to leave them with anyone else, especially Fred. I spent hours playing with them in the one small room, hardly ever going out of the house, apart from the very occasional visit to Ann Sufi. The sad thing was that, although I needed her company and support, I felt incredibly jealous of her happy marriage and family life and the safe environment she enjoyed.

Then my attention was diverted by another problem, one which led to my own situation changing more quickly than I had imagined.

Late one night, my brother David called for me to go to Mom's house. All was not well. Perhaps she had had enough of trying to cope with the old man and all their other children, my brother Henry and half siblings Harry, Billy, Ellen, Derek (David), Marian, Carol and Neil. Nine of them but this did not include my stepfather's two children from his previous marriage who were also living with them. My stepfather had recently had a stroke which had left him paralysed down one side of his body and unable to speak. Mom needed a hand with the kids.

I tore into the house and found Mom sitting in the lounge, surrounded by eight of her twelve children, all of whom were fairly young and jumping all over her. She sat there in the fireside chair like a zombie. I had never, ever seen her look like that in all my life and it frightened me.

We discovered that Mom had cancer, which had advanced to its final stages without any previous detection.

Because of her illness, I made a decision to move out of my home and into my mother's house. The power I felt at having taken this step was overshadowed by Mom's condition, but I still cherished it as the first firm decision that I had ever made. It was a shame that it took something so desperate to urge me into action.

Henry and I seemed to be on a never-ending treadmill of work and multiple calls on our attention as we cared for all the kids and my stepfather when Mom went into hospital. We were visited regularly by a social worker and one afternoon, soon after I had returned from the hospital, she called in. We chatted for a while and soon I found the conversation turning to my own affairs. She asked me if it was too hard for me to cope, seeing that I already had my own family. She supposed that Fred would be expecting me to come home to look after him.

In a fit of fury, I held on to my independence. I told her that I didn't care if things were difficult for me, I would rather stay in this situation, bad as it was, than go home to him. The social worker advised me to apply for a council house if I was certain that I wanted to leave him. So I did.

Later that same afternoon, Billy and I were called to the hospital to hold Mom's hands as she finally slipped away.

I remember thinking how fragile life was, how sudden death. What would happen to my children if anything should cause me not to be there for them? I wondered if I would ever see Laila and Ahmed again before life was taken from me, too. I would have to try. I would tell Fred that I was never going back. As long as Laila and Ahmed were not with me, I would not be with him.

Chapter Six

Things were hectic for a while. The funeral had gone off smoothly. Within two months my stepfather took a turn for the worse. He was admitted to hospital, where he died soon afterwards. Again I worried about the fragility of life and inevitability of death.

In September 1969 I had Tina. She was my biggest baby, weighing in at well over eight and a half pounds. Fred came to see her just after she was born, but the tension between us was still very much in evidence. Just because I had had a baby it didn't mean that I would go back to him. Besides, he would only get me pregnant again. Fred was determined that I would go back sooner or later. I was equally determined to fight him off.

Now was the time to move on. Around Christmas time I managed to find a private house to rent temporarily in Balsall Heath. It felt good making a statement of independence from Fred, if for no other reason than to prove him wrong.

Early in the New Year Fred lost the house in Golden Hillock Road. He blamed me. He seemed to think that because he didn't know whether I was going back he couldn't rent out the house. With less money coming in, he defaulted on the mortgage and it was due to be repossessed. He put doubts in my mind about whether or not I was doing the right thing.

Zana and Nadia were now at school, Ashia at nursery. I had only Tina at home with me all day. I missed my siblings. I felt safe in their company. At first they did their fair share of looking after me, and the kids, too, but gradually it dwindled and I found to my chagrin that this left me all the more vulnerable to Fred.

He was OK, helping me on occasions to take care of the children. You can never know, unless have been in the same position, how it feels to fight for your independence when you are, and have been for a long time, dependent on the person whom you are fighting. Fred and I had lived together for so long now that I was completely under his influence. He knew just how to put me down. With one click of his tongue he could undermine me. He would nag me continually about my spoiling the kids, insisting that I needed his guidance to keep them under control: or rather, in the same state as myself – conditioned.

Fred also had this knack of making people feel sorry for him – including me. I fell for it when he offered to put up a light fitting someone had given me. He moved in and stayed, despite the half-hearted protests I made. He would just suck air through his teeth if I dared to ask him to leave, then tell me that I could not, in any way, manage to look after myself.

In 1971 Fred bought another house, this one in Washwood Heath. He promptly rented it out to a young married couple. It was not that I didn't understand about the financial commitments involved in buying a house, but I felt that I was entitled to have more space than just two or three small rooms in which to raise my family. I needed privacy and security; I needed to be sure that what little we did have, in any house, was for us, the family, not for a bunch of strangers who seemed to be doing their utmost to destroy what was not theirs.

Before I knew what had hit me I was just how Fred wanted me – pregnant again.

Our son Mohammed was born in August 1972. Fred was over the moon.

I was so pleased that Fred welcomed his new son and I was glad that we had another boy. I thought of Laila and Ahmed. Fred had doted on Laila, in particular, so much after she was born – and look at what had happened to her. The nagging suspicion returned to torment me. I asked him the same old question: could they come home now? They had, after all, been away for over five years. When the inevitable reply came, 'Soon!', I was angry and helpless.

After Mo's birth the change in Fred was a sight to behold. He was so different. He became attentive and active in the family, especially as far as Mo was concerned. I found that this gave me a little more time to be myself.

The girls were happy at school and things were settled in the family for the first time ever.

Fred still had a jibe at me when he felt like it, but generally, I thought that maybe it could work after all. I decided that I would give it a go, if only for the kids. Besides, it seemed impossible to decide anything else with Fred around me. In a bid for a fresh start, we evicted our tenants and moved into the house in Washwood Heath. Inside three months, the initial period of settling down was over and we had established a routine. Then Fred dropped the bombshell.

Here we were, five kids at home, and he wanted to

rent out most of the rooms. Oh, it was all right, we would have two to ourselves. The following months were harrowing and depressing as a horde of Arabs took over our living space.

Would nothing ever change? I was so bloody stupid. Self-loathing overtook any feelings of contempt I felt for Fred. I was just fooling myself. How did he con me into thinking that things would turn out for the better? How could I believe him time and time again? It was such a waste of life.

It was always the same scenario. We would find ourselves together. I would endure the trials of Fred's domination, especially his ability to debase me, my efforts and achievements. Our fragile relationship would moulder and rot in a relatively short time. The family ended up back at the bottom of Fred's mental list of considerations.

Now I wanted to leave him again. In truth I had never really wanted to be with him again in the first place. It was not my idea. It was not my fault. It was Fred's fault. We had had a slim chance of making a go of things, if only I could have forgiven him for taking Laila and Ahmed. Impossible. I would never forgive. I would never forget, even though I had spent quite a time being brainwashed by Fred into thinking that they were far better off where they were than they would have been with us. Only one thing was certain: they were better off without *him*!

In 1973, after years of waiting, I was finally offered a council house in my own right in Strensham Road, Balsall Heath. Overcome with excitement, I babbled on to the kids that we would be moving to our own new house. I really could not believe my luck. We all laughed, said it was a sign of good luck, and skipped around the house until it was time to go. I walked the girls to school and then rushed to the Housing Association to collect the keys.

I was too busy to go immediately to see the house. It would have to wait until the afternoon. It was just my luck that Fred decided to meet the girls from school. They told him about the house, and he came home with them. As soon as I saw him I knew that he knew.

He spent ages pointing out my inadequacies, berating me, telling me that I was too weak to look after myself. I suppose I could have shown stubbornness and strode out into the great unknown to prove him wrong but, as he knew so very well, I *was* weak and he was preying on that weakness. I was so inadequate. He talked me into letting him see the house, convincing me that it was his right to see where we would live, that the house was suitable, the area good. Things like that had never concerned him before. All that was different now, he told me.

He won.

He came with me to see the house. 'This is good enough for us all to live in.'

Slowly the penny dropped. I couldn't believe my ears.

'What do you mean, all?' I protested. The house was for *me* and the kids.

He chilled me. 'It's for all of us.'

And so it was. Fred moved in along with us.

I was back to square one.

Chapter Seven

It was especially cold for the time of year. Bitter winds ripped through the house when a door was opened. Fred was spending most of his time either at work or with his Arab friends. The Arab community was buzzing with stories of 'Black September', of letter bombs sent by Arab brothers to Jews and of the introduction of the Race Relations Act by our government, banning colour discrimination in employment considerations. It was all above my head. I tried to keep interested, but the children were demanding and I was more than happy to devote myself to them.

I was tired and had gone to bed early. Fred was still out somewhere gorging himself in the company of his friends. I was half asleep when I felt his cold presence on me, shocking me into full wakefulness. He was already reaching the peak of his sexual fulfilment. Too late I realised that of course he wore no contraceptive protection. I knew immediately that I was pregnant yet again.

I had only had Mo that August. He was now three months old. I cried all night. Fred slept with a smug, contented smirk on his face. Oh, I hated him then, more than I could ever put into words. I was so angry. Not just because I was surely pregnant again, but because it was so soon, and after we had made a concerted effort to play at happy families. I felt as if Fred were trying to kill me.

I was so tired all the time. I sank into a long fit of depression and by the time I managed to get myself to the doctor, I was nearly three months gone. I sat dejectedly in his office, crying my eyes out, spitting out venomous comments about Fred's libido. With a start, I sat up. The doctor was asking me if I had come to discuss an abortion. I had not considered that option. I would never have thought, not in a million years, that I could actually do this. I loved my kids dearly and was so proud of them. I had now had seven babies by this man, and I could no longer relate to him since he had taken two of them out of my life.

'Yes! I want a termination!' It felt strange saying this.

The doctor looked at me with some sympathy. 'Miriam, have you considered having a sterilisation? Or Fred having a vasectomy?'

When he saw the vacant look on my face he explained to me what these operations were. I scoffed at the thought of Fred having a vasectomy. I slumped in the surgery chair. Fred could go on getting me pregnant for years. I was only thirty years old, and likely to be fertile for a few more years yet. Perhaps I would reach the change of life about fifty at the earliest. Another twenty years of being able to produce babies! No, that was it. Enough.

'I want to be sterilised. Now.'

Finally, after having a routine cervical smear and receiving an earnest pep talk, I left, feeling sorry for myself, but adamant. Although I felt awful about being there, wanting the abortion, I knew I had no other option. I tried not to dwell on it, and resolved to get the following Monday over and done with.

Within a month, I was called in for the sterilisation. This operation went well, apart from the shock of my discovering that the small scar I expected was, in reality, a huge hip-to-hip bikini-line gash. This was a minor, although inhibiting, irritation.

I was liberated. Free. Life would be better from now on. I could concentrate on the children I already had and would no longer live with the threat of pregnancy. I could actually build a life for myself and my children; I could plan things without fearing that my plans would be dashed by an unplanned pregnancy; I would have normal breasts, no longer full of milk all the time: I could leave Fred and live my own life to the full.

I came down to earth damned hard.

Two weeks after I had been discharged, a letter from the hospital arrived.

'The results of your smear test have been returned from the laboratory . . .'

I had cervical cancer! I held on to the sink top to steady myself. Cancer! Me? Oh, dear Christ! The kids! The tears flooded down my cheeks. What was I going to do? My worse fear had been realised. Vivid memories of my mother flooded my mind. I saw her again. I had let her down. I had let the children down. I had let myself down. I recalled how her death had urged me to cherish life and how I had forgotten. I felt wretched. I was being punished.

Mo cried. I rushed to him, picked him up and held him tight to my chest, sobbing. It took a long time for me to regain any semblance of composure. I read the letter again and again. The word 'cancer' screamed at me from the paper. My head ached. I sniffed away further tears, got Mo ready and rushed to the clinic.

I was so lucky. By sheer fluke, they had found the cancer just in time, thank God. It was not too late. I had the top of my cervix removed in my third operation and was cleared of cancer, although the doctor did say that it might come back. I would spend the rest of my life having regular checks, but for now, I was going to be OK.

In a funny sort of way I was glad that Fred had come home feeling amorous. It had saved my life. Had the cancer gone unchecked, I might not be here now.

The family unit became a little closer, with Fred playing the attentive father role again. Zana and Nadia were, at eleven and nine respectively, growing fast. Zana was showing great promise at school, paying particular interest to English and Childcare. Nadia was causing a storm – she was an utter tomboy, preferring football to dolls. Ashia would follow her elder sisters everywhere and mimic their actions. Tina was quiet and gentle. Mo would not walk anywhere. He started pre-school at three and I would take him, or rather carry him, there every afternoon then carry him back again. He would then be happy with his box of toys in the lounge while I prepared tea for the kids, who would return imminently from school.

Life was easier. For the first time in years I had time on my hands, time alone. I now had Mo only in the mornings and in the late afternoon until bedtime. It was probably this unaccustomed leisure that prompted Fred to swap the house in Washwood Heath for a fish-and-chip shop on Stratford Road. He came home one day and told me about the swap. We were going to live there, run the shop together and live above it in a large three-bedroomed maisonette.

I was taken aback. Me? Help run a shop?

We went along to see the premises. The shop was quite a going concern, really busy. The maisonette was massive. It boasted the biggest lounge I had ever seen in my life. The bedrooms were big, too. Fred smiled and spoke of decorating plans. There was a school very close by that the kids would attend. Zana was about to change to senior school anyway, and this would be a good move for her as most of her beloved friends were hoping to come to this particular school.

I wondered if I was capable of running a shop. How would I cope with all that burning hot fat? Fred said that, soon after we moved in, he would change it to a sandwich shop and sell tea and coffee. It would be far easier to cope with than fish and chips. He would be with me all the time, opening the shop while I got the kids ready for school, then I would help him until three in the afternoon, when I would 'retire' upstairs, get their tea and stay until they were all in bed at eight. Then I could come down and help again until the shop closed at eleven in the evening. It all seemed easy enough. My naivety has to be forgiven.

I had no idea it would be such hard work. Fred forgot, or declined to mention, all the cleaning involved, and my day expanded from a hard 8 a.m. to 11 p.m. to a grafting 6 a.m. to 1 a.m. Gradually, after a pretty easy initiation, I got involved in cooking bangers and mash, or pie and chips. We offered a limited menu, but I was the cook, cleaner, server, washer-upper and guard.

We introduced pinball machines and I then had to watch the kids with a hawk-like eye. Fred was upstairs, knocking down walls and moving staircases.

The children were very happy in Stratford Road. They

had a settled life and, although it was very hard work for me, it was all worthwhile for them.

Weeks rolled into months, and months into years. Where did the time go? I watched the children grow and flourish. They had plenty of friends in the neighbourhood and we were all very close. Why did Fred have to spoil it all? I will never know.

He had started to gamble heavily, running a card school upstairs. He would play cards all day, all night, breaking only to go to the loo. Fred and his Arab friends kept themselves awake by chewing a mild narcotic called *qat*. It is available in England, being brought in as a herb for cooking, but in fact it is a drug, not unlike an amphetamine, inducing alertness, suppressing hunger and making the chewer feel good about himself in general – the latter benefit perhaps accounts for its popularity in Shamiri circles. It is a bush-like herb, resembling a privet hedge. The leaves are chewed and the pulp stored, distending the cheek into a grotesque protrusion. The sap is then sucked out of the pulp and the flow of this is encouraged by drinking Coke. When you talk to an Arab chewing *qat* all you are aware of is this slimy green pulp trying to burst free at the side of his mouth. Fred and his Arab pals would spend days at a time on *qat*, playing cards and drinking pop. I was spending all day and all night in the shop now, and this soon increased to weekends too. I hated being alone in the shop but would only call Fred down if some of the kids got out of hand. If I was to call him on any trivial matter, like his valuable assistance, he would go into a sulk and take it out on the children, whom I would defend, starting a chain reaction of bad feeling all round.

I was particularly upset to find that he had been betting and losing the daily takings from the shop. I poured all my

36

time and effort into the children and the business; Fred poured all the profits into the ante.

Later that year he was issued with a court summons for non-payment of rates. He was ordered to pay the bailiffs weekly amounts, creating another task for me to cope with: taking the money to the bailiffs. But Fred was completely out of control with his betting and before long there was no money to take them at all.

Fred was taken to court. This time he sent me a telegram saying that he was being held in Winson Green Prison. I was to contact one of his friends to get money and take it to him immediately. Fred was bailed out.

Although he still had the closed game upstairs, he would no longer actively bet but continued to be keeper of the ante. This still left me in the shop alone for most of the time. Times were pretty hard, but a lot easier than they had been in the past.

I was continuously busy. The kids were now less demanding as children, but more demanding as young adolescents. I became accustomed to the hectic daily routine of being a full-time mother, housekeeper and shopkeeper. I didn't really bother chasing Fred for assistance too often. He would only help me for two or three days before wandering off with his friends again, and since his court case and subsequent arrest, he was irritable and moody. It was better that he did wander off and leave me to it. A mutual benefit.

Chapter Eight

Ashia's twelfth birthday was approaching. I had taken a day out of the shop to go to the market and pick up a little something for her present. Nadia came with me and we must have toured the circuit of stalls six or seven times at least. I wanted to buy her something to wear, but Ashia was not the easiest of my children to choose clothes for. She always wanted to express herself in a manner different from everyone else.

I was engrossed, pondering over a couple of jumpers. It was some time before I realised that Nadia had been calling me. She had wandered off to a costume jewellery stall, about five or six stalls up the aisle from me, and was holding something aloft. She was beaming at her find, and in her excitement, began to make her way to me, through the crowd. I was a stall away from her when suddenly a largish man with a withered face grabbed her from the back, pulling her down by her hair. She screamed as she fell to the floor.

'Thief! Thief! Someone get security, quickly. I've caught this bitch nicking from my stall!'

I flew at him, hitting at the hand that held Nadia by the hair, protesting in the strongest terms.

I helped Nadia to her feet. Her eyes were wild and disorientated, her hair dishevelled.

Two policemen arrived and Nadia was arrested, taken into custody because of a small ring. There was no stone set in the silver-coloured metal; a mere pretty pattern adorned the cheap costume jewellery. It was a ring worth perhaps 10p, but handsomely priced at 90p.

Nadia was pushed into a patrol car. The door slammed shut after her. It sped away, leaving me heaving with laboured breath on the side of the road. I watched as they disappeared around the corner.

Nadia was in a dreadful state when I finally got to the police station. A statement had been taken from her and I made one, too, as a witness to the event.

The WPC who had taken our statements explained to me that Nadia had been charged with shoplifting and would have to appear in the local magistrates' court. We left the station with our heads hung low. It was not shame. Nadia had done nothing to deserve this. It was the implications of the accusation.

Nadia sobbed all the way home, telling me of her ordeal: no friendly faces, all alone. I was crazy with anger at the whole episode.

As we entered the shop Fred made to take off with his friends. I ignored him and stomped off up the stairs with Nadia. He was hot on my heels. 'Miriam, I want to go out! Come down!' he called up the stairs.

Nadia went up to her room to sob her little heart out, and I went to put the kettle on. I stood by the sink and lit a cigarette, drawing deeply on the smoke. I was tapping my foot in irritation when Fred entered the kitchen. He was waiting to know why I had not obeyed and gone down to take over the shop; thinking, perhaps, that I was trying to get out of work.

'Fred, Nadia has been charged with shoplifting!'

He raised his eyebrows. His mouth opened in shock. He didn't say a single word as I told him of her ordeal. All the while, I protested that Nadia was innocent.

For a long moment Fred simply looked at me, then he ordered me again to watch the shop, turned on his heel and went upstairs. I started to follow him up to Nadia's room but he turned on the stairs and cautioned me with a single look to stay where I was.

'She didn't do it, Fred, I'm telling you now! I was there! I saw the whole damned thing. Do you hear me, Fred? She didn't bloody well do it!'

As it was, Fred preferred to reserve judgement in this matter. He came down after fifteen minutes and silently left the house.

The day of Nadia's court appearance duly arrived. It was a dreadful morning. Nadia was nervous and I was running on a short fuse with all of the kids, Fred and anyone else who got in my way. Zana, Ashia and Tina wished Nadia the best of luck as they left for school feeling subdued and oppressed. Fred didn't speak at all to anyone. He didn't even say goodbye as Nadia and I left for the court.

It was quite an informal affair. Two capacious oak desks faced a raised rostrum where the Justice of the Peace would sit and, after deliberation, deliver an opinion and punishment or freedom. I hoped for the latter and felt pretty sure that would be the outcome.

And so the case commenced. Nadia was good, despite her nerves, and told the truth. I felt both proud and sorry for her at the same time. My name was called. I went to the court clerk to swear my oath and took the stand. Glaring at the stall-holder, I recounted the events which had brought us to this room to waste the time of the British courts.

Incredibly, Nadia was found guilty of theft, and a supervision order was issued. Now she would serve a probationary period of two years. She was released into my custody but I would have to take her to the Social Services offices every fortnight for a visit. As long as we kept them happy they would leave us alone.

Fred took it badly. I was still in a fury as I tried to explain what had happened in court. He sat cold and stony-faced as he listened to the outcome of the hearing. I sat breathless as I relayed the details. He stared into his tea, swilling the contents around and around in the mug. Finally he looked up and coldly surveyed Nadia, sitting on the sofa beside me.

'So, I have a petty thief for a daughter, do I? She has shamed my good name! How can I hold up my head in the shop, in the street, when I have a convicted criminal for a daughter?'

I stayed quiet for a few moments as Fred launched into a dogmatic attack on Nadia for having dragged his name through the courts, which left me incredulous. Eventually I was obliged to remind him about his own brush with the law, about the rates and his subsequent arrest.

I could see the fury in his face. His jaw worked and his eyebrows were knotted together. He ordered Nadia to her room so that he could vent his anger on me.

I couldn't be bothered to argue with him. As far as Fred was concerned, if the courts found Nadia guilty, then guilty she was. Turning, I stormed out of the room, leaving him alone to rant and rave in Arabic, jumping up and down in a fit of pique.

I went to comfort Nadia.

Chapter Nine

Fred had taken a job in a local factory, working a press hammer. Once again, he left me to run the shop on my own during the day. The shop was doing quite well, so I couldn't really understand why Fred wanted extra work. I was in a confusing situation: pleased that I had him out of my hair but annoyed that I was having to work extra hard. I wondered if he was gambling again, although I said nothing. As far as I could tell, no money had gone astray from the takings. If Fred was using money from a different source I could hardly say anything.

I was cleaning when the shop bell went. I peered over the counter to see Fred coming in, supported by a colleague from work. He sat Fred down at a table and walked over towards me. 'There's been a bit of an accident at work. Fred's hurt his hand. Mashed his fingers up in the press hammer. Don't worry, we have been to the hospital and he's all sorted now. He is a bit shocked, needs some rest for a few weeks, then he will be right as rain!'

In fact, Fred had hurt his left hand very badly. He had lost the tip of his thumb, most of his forefinger and all of the middle finger. The accident had shaken him up, which was understandable.

He made his way to the stairs at the back of the restaurant. 'Gowad is coming soon. He has gone to the chemist to fill my prescription for painkillers. When he comes, send him straight up.'

'Yes sir!'

Fred sucked air through his teeth.

I could hardly leave the shop to run up after him; besides, he would have found the decrease in takings substantially more painful than his injured hand, however quiet we were at that time of the day.

Gowad Abdul Majid arrived within a quarter of an hour. Looking at him, I thought about Laila and Ahmed. Even after all these years it still hurt, but they were hardly mentioned now. What was the point?

Gowad had been a friend of the family for years. All the kids called him 'uncle'. He was in his fifties, about five foot six, and had a slightly rotund figure. He was a kind-looking family man who always dressed casually in trousers, shirt and jacket and didn't mind the kids making fun of his bald patch. He would never shout, always speaking softly to the children. His English wasn't perfect – who would expect it to be? – but I never had to use pidgin English with Gowad, as I did with some of Fred's other friends. Gowad too came from Yemen, although whereas Fred was from Aden, a previous British protectorate in the south, Gowad came from a village in the north. Despite the difference of opinion between the extremely religious and traditional northerners and the fiercely independent, Western-thinking southerners, Fred and Gowad had remained good friends. They were more like blood brothers than brothers of a common country. Gowad had always been extremely polite and courteous to me and the kids. He seemed very gentle and kind, trustworthy and well respected. He was married to a Yemeni woman who still lived in the village of her birth. Gowad used to go and visit her as often as he could. He would come back with tales of his people and report on how well his two sons were doing. His eldest son was the same age as Nadia.

About a month after Fred's accident Gowad came round for dinner. Zana, Nadia and Ashia had gone to their beloved youth club centre for a few hours. I had washed up, and as I waited for the kettle to boil to make tea, I was sneaking a crafty cigarette in the kitchen.

When Fred came in he made me jump. He told me some more of his friends had arrived. I should make more tea. He left as soon as he'd given the order and, for once, didn't nag me about smoking. Perhaps he hadn't noticed, but that seemed unlikely. It was rare for me to be asked to make tea for Fred and his guests if they were going to play cards. No, they must be here for some other reason. I was curious. The only thing to do was make the damned tea and find out. I willed the kettle to boil faster.

Eventually, I joined Fred and his guests, about ten in all, to leave the tea for them to help themselves, as was normal. Surprise, surprise, Fred asked me to pour the tea and sit down. Now I was really intrigued. I made the rounds with the tea. Some of his friends I knew, but many seemed unfamiliar. Fred reminded me of their names. He was in a jovial mood and didn't moan at all at Zana, Nadia and Ashia when they arrived home, late as usual. To make matters all the more confusing, he invited the girls to join us.

Fred and his friends spoke in English, including me and the girls in the conversation. Abdul Khada and his eldest son, Mohammed, were there and struck up a conversation

44

with Zana, talking politely about work and languages. Gowad had whipped out pictures of his wife and two sons in the Yemen. Nadia tried to stifle a yawn as she passed them over to us.

Gradually, in ones and twos, all of his friends left, until only Gowad remained. I went to make more tea for us, and to sneak another ciggie in the kitchen. When I returned and served the tea, my curiosity was finally satisfied.

'Gowad is going to Yemen soon,' Fred announced.

'Oh, really? When?' I asked, handing Gowad his tea.

'Oh, about June, *Inshallah*!' Gowad nodded his thanks for the tea. *Inshallah*, which means 'God willing', is often used after expressing something that is hoped for.

Fred and Gowad exchanged glances, covertly encouraging each other. Fred then voiced the wish that he wanted to go too. It had been twelve years since he had been to see his family. His father no longer wrote to us. Either we had changed address once too often, or something had happened between them, although that now seemed unlikely as Fred was eager to see his family again.

So Fred wanted to go to the Yemen to see his family again. His family in Yemen included Laila and Ahmed. I wondered if he could bring them back now. I started to become excited at the thought. I wanted to ask him about them, but I would have to wait until we were alone. Gowad and Fred didn't seem to notice that I was off in a dream as they chatted together, in Arabic now.

I tried to visualise my two long-lost children. How had they grown? Who did they look like? What were they doing now? I closed my eyes and I could see them, but the picture in my mind was of a four-year-old girl and a two-year-old boy. Laila would be sixteen now, Ahmed fourteen. Fred pulled me from my reverie. 'Miriam! Are you listening?' He tutted his annoyance at me. 'Gowad said that he would take one of the girls to the Yemen for a holiday.'

'One of the girls?' I was astonished.

'Yes! Isn't that a nice offer? I thought that maybe after the compensation for my accident comes through, we could join them and all come back together.'

My thoughts raced back to Laila and Ahmed. It would be so good to see them again. I tried to calm down, until I had Fred on his own. 'Well, it would have to be Nadia. After all the trouble she has been through, she could do with the break. A fresh start.'

'I thought you would say that,' Fred agreed. 'It is the wisest choice, even if she has done little to deserve it. Perhaps the break would do her some good. OK, then. Nadia it is. Besides, Gowad and I already thought she would be the one to go. It will be for about one month, and she can go with Gowad.'

The next few hours we spent listening to Gowad and Fred telling us all about the Yemen. How great it was. Gowad said he had a house in the middle of green pastures, a huge white house with marble pillars and fruit trees around its perimeter. They spoke about the balmy beaches just a stone's throw away from Gowad's house. Clean mountain air, sunshine, palm trees and camels. He told Nadia that she could learn how to ride a horse bareback. Paradise found!

I looked at Nadia. The boredom gone, she was radiant, her eyes sparkling with excitement, a smile so wide it flashed all of her gleaming white teeth, like a Colgate commercial. She folded and unfolded her arms in excitement as she listened, in awe, to the two men describing the land of the Queen of Sheba, a fertile land which produced myrrh, frankincense and spices. Arabia Felix. A land supported by Britain before Independence and one which had become a United Nations member in 1947 and a Republic in 1962.

It all sounded so wonderful and exciting, especially to the young, impressionable Nadia who listened so intently. When Fred said that as soon as he was compensated for his damaged hand, we could all join her, I found myself feeling as highly charged as Nadia.

It was settled, then. Gowad excused himself and left, leaving us to our dreams of paradise. He hadn't been gone ten minutes before Zana and Ashia started protesting to their father.

'It isn't fair, Dad. Why can't I go too?' Zana sulked at him.

'You can go. When my compensation comes.'

'But Nadia is only fourteen. She is too young to travel alone, with strangers!'

'Gowad is not a stranger. How long have you known him, Zana?'

'But it's for six weeks, Daddy. I've never been without Nadia for six hours before!'

'You will live. People have survived worse than that.'

'But if we are going anyway, why can't I go for the school holidays too? If you, Mommy and the others are going to join Nadia in Yemen, we should be allowed to go first together. She can't even speak Arab, can she?'

'Can you speak Arab, then? Or have you forgotten that most Yemenis can speak English as a second language?'

'No, but Nard will be scared all alone, and I don't think Gowad will want to spend all his time interpreting for Nard. And if you are going later anyway, why can't I go early, too?'

'We'll see.'

I think it was the very first time that Fred ever gave the appearance of listening to the reasoning of any of his children. This was a Fred of whom I had no experience, either.

The girls went off to bed at last and I asked Fred if he was seriously considering sending Zana out too. He said that she had a reasonable argument. It was a question of fare money and travel companion, really. I thought it was a little odd that he should consider sending Zana and Nadia separately. Could Gowad not manage both of them? Gowad had made a kind gesture, Fred said, and it would be impolite to abuse his hospitality by asking him to take both girls. I shrugged my shoulders and accepted his reasoning.

Zana was quiet over the next few days. She knew her father well enough not to press the matter too far, for it would risk pushing him in the wrong direction. However, to me this all seemed too easy. Fred was keeping something from me.

Nothing was as important to Fred as money. He must be expecting a huge pay-out for his damaged hand, and keeping it all quiet. At the same time I had to remember that he was going to take the whole family on the holiday of a lifetime to a far-off exotic land. How could I be so selfish as to suspect any wrong in his gesture to his own family after we had all suffered hardship and poverty for so long? My mind was in turmoil, thinking of Yemen and how it had influenced my two eldest children, wherever they were.

A few days after this extraordinary family convention Fred announced, at the dinner table, that Zana was to go to the Yemen early too. She yelped with delight and

Nadia was pleased that her sister would travel with her, until Fred added, after the initial excitement had died down, that she would have to go two weeks earlier, with Abdul Khada Saleh and his son Mohammed. She would stay with them for two weeks, then join Nadia when she arrived with Gowad for a few days before travelling across to the south side of Yemen to be with Fred's family and, of course, Laila and Ahmed.

Abdul Khada Saleh was an impressive man who spoke English like a native. He, too, wore casual dress much of the time and he looked to me like a man of means. He had spent a lot of his time working in oil-rich places like Saudi and Kuwait. His wife, Ward, had stayed in the Yemen looking after their other son, Abdullah, who was a little younger than Zana, and their property. This seemed the norm in the Yemen. Mohammed was married with a growing family of his own.

The only hitch was that Nadia needed the permission of the courts to go abroad. I had to phone and ask if she could go on a much-needed break with relatives, and although they were not going to commit themselves to a reply over the phone, the authorities said they would consider the request and write to us with their response.

Nadia's social worker called round shortly afterwards and said that extensive inquiries had been made into Gowad's background and that these inquiries had been answered satisfactorily. It was all systems go.

The girls were going to the Yemen.

49

Chapter Ten

The music filled the air and drifted away into the warm June evening. I watched Zana and Nadia having a great time at the surprise party held for them by their friends. It was so nice. It gave me a warm feeling to know that friends could be so appreciative and make such loving gestures. Nadia and Zana had that effect on their friends. They were both warm-spirited, good-natured girls, Nadia was a little quieter than Zana, but more of a tomboy than any girl I had ever known. I watched them laugh and sing and dance. Zana became over-emotional and began to cry when one of the organisers made a 'Bon voyage' speech. I left quietly, unnoticed, went home and cried alone in the kitchen. I had never been without the girls before. I was going to miss Zana's sixteenth birthday, a milestone in a young girl's life when she leaves school to make her own niche in the world. At least I would be with them when Nadia had her fifteenth in October. I would be with all my family – Laila and Ahmed too. The thought warmed my soul, and my tears abated. I was still thinking of all these things when the girls arrived home. It was well after midnight. I could hear them from right down the street, singing loud enough to wake the dead.

On the day before Zana's departure, the coach for the airport picked us up just after three. The journey through the night seemed so long. We drove until the first rays of light tinged the early morning sky a dull red. We arrived at Heathrow in plenty of time for our ten o'clock check-in.

Feeling ravenous, we followed the wafts of cooking aromas that drifted into our nostrils. In the restaurant Abdul Khada treated us to a slap-up breakfast. He spoiled Zana rotten, buying her whatever she wanted. I felt much better seeing him treat Zana so courteously. It induced feelings of trust. I was relieved that he would take good care of her until we collected her.

The flight for Yemen was called. Zana and I gripped each other's arms in something like panic, trying our best not to show our fears. Fred said it was time to go. It was as simple as that. We embraced and kissed each other. My daughter walked through to the departure lounge. I strained my neck to watch her for as long as possible, until she was completely out of sight.

All the way home on the coach my thoughts were of Zana. Was she was OK? The parting was over for her, but I would have to endure a repeat with Nadia in a fortnight and I hated the idea of it. But at the back of my mind I consoled myself with the knowledge that Fred was coming good after all these years and was going to take us all to the Yemen to be reunited as a family once and for all.

At last!

As soon as we got home to good old Brum, I started to collect all the cards for Zana's forthcoming sixteenth birthday. Into a large envelope they went. Thanks to Ashia, word had gone around and soon all Zana's friends had given me their cards early so that I could forward them in good time for an extra-special celebration. I could imagine it all: the dancing and the singing, Zana with all her new Yemeni friends having the time of her life.

At the beginning of the second week I had a postcard from Zana. A huge, impressive castle on a rock, thousands of years old, which probably once housed the Queen of Sheba herself. She was OK. They had arrived in Sanaa, the capital, and were going to make their way to Taiz later in the day. It was very very hot, she said. 'Tell Nadia to dress properly. No camels yet, but remember this is the city!'

Nadia grabbed the card and scrutinised it. You couldn't see much in the way of palm trees and exotic beaches but, this being the main city, that was rather unlikely. Her bright eyes lit up. 'Looks like the old Greek cities, or Rome,' she enthused.

I loved the idea of Greece. It was a country I had always wanted to visit, the only place I had ever had a hankering to see. I could envisage Yemen being very similar, with exotic beautiful islands and golden sands. Nadia couldn't wait for the week to finish. She joked around the house all the time, laughing at her own jokes and pranks more than anyone else. She was going to be such a beautiful woman when she was older. She was beautiful now, but soon she would have that serenity that makes a woman glow.

Ashia kept by her side all the time. She missed Zana badly now and didn't like the idea of Nadia going away too.

'But it will only be until we all go,' I kept reassuring her, as I also reassured Tina and Mo and, to some extent, myself.

I was so proud that my daughters were able to have the rare chance to experience another country, another way of life. To share in their father's heritage. Fred boasted all the time that he had sent Zana to the Yemen and that he had got a card from her. Nearly everyone in Birmingham must have seen that card by the time Nadia was ready to travel.

We were still anxiously awaiting news about the compensation for his damaged hand. It seemed to be taking forever.

The day of Nadia's departure loomed closer. I had to go through the motions of being happy for her and her holiday. I was, in a way, but she was younger than Zana. I was glad now that Zana had had the good sense to ask her father to allow her to travel too. She would protect Nadia – she always did; make sure that Nadia didn't play around too much in the heat of the day or spend all day riding on the horses, forgetting about the strength of the sun. Both girls were good swimmers, too, so much of their time would be spent at the beach. I could imagine my Nadia at the top of a palm tree, grinning at her achievement.

Would they ever accept Birmingham again? Of course they would; it was their home and they had so much going for them here. All their friends and family. Zana wanted to be a nursery nurse and planned to go to college. Yes, this holiday would set them up for a long time.

All the way to Heathrow I kept thinking about Nadia and Zana in the Yemen: how they would be when they saw their brother and sister. I could envisage Laila and Ahmed welcoming them. They would be as close as the rest of the family. I bombarded Nadia with messages of goodwill and best wishes for Zana, Laila and Ahmed, all of Fred's family, and Gowad, too.

She laughed. 'Yes, Yes! Yes, Mom. I'll tell them.'

'Yes, Mom, I'll be careful of the horses.'

'No, Mom, we won't swim if there are currents in the sea.'

53

I settled back in my seat, reassured.

Nadia laughed and added, 'I'm going to challenge Ahmed to a game of footy!'

I bet that will surprise him, I thought. She was really good, after all the practice she'd had. By the time the rest of us got out there I would find four of my children laughing and brown and probably sun-crazy. I couldn't wait!

By the time she left for the check-in I was harbouring secret thoughts of paradise myself – and, most important of all, of having my family complete.

Chapter Eleven

A whole month had sped by since Nadia had left and I was missing them as much as the rest of the kids were. I was kept busy in the shop all day and well into the evening. Then, at last, I could relax upstairs with Ashia, Tina and Mo and talk of our approaching reunion in Yemen and the holiday of a lifetime. It was all a far cry from Dudley Zoo and Drayton Manor, our usual less exotic holiday haunts.

I was still a little worried about Zana and Nadia, as mothers are when their children are away from home having an adventure for the first time. But of more concern than this was Fred. His behaviour was becoming increasingly odd, to say the least.

Some three weeks after Zana left he received a letter from the company he had been working for with regard to his damaged hand. Their offer was £3500, which he turned down flat. I assumed that this was why he had started to behave oddly. After all, he seemed as excited as the rest of us at the prospect of our trip.

Whatever the reason, Fred was certainly acting out of character. He had started going out to pubs and coming home late, rip-roaring drunk. He was sullen and brooding over something which, in his usual way, he wouldn't share with me. I gave him the benefit of any doubts I might have had, thinking that his rejection of the compensation offer had brought him financial difficulties. He had told me just before Zana left for Yemen that he had borrowed the fare money from a colleague. In view of the impending compensation, this seemed fairly logical at the time.

We had had no news from Zana and Nadia for a month. Fred explained this away by saying that the girls would be far too busy having fun. Time would prove him right, he claimed.

When I returned from my regular visit to the bailiffs to pay Fred's fine, he told me that he had had a telephone call from the girls, asking if they could stay a little longer, and that he had consented. At first I protested, but his reasoning was that since we were going out there soon ourselves it would be silly to have them return. It was only a matter of time before his money came through.

I had to accept this as reasonable, and continued my daydreams of meeting up with our children very soon.

By the end of the fifth week this view had changed dramatically. It was the start of a battle that would drastically change the lives of my family; a battle that was to take over my life.

Chapter Twelve

It was such an ordinary day really, as I recall it. I was in the shop, watching the kids playing on the pinball machines as I absentmindedly wiped down the top of the serving counter. The door burst open and in barged Mary and her brother. Mary was the same age as Nadia. They were very close friends and had much in common, not least being members of the tomboy sorority.

The usually bubbly Mary was very uptight and belligerent. She came rushing over to the counter – normally she would have made straight for the pinball machines. 'Is it true that Zana and Nadia are married?' She clenched her fists and banged them on top of the counter.

I was taken aback. 'Don't be stupid. What do you mean, are they are married?'

'Is it true?' She was determined to get an answer to her question, however silly I thought it was.

'No, Mary, of course it is not true! What makes you ask that sort of question?'

She looked deep into my eyes; then, satisfied that I was telling the truth, huffed, turned and slammed out as quickly as she had come in, without answering my question.

I dismissed her sudden visit as impulsive, dramatic kids' stuff. As far as I was concerned, that was it. I didn't give it any more thought. Married, indeed! Whoever heard of such a thing?

Two days later, Mary paid another sudden visit. Again she stormed up to the counter, her face red and angry, her eyes accusing. 'Zana and Nadia *are* married!'

I felt so sorry for her, and a little proud that Nadia had such a good, loyal friend. My heart warmed to Mary for concerning herself so emphatically about my daughter's welfare. She must miss Nadia terribly. 'Look, my love, Zana and Nadia are not married.' I tried my best to reassure the poor little mite.

'They *are*! They *are*!' she screamed at me.

I had a vague feeling of dread inside my soul. She was so determined, so adamant. I stared at her, dumbstruck.

'They are married. This woman told us!'

I had to get to the bottom of this. Mary was so sure, so convinced – and so convincing.

'Where is this woman? Who is she?' I managed to ask, still feeling that this wasn't really happening.

'Round the corner!' Mary was champing at the bit, determined to prove that she was telling me the gospel truth, and willing to back up her bizarre claim, too.

I jerked myself back to reality. 'OK, Mary, let's go and see this woman of yours.' I took off my pinny and followed her, leaving the shop wide open.

We hurried through the streets. My mind was buzzing. What on this earth could I say to this woman, a perfect stranger? She would obviously think me raving mad, to say the least, not knowing whether my own daughters were married. At the same time a rising sense of panic was taking over. I tried to keep it out of my mind, tried to concentrate on what I would say to the woman. By the time we reached her door, I was still in a daze.

'Hello. I am Zana and Nadia's mum. Mary here is convinced that you have news that Zana and Nadia are married!'

I could feel my face glowing red as I blurted out my unrehearsed and embarrassing reason for troubling her.

'Yes, that's right. But I thought that you would already know this. I was told by this woman, you see . . .'

'What woman? Where is she?' This was getting ridiculous. Did the whole area know about it?

Without hesitation or question she gave me the address. Mary and I rushed right round there to find out why she thought that my daughters were married and was telling all the locals so.

I intended to approach this second woman a little differently from the first. I had only come out with Mary to call Mary's bluff, to give her a little peace of mind, but in reality it was playing havoc with my own.

'Hello. I am Zana and Nadia's mum. Mary here is convinced that you have news that Zana and Nadia are married!'

It was a repeat nightmare. The conversation was the same as the first – except that this woman added, to my horror, by telling me that two young Arab men who had just returned from Yemen had been to a village where they had met two Birmingham girls, by the names of Zana and Nadia, who were married to locals and living in the village.

'This can't be right.' My mind was reeling. 'It can't be true!'

Thoughts tumbling around at a rapid rate.

The woman was still speaking but her words were lost

in the air long before they reached me. I wanted Fred. I wanted to confront Fred. I raced off to find him, leaving a now thoroughly upset Mary and the open-mouthed woman staring after me.

I don't remember how I got from that house back home, but I do remember being in a right state of panic. By the time I reached our shop, fear and suspicion had me firmly in its grip.

I went in, slamming the door behind me. Fred appeared from behind the counter. 'Where have you been, leaving the shop unattended? We could have been robbed! We . . .' He turned to face me.

'*Frreedd!*' I screamed.

He shut up immediately. Tears rolling down my face, I went right up to him, my fists clenched tightly by my sides, anger choking me. How the words came out I'll never know. 'Are Zana and Nard married?' I stared at him for any sign of knowledge, any indication of guilt. Coolly, he kept a straight face and, God alone knows how, but he actually acted indignant.

'Married? Don't be stupid. Of course they are not married. Why do you say this?'

'Mary told me. And these two women who know people who have just come home from Yemen. They all say it's true!' My voice rose hysterically.

'No, Miriam. They are not married. They're coming home soon. Why do you believe these stupid kids? Did you really go chasing around the streets on the say-so of a silly kid and leave the shop empty for robbers to help themselves to our hard-earned money?' Fred held himself confidently.

God, I felt stupid. I wished the floor would open up and swallow me there and then. Fred was so very capable of making me feel little, insignificant, stupid even. I cringed from my head to my toes, going hot and cold as I thought about what I fool I was. Of course I was a fool.

Fred did enjoy the next couple of days; rubbing it in, making the most of it, making sure I knew how superior he was, how much cleverer than me. How easy it was for me to make silly mistakes, like listening to the stories of a child and leaving the shop vulnerable. He managed to convince me that the girls were not married and were going to come home. But between these bouts of female inferiority I still had this nagging feeling. I kept on at him, asking him time and time again if the girls were married. And time and time again he would deny it and and make me feel stupid all over again. But I was willing to risk my own embarrassment for the reassurances that he kept giving. I badly needed those reassurances.

This went on for three days. On the fourth day I managed to control myself until the evening. Then I broached the subject for the umpteenth time. I had this awful questioning coming from the depths of my soul, and only Fred could make the terrible ache go away with the powerful medicine of his reassurance. It was somehow addictive: each time the pain would disappear but for shorter and shorter periods, as if I was becoming immune to the assurance. Or perhaps it was wearing thinner each time he used the words, 'No, they are not married. They are coming home.'

I thought constantly about the words of the two English-women who told me about Zana and Nadia being in the village, married to Arab men. Who could they be talking about if not my girls? If it was not true, why would they bother to talk about it at all? They even knew their names. How could they be so sure when Fred said that it wasn't true? Could Fred do such a thing to his own daughters? To me? To our family?

I took a deep breath. 'Fred, I can't stop thinking about Zana and Nard. Why would these women talk about my girls if nothing was wrong? Are they married? Fred, are Zana and Nard married?'

'Fred?'

He turned and looked at me from the other side of the huge lounge. He was calm and cool. I waited for the answer, yearning for the reassurance that I needed so desperately. He looked me straight in the eye.

'Yes.'

The electric shock jolted my body into rigidity. I couldn't form a single syllable. I just looked at this man, disbelieving my own ears, because all I could hear was the sound of my own heart thumping, thumping, thumping.

Fred had not moved, neither his stance nor his expression. Cool, penetrating, superior. He just looked at me as I became further entrapped in my own shell of a body. A prisoner of shock and fear, of disbelief and horror. I was retreating further and further into a dark tunnel.

I heard him speak again.

'Yes, Miriam, they are married. They will not be coming back.'

Something snapped. I felt a pain so intense that I could not cope. It got darker in that tunnel. I felt my inner self give in to the pressure and oppression of the darkness. I welcomed the darkness, embracing its mystery, thankful for its protection.

Oblivion.

Chapter Thirteen

It was October 1981. Nadia would be having her fifteenth birthday about now, although whether or not a celebration would be in order, I had no way of knowing. As the thought passed through my mind I started crying again.

I was told that I had had a nervous breakdown. For over three weeks I had been in a world of my own, muttering the names of my children and sobbing in pathetic helplessness. I was now on tranquillisers and sleeping tablets, drifting in and out of reality. I would wake up to the world and remember Fred telling me I would not see my daughters again, that they were lost to me and happy where they were. I would cry and pass back through a veil of mist into the twilight zone and stay there until the tablets wore off. I had not washed, nor eaten. I had not spoken, apart from the inane mutterings of a drug-induced sleep. I had taken no action at this time. What could I do? Who could I turn to? How would I get my kids back home – if they wanted to come home.

I woke up to hear one of my children crying. Ashia.

Was it for her sisters, or was I now a cause of worry for her? I felt my maternal strings being pulled and I fought the fog that hung over my brain. I called her name softly, and immediately she was in my arms. How could I tell her about her sisters, her father's betrayal? She sobbed into my neck and we clung on to each other for dear life.

'Ashia, your dad . . .' The tears took over again and I lost another battle with my emotions.

'We know, Mom, he told us! Oh God, Mom, what are we going to do? Zana . . . Nadia. I want them back, Mommy. Don't let him take them too!'

We cried together until, exhausted, we let sleep protect us from the pain of remembering, of knowing.

The doctor came again. Fourteen-year-old Ashia was given tranquillisers, perhaps a little younger than is normally acceptable. She had taken it as badly as I had. All my children were in a state but, thankfully, Tina and Mo, being younger, were protected to some extent by naivety.

I needed to think. I needed my brain to function properly, to fight. I was weak. I needed to sleep. No, I needed to fight. It was so hard to find the energy or the will. I was weak and found solace only in sleep. I couldn't do it. It was too much. I needed to sleep. It felt to me at the time as if I had two people inside my head, ordering me about, telling me what to do. One said sleep – protect yourself from the pain of reality. The other said fight – get up and fight! Face it and fight it! Then these two 'people' in my head would argue and debate which one of them was right and which was mistaken. I would just sit and stare into space while the argument took place, not caring at the time which one won or lost. I had already lost. It hurt too much to move, to eat or to talk. But I knew I had to fight, and the sooner the better.

Finally, I began to spend more time being aware of the situation. Zana and Nadia needed me. I had to be there for them, no matter how much it hurt me to think about them being there, in Yemen. I had to figure out how this had happened. Why it had happened. There was only one person who could answer that. Fred.

But it was useless. Fred was not going to answer anything. For the first time since he had confirmed that he had no intention of getting Zana and Nadia back home I faced him with a barrage of questions, determined not to be browbeaten.

Initially, I found the words difficult. The sound of my own voice had become alien to me. A high-pitched cracking sound emitted from my mouth instead of the voice I was used to. I licked my parched lips to replace the moisture. They were dry and brittle. As my mouth tried to form words, the skin on my lips stretched and tore into open cuts. I looked at Fred, dishevelled and dirty, in much the same condition as me. He was unshaven. I had this intense need to get him to explain what he had done. I managed one word, 'Why?'

Fred sucked air through his teeth and went out. He had, apparently, been doing an awful lot of drinking lately. Tina and Ashia told me that he had gone out every night, returning in the early hours of the morning, banging about the house. Drunk. He ranted at the three kids constantly, raising his hands as if to hit them for offences that they had not committed but of which they had already been found guilty in his eyes.

Ashia would not speak to her father. She cried continually, and he constantly threatened her into a silence of muffled sobs. Tina tried to mother Ashia and Mo in my place, making simple meals for the three of them, trying to organise some sort of order from the chaos. She found she excelled at cleaning up, tidying. She attacked the house vigorously, perhaps finding the energy well spent, perhaps finding it therapeutic, not giving up until the house was gleaming and spotless. She tried to teach Ashia to find comfort from the same frantic technique of scrupulously cleaning the house, as if scrubbing at a dirty spot, at the pain, until it went away. It never did.

Tina was twelve years old.

Mo kept close to me, guarding me in my state of shock. He watched over me as the drugs induced sleep, never leaving my side. When I reached a bearable state of awareness Fred, who idolised Mo, would try to take him from my side. He wanted Mo to go everywhere with him, even to sleep in another room with him. But Mo stood by me, making his own stand, his own protest for his sisters' freedom. Fred still persisted, unsuccessfully.

I tried desperately to pull through for the three children I had left. They hadn't eaten properly since Fred's awful revelation, despite Tina's gallant attempts. I had not put a morsel past my own lips. Hunger was not a priority for me. I didn't give the shop a second thought, either. Fred would have to attend to that himself. He replaced my 'assistance' by enlisting the help of his buddies. As long as they kept out of my way, I didn't care.

He also had to pay his own fine to the courts. He left a friend looking after the shop while he took the short drive to the bailiffs' office. While he was out Mo came running up the stairs holding a letter which had arrived in the second post. He had managed to get to the letter before anyone else.

It was from the girls in Yemen. Thank God! At long last I had some word. Now I would find out what had happened. The only thing Fred had ever said in his defence was that they had met some boys and fallen madly in love.

66

He said that the girls had asked his permission to marry as they felt that I would not approve and were scared to tell me. I had never heard such rubbish, but Fred still had that way of undermining my view, of making me feel stupid and inferior. I was totally confused.

I grabbed the envelope from Mo and stared at the address and stamp. I smelled the paper and imagined my Zana and Nadia handling the envelope. I missed them so much. But now I had word from them. I would know at last.

A clear thought occurred to me, the first one in nearly a month. I would have to read this letter out of sight of Fred. He would be returning at any moment. If he found that a letter had arrived he would try to take it from me. I decided to lock myself in the bathroom and read the letter alone. I took my first tentative steps towards the bathroom, wobbling a lot, but Mo supported my arm, helping me along. I felt weak and a little dizzy. This didn't matter. I had a letter from my girls and I would read it as soon as I got to the bathroom. Just a little further.

Once inside, I turned and locked the door. I sat on the bath mat and took the envelope from the pocket of my dressing-gown. I stared at it for a long time then, all in a hurry now, ripped it open.

The pages were tatty, torn from an old exercise book from school, which had apparently made the journey to Yemen too. The writing was Zana's. At first glance it looked fine. The borders of the pages were adorned with musical notes and dreams of 'White Christmases'. It was dated 10 November 1980.

Dear Darling Mommy and Daddy and family,
 Mom this letter is for you really, a birthday letter, I don't know where to start but this letter.

I am thinking of you always, this is from me and Nadia, and I think I'm gonna cry:

HAPPY BIRTHDAY TO YOU, HAPPY BIRTHDAY   TO YOU.

HAPPY BIRTHDAY DARLING MOTHER,
HAPPY BIRTHDAY TO YOU.

We wish we were with you to make the day so happy for you cause we love and miss you all so very much and it kills us cause we don't know for sure when we will see you again. Remember when me Nadia and Ashia went camping we cried for you after 4 days and now it's been over 4 months. I don't know how I survive.

I suppose it's because I realise Mom when we were all young we were naughty bad girls and life was hard wasn't it. And now I left school I was taken from you and I could be doing a lot to make things easier for you, but Daddy doesn't want that. When I write to you, I speak the truth, but you lie and make excuses so not to let me be with you. WHY? Mom why, why why?

Don't write and deny that, that you don't let us know anything, why doesn't anyone write? I don't think England exists, Helen, Henry, Billy, what's wrong will it kill you to pick up a pen and write?

I really am going crazy. It's no good crying. Just a pen and paper. Say come home. Everyone will be happy then. See it's easy.

You're my Mom mom mom mom mom mom mom. Where is she. Where?

Mom do you know what the 10th of November is? A very special day. I was gonna come home to you. Abdul Khada brought me and he had a good reason for coming so he should bring me. He's got a cousin named Mohammed Hashem. He's got a big family in the village and a son who is 12. When he was young he had an accident, his left hand is something like paralysed. So the doctors in Egypt advised Mohammed Hashem to take his son to England cause they have the best surgeon but he said I can't speak English, so he asked Adbul Khada and he said Yes. But when we told Gowad he said, 'I'm warning you don't take her, otherwise you will be in bad trouble from Muthana!'

So A.K. said I don't know, so we never come and that poor boy is suffering. I was only coming until the boy had had his hand fixed and then if Nadia couldn't come with me, I come back to her. You know she is the only reason why I came, so I can leave for a while. She didn't mind. So A.K. wrote to Daddy and explained this matter and we want to see what will happen. He wants to take that boy and me for a little bit and then we come back, you see. So now we wait for a letter from you and if Daddy said bring her and the boy we might make it for Xmas. OK or is your daughter asking for too much?

Uncle Henry, Billy, Auntie Helen TELL MY MOM & PLEASE SOMEBODY TELL HER before I kill myself, I mean it Mom. Don't think I'm mad. It's better to have me now or later LOSE ME cause I won't come to you.

Mom this is the last page. LOVE YOU ALL ZANA xxxxxxxxxxxxxxxx

Mom it wouldn't matter if I left Nadia for a bit cause I'm not with her anyway, she's in the village and I'm in hays. So I don't want that for an excuse. No more lies, no more excuses please. I'm not on the moon you know. Arabia is very close to England. So Mom what

69

would Daddy do if I came for a little while you know I'd never leave Nadia for long. PLEASE let me know.

My handwriting is funny cause of the pen, I hope you can read all of it and understand I need you. Now don't tell me to wait any LONGER. I'll wait with you only or in heaven. Mom. Don't send me no Xmas present or I'll send it back. Keep it until we're together like I'm keeping yours for our house. Honestly.

Elvis song Dad!! DON'T BE CRUEL.

I want to come home to yous. Maybe not tomorrow but it will be very soon.

Mom isn't this a lovely name for a baby GIRL. SARAH VICTORIA. I LOVE IT MOM. This song especially. I'M DREAMING OF A WHITE CHRISTMAS (WITH MY FAMILY)

You're always on my mind.

Don't cry daddy.

I love you because you understand mom. Most of all I love you cause you want me NOW. DON'T YOU?

These are just some that keep rolling through my head if I was with you. You can control me. 5 months mom. Can't wait on earth ANY LONGER Pains all the time. Headaches. Only Mommy can stop it.

PLEASE NOW MOM.

I'll make it for Xmas. Sisters Ashia Tina. Tell Mom I wanna come home. TELL HER Please Ashia.

The words swam before my eyes, lifting themselves off of the paper to hang in the empty air before me, like a banner behind a plane dancing slowly before shooting off like a comet into space. Each word flashed like a neon, pulsating. Desperation. Confusion. Desperation.

70

Confusion. I was being attacked by the words written by my daughter, pounding into my brain, taunting me into a rage.

'Bad trouble from Muthana . . . Tell her before I kill myself . . .'

I found myself standing up, facing the mirror. Was that woman really me? Surely not! But I had little regard for this shell before me. I had fallen into a trap, set by Muthana. I didn't even see it. My girls, my poor girls, were victims of Muthana's bloody-minded selfishness. Their only salvation was me. I had unwittingly allowed them to be tricked into going to Yemen – and the girls blamed me! I had inadvertently allowed Muthana to manipulate the three of us. Why didn't I see it? Even now I couldn't figure out what had happened. Why had the holiday of a lifetime become a suicide bid for Zana? What was she referring to? What lies? What excuses? Why would Abdul Khada be in bad trouble from Muthana? What was happening?

The tension and frustration mounted. I was devastated. Angry. I saw the scissors on the bathroom windowledge. I picked them up. They were cold and hard. I wanted to share the suffering of my daughters, alleviate their pain by taking some of their burden.

I began to hack at my hair. Long black locks fell into the sink and on to the floor as I cut to the scalp, leaving odd bits jutting out at all angles. The scissors were blunt. What I couldn't cut I tore from my head, leaving bloody patches, feeling no pain from the ripped follicles. Mental anguish overcame physical pain. I was crying, screaming. I had no control over anything any more. It would be so easy to die. So easy to die.

The words from the letter dimmed. In their place was a

71

darkness. That black tunnel, that welcome familiar refuge, my sanctuary.

I was falling into my oblivion again and I was so glad of it.

It was all too much. Too much.

Chapter Fourteen

On waking I looked about the room with a sense of unreality. It had happened again. My second nervous breakdown. I knew I had slept, then nothing! I tried taking in all that should have been so familiar, yet which now seemed a link to a past that I could not believe I had endured. I shuddered as memories came of Fred smiling, telling the kids about this paradise of Yemen, then luring them into a hell that wanted Zana's life as a price, like lambs to the slaughter . . . Mom mom mommmmm . . . Where is she . . . where . . . The words came floating back before my eyes. Another shudder; I gulped frantically at the stale air in the room to save myself from drowning in the darkness again.

The doctor had been called when I was found in a zombied state of shock. I was dead inside. Again I was on tablets, this time a stronger dosage.

My brother Derek came to stay. He said he needed a place to live, but this was a transparent excuse, as transparent as my need for him then. For the first time in ages I had a 'cuppa'. Ashia made tea for me and Derek and put a few biscuits by the side. Slowly I sipped at the brew. It tasted good. We sat in virtual silence for a while until Derek, obviously feeling a little awkward, felt obliged to make small talk. I didn't take much notice of what he was saying. My thoughts were on Nadia and Zana. Zana and the letter.

The letter!

I felt in my dressing-gown pocket for the letter. It wasn't there. It must still be in the bathroom. Fred would get to it. I had to get up and go to the bathroom, to get the letter before Fred did. I staggered upright. Derek shot a puzzled glance at me.

'Bathroom!' I whispered. Where had my voice gone again?

He almost carried me to the bathroom, pushing the door open with his foot as he leaned me against the wall. 'Do you need help? Shall I call for Ashia or Tina to come and give you a hand?'

I just shook my head, not trusting my voice to try actually speaking.

'I'll be right outside, Miriam. OK?'

I put my hand against the bathroom wall for support. My legs wobbled as they tried to carry me in far enough so that I could get the door closed behind me. The door felt as if it were made of lead rather than plywood. I reached down to slip the tiny bolt into place. It was gone. Just the torn holes remained where the screws had held it firmly to the door. The wood around the frame was buckled and split. I fingered the splintered wood, wondering how it had happened, when it had happened. No matter. I wanted the letter. The door was forgotten. I looked round the bathroom to see if I had dropped the letter on the floor. It was nowhere in sight. I was on my hands and knees looking under the sink, between the loo and the wall. Nothing. Where was it? Damn it!

Maybe Ashia or Tina had picked it up. They must have been cleaning the bathroom while I slept. Yes, it did look very clean. I hauled myself upright. I felt nauseous and a little faint.

I ran the tap and cupped my hands to catch the cold water, splashing it on to my face. It was freezing cold, but it blew some of the cobwebs away. It felt good. I grabbed the towel, pulled it from its perch and patted my face dry, rubbing my eyes gently. They felt sore.

I looked in the mirror. I gasped aloud at the awful sight. It was me! My hair! What happened to my hair? Then I remembered. It came rushing into my mind. Unwelcome. Horrifying.

'My babies!' I sank to my knees on the bathroom floor, sobbing inconsolably.

Derek rushed into the bathroom and gently put his arms around me. 'Shhhh, there there, Miriam. Come on, I'll get you back to the lounge.'

He picked me up and carried me to the lounge, placing me on the sofa. He tucked a blanket around my legs and handed me a cigarette. My hands were shaking as I took a light. I inhaled deeply, immediately coughing to expel the smoke from my lungs. The coughing fit seemed to last forever. Ashia ran to get me water, but I had recovered before she came back. It felt good just to have the cigarette between my fingers. Like a comforter. I was a little afraid to have another puff just yet.

'Do you want some more tea, Mom?'

Ashia looked awful too. The bags under her eyes were dark and deep, blemishing her clear, soft skin. I looked at her with the same expression as she used with me. Shock, I think.

'Well, how about a little hot soup?' Derek offered.

'I'm not hungry,' I said, quite truthfully.

'But it's been a long time since you ate anything, Mom.' Ashia was concerned.

'Really, I don't think I could eat just yet,' I protested.

'What do you mean, "Just yet"?' Ashia demanded angrily. 'You haven't eaten properly for two months!' The tears rolled down her cheeks as she stamped her foot to add emphasis to her words.

'Two months?' I could not imagine what she was talking about. 'I had some toast, didn't I? This morning.'

'No, Mom! You didn't!'

Mo and Tina came into the lounge, attracted by Ashia's hysterical behaviour.

'Mo, didn't I have toast this morning? Just before the letter. Remember?' I looked at Mo and Tina for support.

Tina ran out of the room crying and Mo looked down at the carpet. Had the kids found the letter and read it for themselves?

'Mom, that was over two weeks ago. You barely touched that and nothing else has even been looked at for eight weeks. You had another breakdown. You've been in a world of your own since Mo found you locked in the bathroom. He called the doctor and they kicked the door down. You were cutting your hair off. The doctor had to inject you to get the scissors out of your hand. You've been ill ever since!' Ashia sobbed.

I stared at the floor. Two weeks, gone. Oh, God! I felt like crying, but the tears would not come. I clenched my fists, breaking the cigarette. Derek took the pieces from me.

'How about that hot soup, Miriam? Huh? Just a little bit?' he cajoled.

76

'OK. Just a little bit,' I relented and Ashia quietly left the room to prepare it.

'Listen, Miriam. I don't know what is going on. The kids have told me that Fred has done something to the girls in Yemen. They said Zana and Nard can't come back. Is that true?'

I didn't answer. I couldn't find the words to begin to explain.

'Look, you don't have to tell me if you don't want to. It's really none of my business, but you are my sister, and I can say, truthfully, that I have never seen anyone in such a state, let alone you being my sister. And I don't like it, Miriam! You can tell me to shut up or mind my own if you like, but I love those kids too. If I can do anything, you have to tell me what is going on.'

It was still hard for me to gather my thoughts, to work out what had happened myself, let alone tell anyone else. I was so confused that my attempt at explaining it to Derek sounded garbled. But condensed into a few sentences, it could have sounded like a mere misunderstanding, trivial and unimportant. And it wasn't. Far from it.

'Where is this letter?' Derek offered me another cigarette.

'I don't know. I remember reading it in the bathroom, then it was gone.'

'Have you asked the kids?'

'Well, no, not yet.'

'I think you should. This letter could be important.'

He lit my cigarette and this time I was grateful for the nicotine in my system.

'Have you asked Muthana about it, Miriam? Maybe if he knows that the kids are suffering, he will tell them to come home immediately.'

'Could it be that easy, Derek?' I recalled Laila and Ahmed.

'You have to try it to find out.'

I drew in the smoke from the cigarette and thought about it until Ashia came back into the room with the soup. 'Have you seen your father, Aish?'

'You're joking, Mom. He's been out every night for months now. He comes in blind drunk at three or four in the morning and sleeps until he can go out again.'

'What about the shop, who looks after that?' As if I really cared about the shop! It was more curiosity.

'Well . . .' Ashia thought about it for a few moments. 'Dad for a while, then these friends of his take over and play cards behind the counter while he goes out and drinks himself stupid.'

'That shouldn't take too long, then!' I muttered resentfully. 'Where is he now? What time is it? What *day* is it?'

'Well, it's Wednesday, December seventeenth. It's half-seven. He left for the pub when he heard you were up and about. He won't be back until about four in the morning now. And he'll be home drunk as usual, I guess.'

'Do you know which pub he goes to?' I had an idea. Derek quickly stopped it in its tracks.

'What do you think you're going to do, Miriam? Go to the pub and have it out with him? You haven't got the strength for that, and you know how he is with you. Leave it, Miriam. It's not a good idea.'

'Well, what the hell am I supposed to do, Derek? Let it go? Did you see the letter? Zana wants to kill herself. She can't come home. It's his fault. He lied. He lied to me, he lied to the girls and he's still lying! They think . . . they think it's my fault. They are blaming me! What's he said, Del? What's he said to them, that they think I had a part in this? Why is he tormenting us all like this? Why? I can't let them suffer, Derek. It's killing me.' I was losing control. 'Do you hear me? It's killing all of us!' I was hysterical.

Derek held me tight. 'Oh my God, Miriam. I don't know what to do. I don't know what to say. But . . . but we will find something – someone! You've got to hold on, Miriam. Hold on!' His grip tightened and he rocked me back and forth, as if I were a baby. I let his care comfort me.

After a little while he spoke again. Softly he asked me what I intended to do. My thoughts were filled with memories of Laila and Ahmed. I didn't know. I really didn't know. Fred: why?

Chapter Fifteen

I sat up all night, just staring into space, trying to figure a way out of the mess. But each time I strove for an idea, my mind was invaded with thoughts of the letter, of Laila and Ahmed, of Zana and Nadia.

I was aware of the morning sun trying to filter through the clouds of the cold December day. It reminded me of myself, fighting the oppression that surrounded me. I willed the sun to win and shine through, but the heavy rain-burdened clouds blocked out the rays and hid the sun from view. I took it as an omen. It was a fact of nature, but not the way I read it.

I was brought back to reality by the sound of banging and belching. It was Fred, staggering up the stairs, home after another night on the binge. I looked at Mo, sleeping on the camp bed at the other end of the room, guarding me. He was awake now, looking at me. I saw fear in his eyes as he tried desperately to read my thoughts and anticipate my actions.

'I'll do nothing now, son. Soon. I will very soon. As soon as I know what to do.'

Fred called out for Mo. Mo shot a worried glance at me and put his finger to his lips to say 'Shhhh!'

Again Fred called, telling him to come to his father. Mo sat rigid in his bed, not moving a muscle, not making a sound.

The door handle wiggled and jumped as Fred tried to turn the knob and slip the bolt from the latch. Mo gasped.

Enough! I jumped up from the sofa, then had to stand for a moment while the dizzy spell subsided.

'No, Mom!' Mo's cry was nearly drowned out by the sound of heavy footsteps thudding on the stairs. I got to the door and tore it open, just in time to see Fred disappearing round the corner at the top of the stairs into his hidey-hole.

That mere glimpse of him made me crazy with anger. It was the first sighting I had had of him since he confirmed that the girls were not coming back. Now I was shaking with rage, but there was little I could do at this point. I had to concentrate on protecting the kids I had left.

I told Mo that from now on, he would have to sleep in the girls' room, with Ashia and Tina. They had the only room with a lock and the room was the closest to the lounge. I said to Mo it was to protect Tina and Ashia, just to make him feel that he was still being a protector. But he was no better off than his sisters. He loved his father deeply, but was saddened because, instead of the man who doted on him, here was this creature who had taken his sisters away from the remnants of their family, who could spark violence in me with mere words, even if this was a reaction to his inhumane deed. Their world had been turned upside-down, as mine had been, but they were too young to understand, to comprehend the enormity of this barbaric act by their own father.

I could not fault Mo for his efforts. For his age, he was

being more of a man than his own father ever was. With Derek staying in the house, sleeping in Zana's and Nadia's old room, I felt a little better about being under the same roof as Fred, who seemed to show little or no conscience about what he had done.

The day dragged by, but the kids were a little happier now that I was at least semi-conscious and aware of my surroundings. For the first time in ages Ashia and Tina had gone to school but Mo stayed with me just in case I needed him. I sat on the sofa most of the day, as usual, thinking.

After what seemed an eternity, the kids came home and Ashia got their tea ready. Tina fussed around the house, tidying and polishing what Ashia already had made spick and span that morning before school while Tina had prepared breakfast. I told them to go out and see their friends, play up at the centre, or something.

They had obviously had a conference about it over their tea. It was decided that Tina would go and see her friends, Mo would go out to play footy, and Ashia would stay in with me until Derek came in. Ashia explained all this to me when she brought me a bowl of soft noodles and chicken sauce. She supervised while I ate as much as I could and then said that she wanted to talk to me. Lighting a cigarette, I puffed smoke into the air as she tried to talk about her other sisters, Zana and Nadia.

'Mom . . . I found the letter. It was in the bathroom. After Mo and the doctor kicked the door down to get you out, I cleaned all the hair out of the bathroom. I found this letter on the floor. I'm sorry Mom. I read it. I was so pleased to see Zana's writing. I couldn't understand why you had chopped off all your hair, though. I tried not to read it, I really did. I wish that I hadn't now, in a way.'

She reached into her pocket and took out the letter. She handed it to me. It was crumpled up and battered, but the message was still as potent as ever. I could not find any words to explain, or give comfort to her. I looked at her face. It was older than I remembered. I was sure that she could not have aged so in just a few months. It had affected her badly. I could see that now. Why could Fred not see that too? Or didn't he care?

'I miss them, Mommy!' she sobbed into my arms.

Chapter Sixteen

Tina, Ashia and Mo were asleep, safely locked in their bedroom. After a good cry I felt a little better but I had by no means forgotten the enormity of the situation. I didn't like the idea of the door being locked. I was aware of the nightmares that Ashia was having. She would whimper and call out in her sleep, unable to wake because of the medication prescribed by her doctor. It was a Catch 22 situation, sedation or no sleep. And she needed rest. Could the dreams really be as bad as the reality? There was nothing to be done when she called out. We all felt so helpless and vulnerable, trapped in a living nightmare. There it was again. Ashia calling out to Zana and Nadia. A cold feeling lingered in the pit of my stomach. I turned on the television for the first time in ages, feeling guilty about trying to drown out the sound of Ashia's moans.

John Lennon had been shot dead and there had been some sort of tribute to him in Liverpool. I wondered if people would feel the same about my kids if they knew. Bombs had been going off in London and the people that they had caught and imprisoned for it had escaped from Brixton Prison. Again I thought of Zana and Nadia trying to escape from their prison in Yemen.

Time quickly passed as, locked in these thoughts, I worried about the children who had been taken from me by their evil, scheming father.

Someone was in the room. Watching me.

I turned round. It was him. Muthana. Revulsion passed through my body, and anger competed to take over. He staggered across the lounge towards me. I could smell the alcohol before he got within four feet of me. I was petrified. All I could do was look at this pathetic excuse for a man as he swayed before me.

'I've been out!'

His half-closed eyes blinked slowly as he licked his lips. With his hands in his pockets he adjusted his pelvis left and right, back and forth to keep his balance. He belched. The gust of stale breath almost took my breath away. Saliva trickled down his chin from the left corner of his mouth. He took his hand from his pocket and wiped the sleeve of his jacket across the slimy trail on his face. His hand went back to his pocket.

'Why, Fred?' I could hardly speak.

'Why? Why? Huh!' Fred sniggered at me. 'What kind of wife are you, that a man has to go to – to a strip club to have fun?' He belched loudly. 'You know what they did? Oil. Baby oil. Took everything off. *Everything*. We put the oil on them ourselves. Slipped all over, they did!'

He leered as his hands escaped from his pockets to demonstrate how he had applied oil to the breasts of the strippers. He laughed and gulped air at the same time. I thought he was going to throw up.

'Then we went home with them. And they did it again. Walked round and round with nothing on. Let us touch whatever we wanted. Beautiful!' His eyes rolled lasciviously as he trailed his hands over his body.

'Touched them all night! *Everywhere*!' He lolled his tongue and laughed lewdly. He raised his hand to his face, sniffed at his fingers, laughing hysterically as I cringed. I felt sick.

'It's only . . . baby oil, I think!' He sniffed again. 'Yeah!'

I clenched my fists in frustration. 'Why did you do it? To Zana and Nadia?'

'Bah, why?' His mood changed; darker, more foreboding. 'What kind of mother are you, letting them talk to black men? I ain't gonna let *my* girls be whores, with blacks sniffing around them. Huh! Let the white women around here be the whores, like those tonight!'

Again his mood changed. He became maudlin. 'You know, all those years, I kept you pregnant just to tie you down? You gave me nothing but *girls*, cost me money for husbands. Lots of it. I got round that! But you can't even have babies now can you? So what's the use of you to me now? Look at you. A mess! You can't be a mother. I got lucky with them two. Now they have gone and they ain't coming back here. Gonna send Mo out as soon as he is old enough to be in the Army. After Ashia and Tina!'

'I have spent their whole life being a mother to them, Fred.'

'You ain't no mother, Miriam. You couldn't be a mother. Or a wife! Look at this shop. Nothing but blacks everywhere.'

'You stupid bastard! It's your shop, you chose to bring us here. There's nothing wrong with the girls' friends, they are all nice people, coming in your shop to fill your pockets. You can't choose the girls' friends! No more than they could have chosen their father!'

'Oh, feeling brave are you? Calling me names, arguing with *me*!'

Muthana walked across the room and jammed a high-backed chair against the door knob, effectively locking us in and the kids out of the room.

'What are you doing?' I hissed at him. I was frightened.

He turned to face me, staggered a little, them sauntered across the room. I recognised the leer on his face, although I had never seen him quite as crude as this before. I tried to think. I had to get him to respond to my questions about Zana and Nadia.

I reached into my pocket and pulled the letter free. 'Look at this. Zana wants to kill herself. She said Abdul Khada wanted to ask you to send her home for a while, but Gowad warned him you would be angry. Why, Fred? I want them home. *Now!* Both of them!'

'Shut up! Who cares about them? They are out of your life now. Forget them. You should be worried about pleasing me. Now you can't have babies you will have to make up for it – in some other way. I had to go to prostitutes to have a little fun. Call yourself my wife? Huh!'

He was close now, leaning towards me, his beery breath engulfing me. I sat, terrified, on the sofa. He came closer and held out his hand. I slapped at it furiously, hoping he would go away. Instead he pulled me up, his good thumb and middle finger around my throat. I fought him off, pushing him to the floor. He grabbed at my dressing-gown in a vain effort to save his fall, pulling the material apart, tearing it down its length. As I stared disbelievingly at his prostrate form I was aware of banging on the door and Mo's frantic calling.

Muthana sniggered. 'Make one more sound and I'll make him watch. He will need to know how a man has sex soon!'

I could not believe my ears. He reached up and tore the rest of the gown from me. I yelped in horror.

'Mom! Mom!' Mo was banging again.

I looked down at Muthana.

He sneered at me. 'I mean it, Miriam!'

'It's all right, Mo, it's the TV. I'll turn it off. Go and get some sleep. I'm OK.' I tried to reassure him, for his own sake.

'Mom, can I stay in your room?'

'No, Mo. Go and look after Ashia and Tina, please. I want to be alone.'

'Aw, Mom!' The disappointment was evident in his voice.

'Take your clothes off! All of them!' Muthana growled deeply.

I had only ever done that once or twice, in the early years. After that he was just too eager to wait until I was undressed. Now, after all this time, he wanted me to strip before him. I was riveted to the spot.

'Take them off, now, else I go and get Mo!'

Well, if he thought I was going to make this into some fantasy trip, he was mistaken. I flung my nightie into a heap on the floor, contemptuously. His eyes travelled over my body, settling on the scar from the operation to sterilise me. He reached out and touched the scarred flesh. Instinctively I slapped his hand away. He laughed and touched it again. I went to slap at his hand again when, suddenly, he grabbed my hand by the wrist and pulled me sharply to the floor, rolling me over onto my back and jumping on top of me immediately in a quick movement.

I scrunched my eyes shut and clenched my fists at my side. I lay rigid on the floor as he indulged himself, crying out in his pleasure as I cried out in my shame.

It was over. He rolled off me and I crawled away to collect my torn and crumpled dressing-gown. I tried to pick it up. My hands hurt. Looking at them I realised that I had dug my nails into my palms with such force that they were bleeding in eight little half-moon shapes across the flesh of both hands. I pulled the cloth of my gown around me and staggered to the door. It was still jammed shut. I struggled with the chair, pulling at it.

'What are you doing? Where do you think you are going?' he hissed.

At last the chair was free. I opened the door and glared back at him.

'To get Derek, you bastard!'

Muthana leaped up, drunkenness forgotten, and flew across the room.

I held the chair out in front of me. 'One more step, Fred, and I swear . . .'

'Swear what?'

'I'll kill you.'

I spoke quietly, slowly. It was the first time I had ever answered him back, let alone threatened him. But I meant it and he could see that. He backed off and let me go. I walked steadily out of the room, into the hallway, making for the stairs and Derek.

Before I had got to the third step, Muthana was away down the other stairs leading to the shop. I listened to the sounds of the house and heard the bolts being thrown back on the main shop door. He was in the street now, away into the night, no doubt to the sanctuary of his friends.

I hurried down to the foot of the stairs and stopped at the

door, listening for any sound, in case Muthana had tricked me. For several moments I held my breath as I listened intently. Nothing. I flicked on the light and scanned the area for movement. Cautiously I tiptoed across the shop to the door and threw myself against the cold wood, slamming it shut with my body weight. I bolted it top and bottom, clicked the latch so that even the key could not get the door open from outside and secured the safety chain. The floor was cold on my bare feet and I realised that I was practically naked, save for the scant cover of the now-tattered dressing-gown. I went to the back door and did the same thing, locking us in and everyone else out.

I needed a bath. I felt so very dirty and degraded. I made my way back upstairs to the bathroom. I regretted not having a lock on the door but I felt fairly safe now anyway. The shower was steaming hot and I gasped as I stepped under it. It was only then that the tears were allowed to flow, mixing with the water of the shower, along with my sobs. I stayed in the shower for over two hours, just sitting in the tub and letting the overhead water cascade over me, cleaning my abused body, washing him away, washing away his touch and the awful smell of him.

Eventually, exhausted, I turned off the water and climbed out to dry myself. I wrapped the remnants of my gown around me and went to the kitchen to make myself a pot of tea. I needed a cigarette and I didn't have any. I crept up to Derek's room, silently slipping the door open. I needn't have bothered. He wasn't there. I bit my lip, thanking God himself that I had not called out for Derek's help. I could imagine what Muthana would have done if I had called Derek and Muthana had discovered that he was away for the night. He certainly would not have run for it.

I switched on the light and looked around. The room was just as Zana and Nadia had left it, with the exception of a few things which belonged to Derek. It still smelled of the girls. I breathed in the essence of the room, the essence of Zana and Nadia.

I would get them back. I vowed it to the empty room. Their room. I vowed that I would get them back even if it cost me my life. Somewhere deep in my heart, I knew it probably would not come any cheaper than just that – my life.

Chapter Seventeen

I slept in that room for the rest of the night. With the vast collection of reggae records and trinkets. With Nadia's football paraphernalia and mountains of denim jeans; Zana's Mills & Boon library and heaps of read and re-read magazines. I felt somehow closer to them in here. Ashia and Tina had been cleaning the room. They would never have thrown anything away, but they had made sure it was polished and hoovered. I think that they, too, used to spend a few quiet moments in the room.

Mo came and found me, telling me that Tina had made me tea. They were all curious as to why I had actually moved from the sofa in the lounge. I followed Mo down to the kitchen and sat down at the table. Ashia came up behind me.

'Mom, you left this in the lounge. You really should be careful with this, it could be important. What if Dad gets to know about it?'

She handed me the letter. Thank goodness the kids had no idea of what happened to me last night. But that was precisely what Fred was banking on. My silence.

Soon enough it was time for the girls to go to school, leaving Mo home with me. I hated him missing school but

I was also glad of his company. Derek came home around midday and we sat at the table together in the kitchen, talking. We were still talking when Mo announced that Nadia's social worker was at the door. Derek excused himself and went out with Mo for some fresh air. I didn't feel much like chatting to a social worker just then.

Mary Burchell was a small woman with mousy blonde hair, dead straight with a fringe nearly hiding her bright eyes; a warm and friendly person who oozed confidence and informal professionalism. She sat at the table and prattled away. I just nodded in the appropriate places and added a few grunts and groans for good measure. It was just a matter of time before she would ask me where the hell Nadia was. She had come to counsel Nadia, as set down by the orders of the court as part of her fine for 'stealing' that blasted ring. I was trying to think of a way of telling Mary about the trip to Yemen, their supposed marriage and the fact that Fred said that they were not allowed to come home. She had been droning on and obviously I had made a polite groan in an inappropriate place. She knew now that I had not heard a word.

Gently, she placed her hand on my arm. 'Miriam. Miriam, listen to me. Miriam!'

Slowly I looked her in the eyes. Her eyebrows knotted as she frowned at me.

'Miriam, I've been talking to you now for over fifteen minutes and you haven't heard a word I've said, just like on my last two visits!'

'Last two visits?' Had she come before?

'Uh-huh. I have been here three times now and each time I've seen you deteriorating more and more.'

'I – I don't remember. You came before?' I had no recollection of it whatsoever.

'Well, you take my word for it, dear, and if that's not good enough, ask your Ashia and Tina. Listen, that's not so important at the moment: what concerns me is you.' She squeezed my arm. 'I know that there is something wrong, Miriam. Has it something to do with Nadia and Zana not returning from their holiday yet? You don't have to tell me if you don't want to, but you might find it makes you feel a little better and a problem shared is a problem halved. Won't you tell me, Miriam?'

She looked so concerned. Could I tell her? Could I find the words? Could she help? I was taking my time thinking about this.

'Miriam, look at yourself. You look like a refugee from Belsen. How much weight have you lost? Look at your hair! Look at Ashia! Please Miriam, tell me, what the hell is going on?'

I took a deep breath. The whole story poured out. Nothing was omitted. I told it as it happened. I watched the look of deep concern on Mary's face turn to one of shock and horror.

For a long time she was silent, taking it all in, digesting it, analysing the facts. I jumped a mile when she thumped the kitchen table, suppressed anger in her voice. 'My dear God! I can't believe this, Miriam. Are you sure, dear, are you really sure?'

How could I prove it? Fred would never confess to someone like Mary. It was a little difficult to contact Zana and Nadia to confirm my story. But there was a way. I reached into my pocket and handed her Zana's letter. She unfolded the worn pieces of paper on the kitchen table. I lit a cigarette and watched her read the letter, her eyes widening in disbelief and amazement.

After reading it a second time, she put the letter on the

94

table and meticulously straightened the edges, her mind on its contents. She was silent. I thought for one horrible moment that she would have about as much of an idea of what to do as I had – none!

'You need a cup of tea!' she decided. 'And so do I.'

I started to get up. Mary held up her hand. 'Oh no, my dear, I'll see to it. You take it easy.' She walked across the kitchen and busied herself with the kettle.

'You need to get Ashia, Tina and Mo on your passport, Miriam. Do you have a passport?' Mary was looking out of the window, across the loading area of the shop, seeing nothing.

'No, I don't have a passport!'

'I'll go and pick up an application form from the Post Office and we'll fill it in today and send it off. You will need a passport photograph of yourself, and I should imagine it will have to be endorsed by your doctor to say that it is an accurate likeness. We will have this cuppa and we'll go and get it all wrapped up. That's the first thing to do. Secondly, I think we should make an appointment to see your local MP. Maybe he can help.'

'Who is my local MP?' I was raring to go.

'Roy Hattersley. He has a surgery in Sparkhill which covers Sparkbrook. We can get the number from the library. We will do that on the way home from the doctor's.' Mary stirred the tea and brought it across to the table.

'You will need to get the kids' birth certificates, of course, for the passports. Do you have them at hand, Miriam?'

I nodded. I knew where they were. It was not all that long since I had done the same for Zana's and Nadia's passports. I went into the lounge and took them from the centre drawer in the cabinet. I gave them to Mary, not trusting myself to be able to look after them until we had completed the task in hand. She put them in her bag.

'What about yours, Miriam? Where is your certificate?'

'Jesus, Mary. I don't have one. I never have.' I slumped into the kitchen chair, put my elbows on the table and cradled my head in my hands.

'Not to worry, Miriam. We can get a copy from the Registry Office. You were born around here, weren't you?'

I nodded.

'Well then, there is no problem.'

She smiled. It warmed my heart. Thank God for Mary Burchell. At last I had hope, and she was the source of that vital commodity.

After gathering all the relevant information, we set off in Mary's car to get the forms and the photos. Next we went to see my doctor. The people in the waiting room just stared at me, as if they feared I was going to throw a fit at any moment. They probably thought I was a mental patient. No disrespect intended, I certainly looked the part.

The receptionist called my name. The doctor gasped aloud as I went into the surgery. The first thing he did was make me stand on his scales. 'Miriam, you have lost over three stone. This is not good. Do you know that you just tip the scales at six stone? I must insist that you take care of yourself. I know the position you are in, but if you lose your good health you will not be able to survive to fight the battle. Is that understood?'

He insisted on giving me a thorough check-up, prescribing vitamins and tonics, before he would even consider looking at my passport photo. He called Mary into the office and spoke at length to the two of us. He was very concerned for

Ashia and myself. Mary voiced the opinion that I should not stay in the house with Muthana and the doctor gave his full agreement. He added that he wanted to see me again in one week; Ashia, too.

From the surgery to the library, where we picked up the contact address for Roy Hattersley and a list of housing associations. One was really close by, so Mary took me to make a personal application there and then, so that she could support my need for urgent rehousing.

I admired Mary Burchell so much. I know that if it had not been for her professionalism and cool confidence, I would have remained a zombie, sitting in my home, fretting for the kids, but not actually doing anything, because I had no idea of what to do. I knew something else, too. If it had not been for Mary Burchell, I would have probably died, either by my own hand, or by burning out completely.

Chapter Eighteen

I had a lot to look forward to now. I found myself coping a little better, armed with the hope that Mary had given me – and my diazepam tranquillisers. Every morning I looked forward to receiving something in the post, either my passport or a letter from the Housing Association to say we had been given a new home. Ashia was a little better; seeing me hopeful of getting the girls home and safe and us away from Muthana helped enormously.

Eventually a letter did arrive, but not from the Housing people, nor the Passport Office. It was from Zana.

Mo gave it to me in the kitchen and suggested I should be careful as his father was about. Regardless of this, I opened it and leaned against the kitchen sink to read it. Ashia and Tina were with me in the kitchen. Ashia put the washing away and Tina disengaged the ironing board, leaning it against the pantry door, eager to hear me read the letter to them. I scanned it first to see if it was in the same vein as the last one.

'Well, read it, Mom!' Tina insisted. 'We want to know everything, good or bad.'

'Yes. Please, Mom. We miss them so much and we want

to know what is going on. It's not just you, you know. They are our sisters. Please read the letter, Mom!'

I suppose I really hadn't scanned the letter sufficiently. I had skimmed over the words, but they obviously hadn't registered, what with Ashia and Tina going on so. The letter started off fine. The usual greetings from Zana, with no mention of the last letter, no expressed disappointment at not being allowed home by her father.

I started to read the letter aloud. I stopped suddenly in horror. This letter was frightening. Zana knew of a Yemeni prostitute who had been talking to Muthana, via Gowad. She was on her way to the UK to get my Ashia and take her back to the Yemen. 'Look out for this woman, Mom, she means to get Ashia here, and Dad has said OK!'

Suddenly, the letter was torn from my hands. The girls recoiled, screaming. We had no idea that Muthana had come into the kitchen and heard me reading it to the girls. He backed across the kitchen, reading. His eyes widened as he realised the contents were damning for him and his dear friend Gowad. He stood there defiant, smirking, tearing the letter into ever smaller shreds. When he was apparently satisfied with the size of the shredding, he spoke. Coldly. Menacing utterances that chilled me to the bone.

'This is the last letter you will get from Zana. She is nothing but trouble. Gowad knows who her contact is and has been watching her, while Abdul Khada makes her feel safe. Clever, that! You will not be able to write to her. All your letters have been stopped at the Post Office by Gowad's agent. She is *not* coming back; nor is Nadia. Forget them, Miriam. I have legal marriage certificates and twenty Yemeni men as witnesses. I have also accepted money for them, so it's settled.'

I screamed in anguish. The girls were crying. It tore me to the very core of my soul. 'How could you? They are *my* babies! They are mine! They are your daughters. And you *sold* them?' I felt sick.

Muthana looked at me, smiling malevolently. 'Prove it!'

'I'm going to get them back. I will get them back!' I paced the floor.

He laughed. He was playing with me like a cat with a mouse. 'You try it, Miriam. There is nothing *you* can do. They have gone! As for Ashia . . .' he turned to her. 'Yes, you will be going to Yemen soon, very soon. I have arranged it all and there is nothing you can do about it, either.'

Ashia screamed. Tina put her arms protectively around her.

'I am their father.' He jabbed his chest. 'I want it this way. Ashia will join her sisters. Then Tina.'

Tina gasped. She clung to Ashia.

'Mo will stay with me until he is old enough to go into the Yemen Army. You can leave whenever you wish, you are of no use to me now; you never were. My daughters will obey me. They have no choice. It is all arranged. A woman will come for Ashia soon, so you had better get used to the idea. It is a little less expensive than me taking them all as I planned to do with my compensation.'

He laughed, then added: 'You didn't think they would be coming back with us, did you? Oh, no! I was going to take them all in one swoop. Never mind, it can still be done and it will be done, and you, English whore, can do nothing about it. Nothing!'

I heard a scream that was more like a growl. It must have been me. I grabbed the discarded ironing board and flew at Muthana. He turned to run, but with all my strength I swung the board at him and hit him full-force in the small of the back. The impact tore the board from my hands. It broke in two as it made contact with his flesh and bone. He screamed in pain and fell to the floor, writhing in agony. I leaped on top of him, hitting him again and again, tearing at his skin. Mo, Ashia and Tina were on top of me, pulling me away from him. They screamed and cried aloud as I fought them off to get at Muthana. They pleaded with me, gripping my arms, so I attacked with my feet, kicking his body as he lay helpless on the floor. I was in a frenzy, too scared to let him up, terrified that he would beat me to death. I wanted to finish the job while I had the upper hand, to save my kids from him and the Yemen. To save myself.

Suddenly I was lifted into the air. Derek tucked me firmly under his arm. All I could think of was the letter.

'Get the bloody letter! Get it!' I screamed.

Ashia dived on to Muthana's hand and prised the pieces free from his fingers. He grabbed her wrist as best he could with his damaged hand. She was transfixed by her own fear. 'You're next, Ashia! You're next!' he spat at her.

Ashia squealed in fear. Derek, still holding me aloft, stepped menacingly towards Muthana.

'Leave her be, Fred. I'm warning you. Let her go. *Now!*'

Muthana, with utter contempt for his daughter, threw her hand away from him and slumped to the floor.

'For now. For now!' I heard him muttering as Derek humped me out of the kitchen and into the lounge. He put me, none too gently, on the sofa and ushered in Tina, Ashia and Mo before slamming the door, closing out the sounds of Muthana's moans and groans.

I was still shaking with temper and trying to control myself as Ashia flew into my arms, crying hysterically. 'Don't let them take me Mom, please. Oh, don't let them take me too!'

Derek slumped into the armchair. He was as shaken as the rest of us. 'I think I had better keep a close eye on things here, for a while,' he decided.

For the next two weeks we were all on tenterhooks. Ashia wouldn't go out alone, for fear of someone grabbing her in the street and carrying her off to Yemen. I told Mary about the letter and that I had flipped and attacked Fred with an ironing board.

If ever I saw his face I would become instantly enraged. While we both tried to keep out of each other's way, inevitably there were times when we met. On one occasion we passed in the hall downstairs. He taunted me about Zana and Nadia, telling me to forget them. He said he had four of our seven children and, as sure as day, he was going to get Ashia soon, then Tina and Mo. I flew at him again but, from out of the blue, Derek appeared and held me off. In utter frustration, I hit out at the wall and went at it until my fists bled and the skin tore away from the bone, smearing the hallway with my blood and skin, all the while screaming like a wailing banshee, until I was exhausted. Derek managed to drag me off to settle down, somewhere well away from Muthana. But he got the message. He realised that what I did to the wall I could do to his face – and would, given the chance.

Derek did his utmost not to give me even half that chance, but he couldn't be there all the time.

Chapter Nineteen

The nightmare became so awful I woke up. I had been dreaming about Ashia and Tina being dragged off in a car being driven by Muthana to the airport. I was groggy because of the pills. They helped me to sleep but they did not stop me dreaming; in fact, they made it harder for me to pull myself from the deep slumber into the safety of being awake. I was always terrified that Muthana would make off with the kids while I slept.

It must have been about four o'clock. I was sitting in the dark waiting for one of the children to cough or something, so I would know that they were still there. I wasn't going to settle again until I was certain that all was well.

Hearing no noises, no sleep-talking, not even breathing, I left the sofa and crept across the floor of the lounge. Quietly, I slipped across to the kids' room. The door was open. My heart skipped a beat. I held my breath in fear. I stabbed at the door with my finger and silently it breezed open. Into the room, straining at the darkness, seeking the familiar outline of a sleeping child.

Tina coughed. I nearly jumped out of my skin, releasing my breath in a gasp as I crept to their beds. Tina was wriggling her sleeping body into a more comfortable position.

Ashia? I crept over to her bed and gently prodded the blankets. They moved in protest. I eased back the top blanket to reveal the tussled hair of a hot Ashia. I sighed with relief.

Mo? Where was Mo? *Where was Mo?*

The camp bed was empty, the sheets stone-cold. He hadn't been here for a long time.

I stormed up the stairs to Muthana's room and barged inside. I could smell booze, the stale smell of beer. On the bedside cabinet was a beer bottle, half full. He had been drinking again and now he was sleeping it off. I kept as quiet as I possibly could as I approached the bed. Cradled in his arms was Mo. I bent to lift Mo out of the bed.

Muthana grabbed my hand, making me yelp in surprise.

'Forget him too, Miriam. He is mine. I am going to take him to my parents as soon as my compensation comes through.'

'Over my dead body! Do you hear?'

'Yes, I hear.'

'Bastard!' I screamed at him. 'I swear, Muthana, you come near me or the kids, I will kill you.' I dragged Mo from the bed. 'I'll kill you!' I screeched again over my shoulder at Muthana as I fled from the room with Mo.

Outside Ashia and Tina were waiting on the landing, hugging each other as they peered through the darkness to try to see what was happening.

'Lounge – quick!' I shouted. They scurried in as I flung a shocked and disorientated Mo to them. I rushed to the girls' room and hauled blankets and pillows off their beds, dragging them into the lounge. I jammed the door shut behind me and then barricaded us in with the heavy old oak sideboard, panic increasing my strength.

I sat there, trembling, looking at my shaking hands, clenching and unclenching my fists, trying to steady them.

'How did I get into his bed, Mom?' Mo was visibly shaken.

It had been all too easy for Muthana to creep into the bedroom, sneak Mo out and get him to his own room without even waking the boy. Was he trying to take my mind as well as my children?

Ashia and Tina cried themselves to sleep. Mo sat staring into the night through the lounge window. He was silent for a whole hour, then he suddenly announced that he had seen Muthana leave the shop and walk down the street. Peace of mind restored, he curled up in the chair and fell asleep within moments.

I sat awake for the rest of the night, guarding the children in case their father returned, watching them in their fitful sleep. They were scared. How could Muthana be so cruel? Why? Why?

We couldn't carry on like this. The kids were shattered and scared out of their wits. We would go to my sister Ellen. At least there we could get a good night's sleep. We left immediately they woke. We didn't stop for breakfast – we wanted to be away.

Ellen and I had been talking seriously all day and now, as evening drew in, we began to settle the children down to watch a little television before dozing. Mo lay on the floor in front of the TV, sleeping. I didn't know how he had managed to stay awake for so long.

My eyes burned with fatigue; my body felt strange, alien. Ellen poured a beer as we condemned Muthana, Gowad and Abdul Khada.

There was a knock at the door. We sat in silence as we strained our ears for voices. Ellen was renting rooms in this house, which belonged to an Arab friend of hers. She was expecting Saif, her husband, and presumed that the other occupier of the house had opened the door.

It was Saif all right. With Muthana.

Ellen went crazy. 'Why have you brought him here, Saif?'

Saif had no idea of what had happened over the past few months. Ellen got up, tugged his arm and dragged him to her other room to fill him in on a few details.

Muthana plonked himself down in her chair, grinning and leering at us. I could find no words to express my anger or contempt for him. It got worse by the minute. The girls sat silently on the sofa; Mo still slept on the floor just feet away from Muthana. Muthana turned on the girls, telling them that their mother was mad, insane, only good for one thing – sex.

I began to shake uncontrollably as the girls began to cry.

'Shut up crying and you' – he leered at me, adjusting the crotch of his trousers – 'get in the bed!' He swiped Ellen's beer bottle and drank straight from it.

I stared at him. He was sick. Evil!

'Get in the bed, now!' He wiped the dribble from his mouth with the back of his hand, put the bottle down and, sitting forward in the chair, snapped his fingers and pointed to the makeshift bed on the floor at the back of the room.

I really didn't know what to do. I was concerned for the children but I couldn't have a repetition of what had happened only days ago.

'The kids . . .' I started to protest.

'No matter about the kids. They will be doing this themselves in just a short while. When they all go to

Yemen! Don't worry about taking off any clothes, Miriam. This won't take long. Get in the bed or else!'

'Or else what, you sick pig?' I spat.

'Or else I take you right here!' Muthana put his hands on the arms of the chair, to haul himself up.

Moving like lightning I grabbed the beer bottle and in a sweeping arc smashed it into the side of his head.

Glass, beer and blood sprayed all over Mo, jerking him from his slumber. He screamed, thinking it was his own blood, then realised it was his father's. He screamed again. I grabbed his hand and pulled him away.

Muthana cradled his damaged head in his hands. Blood oozed between those fingers he had left. The light caught the tiny shards of glass, bringing them to life with a hundred glistening twinkles. He groaned softly. I watched him suffer, gloating over it.

Ellen and Saif came running in, responding to the sound of breaking glass and the screams of the children. Their horror at what they saw quickly spread across their faces. Ellen rushed at me and the kids, took Tina and Ashia by the hand and told me to get Mo.

I stood rigid.

'Quick!'

Her shout moved me. I pulled Mo and ran after her to the other room, where she locked us in for safety.

'Saif, get rid of Muthana,' she yelled through the door.

We cried long and hard. There was still to be no peaceful sleep for my kids. Again, I sat awake and guarded them from their father.

In the small hours of the night Ellen and Saif came to the room. They told me that Saif had taken Muthana to friends who would take him to hospital. He was hurt pretty badly. 'Not badly enough!' I muttered, unconcerned.

Early the next morning we returned home. I had to find a way out of this nightmare. I felt as if we were all in a maze, lost and confused. We went into the lounge and I hauled my makeshift barricade back into place. It seemed like hours later when Mary Burchell came round. She was rather taken aback to find us all barricaded in and horrified when she was told what had been going on. After the whole story had been gone over with corroboration from the children she insisted I go with her to see my doctor. Right away.

In a fit of tears I went over the latest events for the doctor's benefit. 'Please, Doctor, help me get out of there before I kill someone, either Muthana or myself! I can't stand it any longer.'

He gave me a prescription for more tablets and then, in front of Mary and myself, he wrote an emphatic letter to the Housing Association.

Chapter Twenty

Muthana had had another accident. He had been out, drunk as usual, when a car had hit him full-force. The impact had broken both of his legs, splintering the bones. The ambulance brought him home, both his legs in plaster, after hospital treatment.

I grinned. Serves him right! I thought, while silently cursing the driver for not going the whole way and killing him, though not until he had suffered excruciating pain and agony.

I had absolutely no sympathy for him. I cursed him for having nine lives, like a cat. On the contrary, I drew comfort from knowledge that he could not steal off into the night with another one of my kids. Nor would he be stealthily sneaking around the house in the dead of the night to take Mo out of the house to the waiting arms of the Yemen Army. Muthana was out of my face for the time being and I could breathe easily for a little while.

But it didn't last long enough. They say the Devil has all the luck. Muthana became quite adept at hobbling around on crutches. I wouldn't go near him; nor would the kids. It wasn't too long at all before he was up and about again, to my utter chagrin. Maybe I would have to grease the stairs and finish the bastard!

Each time I saw him I would launch an immediate attack on him. He, in return, would taunt me to distraction. I was more scared of myself now, so totally consumed with rage that my tranquillisers proved inadequate. Or was I under their influence enough to have some control at least? A frightening thought. He was pathetic, hung-over for much of the time. Should our paths cross in the hallway or the kitchen he would set me off by giving that lopsided half-smirk and try to block my way past him, so that I would have to acknowledge his presence. And that inane look on his face really got to me. I would verbally attack him then, and he would counter the attack with threats to Ashia, Tina and Mo, and sing his own praises about how clever he was to get Laila, Ahmed, Zana and Nadia, especially Zana and Nadia. I wondered if this apparent death wish of his was for his own demise or if he was trying to push me into a heart attack.

The only real concern he ever showed was over Mary Burchell's involvement. His face would darken and deep lines would crease his brow in a frown when she appeared. To him she represented authority. He hated authority. It intimidated him. And worse, of course, Mary was female authority. I wondered if Muthana had done all this because of Nadia's court case. But how could he, when he himself had been through the courts – although in his case, justifiably. It wouldn't account for Zana, either. I decided it was not worth the effort to try to account for his actions. Only he could ever give the true reason. Still, he was afraid of Mary.

Muthana and I were midway through a massive, explosive argument which was dangerously close to becoming a physical confrontation. He was enjoying teasing me with a little information – a rarity indeed. I would never get the girls: he had marriage certificates for them, issued in Birmingham. It was all legal and above board.

I didn't really think about what he had just said – I was intent on ripping his offending face off his head – but at that moment Derek put paid to any further contact between us, either verbal or physical, by collecting me from the corner that Muthana had me in and hauling me into the kitchen to speak to Mary.

I had had no idea that Derek and Mary were in the house; nor had Muthana. I could tell by the expression on his face that he was wondering what they'd overheard. I gleaned some satisfaction from seeing him squirm with regret at losing control of his big mouth. Still, I would have liked to rip his lips off.

It took me several cups of tea and at least four cigarettes to calm down. Why didn't that damned house come through? Someone was going to end up dead the way things were going.

Mary was silent for a long time. Although she knew what had been going on she was shocked at the scene she had walked into, and she was scared for me, scared that I might lose control totally. No more scared than I was! She wanted to tell me something, out of Muthana's hearing. Derek, at her request, looked up the hallway to see if he was lurking. It was all clear.

'I've got good news, Miriam. The Housing Association phoned today to say that I could collect the keys for you. I took the liberty of picking them up before I came round.' She opened her bag and put them on the table. Two lovely silver keys, held together with a piece of string with a brown tag attached. In neat black print on the tag was salvation – our new address in King's Heath.

I was so pleased. My first thought was that her announcement might be news about the kids, however . . . 'Mary. I'm going to move – now!'

'Wait up there, Miriam. How are you going to arrange that? I don't have a car!' Derek spoke softly, keeping his vigilance at the kitchen door. 'Besides, I think you would be better off biding your time.'

'What do you mean, biding my time?'

'Well, wait until he goes out. One of his cronies will be here later to take him to the pub or whatever. You'd better wait until he goes out and leave before he returns. It might be better for the kids, you know. He'll only make a fuss, make the kids feel uncomfortable by having another go at you or something.'

He was right. I nodded my agreement. 'Yes, but how will I move?'

'Henry's got a car. I'll go and see him later today. OK?'

'Now! Will you go see him now?' I wanted Derek to see our brother as soon as possible, so that I could relax a bit.

'Right this very moment, if it makes you feel better. Back soon!' He winked and left.

Derek seemed to take forever but, in reality, he was gone just over a couple of hours. We sat in the kitchen waiting for Muthana to be collected by one of his buddies and taken out for the night.

Mary had to leave before teatime. She gave us her best wishes for success, and said she would give us a couple of days to settle in and would come around at the start of the next week.

I couldn't do a thing until Muthana had gone out. I made mental lists of what we'd be taking with us and sent Derek out to buy some large black bin-liners to carry the stuff in. To Henry's consternation, I paced up and down, up and down for a further two hours until this friend of Muthana's arrived, and then we had to wait in suspense for a further hour and a half while they sat talking over cups of tea. All the time I fingered the keys to my new home – and liberty.

Finally he was out of the house.

We didn't take a lot: a couple of single beds for the kids and our clothes; two saucepans, four bowls, four spoons, four mugs and an old kettle, an assortment of bed linen and some of the stuff that Zana and Nadia had left behind. Finally, I grabbed their birth certificates, my passport and our medical cards from their hiding-place and stuffed them in my bag along with the two letters Zana had managed to get through. Henry and Derek tied the beds to the roof-rack on the small Escort and somehow crammed the rest of the stuff inside.

Derek organised a taxi so that the kids and I could follow him and Henry. Within an hour of Muthana going out, I was finished and eager to leave. We got into the taxi and I gave the address.

Our new home.

I put the key in the lock and opened the door. 'We are home, kids! Safe!' I swallowed back a few tears. The children tore inside to explore.

The house was smaller than I had expected, but even so it was a palace to us. Ashia was running round the back garden, letting the cold January night air blow through the house. It blew out the damp smell of emptiness. Outside, on the the main road, Derek and Henry were trying to

113

undo the sophisticated knots they had managed to tie to offload the two single beds.

Mo found a cleverly concealed door which led upstairs to three bedrooms and a bathroom. Tina charged up the stairs after him to claim her room before he could claim his. All in all, it was a good house; not just for its design, size and location, but for its meaning to us: freedom. The kids were ecstatic. I had an enormous feeling of relief, a feeling I shared with my three children upstairs. A great weight had been lifted from our shoulders. We might not have had anything to sit on, or eat from – hell, we didn't even have a cooker – but this was our home, and Muthana would never cross our threshold.

Henry stayed the night, sleeping on the bare floorboards in the front room. Derek went back to the shop to pack his own things. He didn't feel it was right to stay there now: it was time for him to move on. He would stay with me for a while but he would now spend more time looking for his own place.

For the first time in God knows how long I slept deeply.

The very next morning I went the the local Social Security Office and applied for income support. They gave me a grant for a cooker and a three-piece suite and a couple of clothing grants, which we used for curtains. Within a week, the skeleton of our home had a bit of meat on its bones.

The kids quickly settled into a new school, the final year for Ashia, and we were all comparatively happy. Now I could concentrate on getting Zana and Nadia home. Mary Burchell came round to see us the following week. She was surprised at how quickly we had adapted to our new surroundings. With peace of mind restored we set about writing to the Foreign Office and seeing Roy Hattersley. Together we wrote a lengthy letter to the head of the Consular Division at the Foreign Office. All we had to do now was wait. It could only be a matter of time.

Chapter Twenty-One

It was nearing the end of November 1982. I must have written a thousand letters by then to various authorities and organisations. The response was always the same heart-breaking answer: the girls were considered Yemeni and would only be permitted to return with their 'husbands'.

I lost count of the letters I had written to Zana and Nadia. I was still writing to the PO box number I had been given, hoping that the letters would get through, despite Muthana's claim that he had alerted Gowad and Abdul Khada to warn their agent to stop all contact with the girls. I had to hope that one would get through. I had no way of knowing if that would ever happen. Was Muthana's boasting true? And even if it were not, could the girls write back if I was lucky enough to get a letter through to them? Waiting and surmising was the worst part. If I wanted to get a parcel to them for Christmas, I would have to post it soon. No matter what Muthana said, I felt a whole lot better if I tried to maintain some form of contact.

It was half-past ten. Tina and Mo were safely tucked up in their beds, sleeping soundly. Now I could slip out to the phone box across the road and phone my sister Ellen. She knew people from Yemen so maybe, if anyone was going home soon, they could take the parcel out to the girls. Ashia was still up and I enlisted her help to find a coin for the call. It took us ages to find a 10p piece. I didn't have a single coin in my purse. After tipping out the entire contents of my bag on the front-room floor, I found a toffee-encrusted coin in the lining of my bag. I cleaned it up.

'I won't be long,' I told Ashia as I went out. It was 10.45 p.m.

I rang Ellen's number and heard her answer the phone, but just as I said 'Hello' the phone went dead. 'Damn it!' I cursed the phone aloud, slamming the receiver into the cradle. Now I would have to call the operator and tell her that this coin box had just eaten my only coin. I dialled the three numbers.

There was a screech of tyres and the phone box filled with bright, blinding light. An enormous bang vibrated through my body. Then a raging sea, the crash of waves, the roar of the angry surf hitting rocks; spray splashing my face, its pin-sharp droplets embedding in my flesh, melting and trickling down my face. I was tossed on a sea of colours, swirling and psychedelic patterns. I fought against the strong currents. There was a mighty crash and pounding footsteps. The sounds of the sea faded into murmuring voices. For a few moments I wondered if I had died, but the pain told me I hadn't.

A woman was speaking as she gently put a coat around my shoulders. I was sitting on the pavement. I looked around me. I knew then that I'd been hit. I had been blasted through the closed door of the cast-iron telephone box. Glass was embedded in my skin; my right kneecap flapped beside my leg, wrapped in torn ligaments and bloodied flesh. The woman was still talking soothingly.

'Please tell my kids!' I pleaded with her, giving her my house number.

Then the police arrived. They had heard the crash from a quarter of a mile away and had gunned into immediate action. Something trickled down my face. 'What's that?' I asked the policeman.

'That's nothing, love, don't you worry about that. There's an ambulance on its way.'

Ashia came screaming down the road and the copper had to keep her from throwing herself at me. She shrieked when she saw the state of me, but all I could do was clench my fists at the pain in my leg.

The ambulance arrived. The medics inflated a plastic bag and placed it under my leg for support. I was wracked with pain. Ashia ran back to the house and asked the neighbours to watch over Mo and Tina until one of my brothers came. She returned to come with me in the ambulance.

When we got to the hospital, the doctor decided that I needed an immediate operation. I had fourteen stitches in my face, starting from the very corner of my right eye. My kneecap had been crushed and fragments of bone were inside my flesh. The pain was incredible. I was so lucky, he said. Yes, I thought, I was very lucky.

I woke late the next day to find my leg in a half-cast suspended from a traction unit. In the afternoon, a policeman came to take a statement. He told me that the booth had been hit by a car. The person driving was, so far, eluding them but a bag had been found in the back of the abandoned car. The phone box was completely crushed to the ground. He took a few details from me and said he had taken statements from the people who had rushed to my aid. Ellen, my sister, was with the kids.

He assured me she would look after them until I got out of hospital.

On the third day the policeman came again. They had the driver of the car in custody. He had gone to the station and confessed to having 'hit and run', colliding with both me and the phone box, and leaving the scene of the crime.

The policeman was so nice. 'Now we have apprehended the man, you can instruct your solicitor to initiate the compensation claim.'

My jaw dropped. 'Compensation?'

'Yes. You can claim on his insurance for compensation. We have all the details at the station. You rest up a while and when you are ready your solicitor can contact the station for the details. We will do all we can to help. Hit and run is a serious offence, especially when so much damage is caused. You should get a pretty penny for this.' He smiled and excused himself.

I didn't even see him go. All I could see was a chance created by my predicament – finally a chance to get Zana and Nadia out of Yemen and back home.

Time flew. I was in a world of my own, wondering how much money I would get. The pain had somehow reduced to a fraction of what it had been as I planned a trip to Yemen to get my girls. Hope was a powerful medicine. Then the doctor came and told me that he would have to keep me in hospital. I was mortified. I gave him a brief explanation of just why he was wrong to keep me there, trussed up and helpless in a bed, when I could be doing so much to get to my kids. He was sympathetic and made me promise to rest up if he let me go home.

I gave him every assurance but I think we both knew I couldn't keep that promise. I was given painkilling 'bombs'

119

which I could take when my knee played up too much. Another addition to my cocktail of drugs. Tranquillisers, sleeping tablets and now painkillers!

Back at home, Derek and Henry had brought a bed down to the front room for me. The girls fussed around me. The problem was that the only loo was upstairs. I had to shuffle up each step, one at a time, on my rear end, and bump back down again. Carpet burns on my backside were a trivial but relentless pain in the rear, so to speak.

I was in that plaster cast for three months before I could get out to the solicitor's to initiate a claim. They hoped to have the whole thing finished with by the end of the year. I thought that was an awfully long time to wait and wished things would hurry along, but with the insurance company insisting on various medical reports and photographs and claiming, quite reasonably, that they would have to wait a while to see if I suffered any long-term damage as this would be reflected in the offer of compensation, it could take even longer than that. In the meantime I busied myself with writing to Mr Cantwell of Defence for Children and the Foreign Consulate Officer, the Yemen government and the girls in Yemen.

Mary Burchell had been writing to Mr Cantwell in Geneva. She had done this in her own time, not her employer's, although they had found him for us. Mr Cantwell was fantastic, giving me much hope. He tried to approach both governments. The well-worn answer came back: the girls were dual nationals. He was the first of many to point out that in fact they were British and nothing else.

A whole year passed and still I had heard nothing positive. Nothing from the girls, nothing from the FCO, nothing from the insurance company. Was there anybody out there? Why was it all taking so long? Time was ticking away. Each day the girls would have lost another day of their life, suffered a day longer. I was becoming frantic and totally despondent at the length of time that it was all taking.

Mr Cantwell got the Red Cross to go into Yemen to visit the girls. They were so very nearly successful until, halfway into Mokbana they were turned back by police command 'on government orders'!

In my own way, I tried to exert as much pressure as possible at every opportunity which presented itself. I felt as if I were climbing a mountain which had been smeared with grease. Slowly, methodically, I would launch my assault. Sometimes I would gain a foothold and precariously balance on the edge; other times I would slide down, plummeting towards a precipice. But no matter what, I would keep on climbing.

Chapter Twenty-Two

March 1984. I was still eagerly awaiting the compensation money for my accident. I had contacted Defence for Children in Geneva and asked them for advice on a visa application. I still intended to go to Yemen as soon as my compensation came through. They had warned me that it would not be an easy task, but conceded that it could be well worth a try. They gave me a few suggestions on how to obtain a visa when the time was right.

In the lull of the waiting Ann Sufi and I went to see Gowad to plead with his better nature. I had known him a long time, through Muthana. I expected him to be his usual courteous self. I believed at the time that Muthana had fooled him, as the rest of us had been fooled. I was wrong. I realised it the moment that Gowad opened the door. His face showed surprise at seeing us there, but that soon turned to an uncomfortable agitation in his manner and the way he spoke.

I came straight to the point. I told him that I had had a serious accident and was due compensation. I wanted to pay for tickets for Zana, Nadia and the two 'husbands' to come to England. There was no need for Gowad to concern himself with money. I would pay for everything. Let them come.

Gowad laughed in my face. 'They are not your daughters, Miriam. They are ours. Mine and Abdul Khada's. I paid good money for Nadia to bear children for my son, as Abdul Khada paid for Zana. They are nothing to do with you now. Why can't you understand that? Muthana knows this. He knew this when we struck our deal, he has no problem with this. You, on the other hand, seem not to accept it.'

'Gowad, I had no idea that you, Abdul Khada and Muthana were planning this. Do you think I would allow this? The sale of my own daughters?'

'What is it to do with you, Miriam? This is a man's business, nothing for a woman to concern herself with. Besides, it is none of my doing if Muthana had no talks with you.'

'You promised to look after them. You promised me that, Gowad!'

'Yes, yes, yes – and I am. So this is why you came? I am afraid you are wasting your time, Miriam. I have no intention of wasting all that money, or turning the events around against Muthana's wishes.'

Ann was in tears. 'OK, Gowad, if you are not going to help, we will do it all ourselves. You do what you want. Miriam will do it her way, then you can see what you will do. You and Muthana!'

'You can't do anything. You are only women. Anyway, a deal has been made. That is that! They are not even bargains, are they? No, they are nothing but trouble.'

'Then let us have them back. How much did you pay for them? I will give you your money back, and more if need be.'

123

'Muthana would be most upset. They will settle, even if we have to knock sense into them!'

'You lay one finger on them and . . . and . . .'

'And what, Miriam? I told you already, they belong to me and Abdul Khada. They should be having sons for us at any time.'

'I never thought you could be like this, Gowad. You were like an uncle to the girls.'

Gowad laughed. 'Well, now I'm an owner instead!'

There was little else I could do now other than wait for this compensation money. When we got back to my house Mo told us that his dad had had a letter from the girls and was bragging about it to all and sundry in the shop. I dismissed it as Muthana's lies and made for the kettle. After a little thought I decided it might be true – after all, they would have no idea I'd left – so I asked Mo and Tina if they would go to the shop, sneak up to their father's room and scout about for a letter with an address. If there was one, I could write to the girls and even have some idea of where they might live for when I went to get them out of Yemen.

They agreed to do this for me and their sisters. I reiterated that they should act with caution, taking the utmost care not to get caught. Mo, in a voice that had just broken, said it was no problem. Mo and Tina entered the shop. Their father was alone, and pretty busy, too. None of his pals were about. Mo and Tina had surprised him, but he seemed very pleased to see them, Mo especially. After a short while they came running home from the shop.

'Did you get anything?' I asked Mo.

He fished around in the pocket of his anorak and pulled out an unopened letter and a tape cassette with Arabic

124

script printed across the top. He gave me the letter and ran upstairs to fetch his cassette player.

Like the others, this letter was written on paper taken from an old exercise book. It was in Zana's hand-writing and a little calmer in tone than the previous one, although I could read between the lines.

I started reading the letter aloud. 'Nadia has had a baby, a boy. She has called him Haney.' I looked at my children around me. Normally we would have been overjoyed, but this had serious implications which cast a shadow over the news.

I began to panic. I couldn't help but feel resentment. I felt that Nadia had been forced to produce children whom she would not normally have had. A bit like myself. I understood perfectly. Still, this child was part of Nadia, a little part of me, and I loved him as I loved her.

Reading the letter was strange. The relief that I had some news was tempered by the underlying message. The girls were in trouble and needed me now more than ever. This compensation money couldn't come a moment too soon. I knew now, as I instinctively felt before, that I had to get out there. I *had* to.

Zana said that I could write to her via this doctor she had made contact with who had agreed to let us use his PO box number. At last I could write to the girls and be fairly sure that the letter would get through. I would write today and get it posted by this evening.

Mo plugged in the cassette player and inserted the tape. He looked deeply into my eyes. I felt him saying 'Be strong, Mom!' yet he uttered no words. I gave him a slight nod and he pressed the play button. Crackles and hisses boomed out of the machine and in the background coughs and Arabic words were hushed with a single command.

Zana spoke.

Hello Mom, Dad, Ashia, Tina, Mo. We are talking to you from Yemen. It's really nice here but we miss yous all. We have settled and are happy. Yemen is nice. We are starting to learn Arab now. I live in a good house and Abdul Khada is good to me. We are going to slaughter a lamb to celebrate and I am very happy. I am happy here, in Yemen with my friends and Abdul Khada's family. They are like family to me. I miss my friends in England. If you see them, tell them I said hello. I am happy here. Very happy. Daddy, you are a good man to send us here, a very good father. Yemen is better than England. I am much happier here. Thank yous, Daddy, for sending me. I am lucky. Yemen is good. Write soon. Love you all. From your loving daughter Zana.

A loud click filled the kitchen where we all stood around listening to the tape. Zana sounded robotic. Her voice was monotone: no real emotion, but a quiver in her voice told me she was upset. I knew right away that this tape was a set-up. There was another series of hisses and crackles and Nadia's voice came booming out.

Hello Dad, Mom, Ashia, Tina and Mo. We got to Yemen as you can see. We have been here just over a month. It's a bit different to what we thought. It's nice. Lots of nature around us. Gowad and Salema are looking after me. We are married now to really nice boys. Me and Zana are happy. We have each other and spend lots of time together. Thanks, Daddy, for sending us out. It's better here than England. We are

126

lucky to have a good, caring father, and good husbands. Yemen is very beautiful. I miss yous all. I am trying to speak Arab and be a good Muslim. We have lots of things to do. It's better here than in England, better than Birmingham. Say hello to all the uncles and aunts. *Ma sallami* – that means goodbye – from your loving daughter Nadia.

The silence positively vibrated around the room. You could hear the proverbial pin drop. Mo, Tina and I all had tears streaking down our cheeks. The girls sounded so sad. Mo put it into perspective in a simple sentence. 'They are being forced to say those things, Mom!'

We worked out that the recording was at least three years old. Nadia had said that she had been there about a month. It would have been about the time I received the letter from Zana, the one in which she wanted to come home, the one in which she said she wanted to finish her life. Now we could be sure that this tape was bogus. I had to write to them. Now!

I wrote to the girls as soon as Ann left. I think I must have broken all records for the longest letter ever written. I told them that I had heard the tape and I just *knew* there was something wrong. I went back in time, over the previous three years, and explained everything that had happened: that I had had nothing to do with them being in Yemen, apart from saying that they could have a holiday. I told them about little Mary telling me about the marriage and going to see the women who knew more about it than me, their mother; about all the people I had written to, and the answers I had received, some good, many not good at all. I told them about my accident and how I was doing everything possible to bring them

127

home. The most difficult part was telling them about their father, this 'good' man who had sold them as baby-making machines to their own 'uncles'. I covered all the ground I could think of; most importantly, that I had left their father and had a new home with Tina, Ashia and Mo. They should write to me here, not at the shop. I tried to exercise the same caution Zana had, using the same kind of code system. I knew she would understand, would read between the lines, as I had done with their latest letter and even the tape.

I felt a whole lot better knowing that I would soon be in a position to initiate my own actions. Then the world could go to hell as far as I was concerned.

Chapter Twenty-Three

Hallelujah! The compensation money had finally come through. In the two months since I had written to the girls I had chased the solicitors incessantly. I had to have the money, as soon as possible. Now that Nadia had had her first child I had to get there and rescue them quickly. I had to do it myself. All this time I kept getting the same negative responses from the Foreign Office and the Yemeni government: 'The girls are deemed to be Yemeni citizens.'

I had decided, against my solicitor's advice, to accept an out-of-court settlement for what they said was only a fraction of what I could get if we went the whole distance. It mattered not one jot to me. I had to get to Yemen. They would never understand. Mo was to come with me. He had gone crazy at the thought of me travelling alone, for the first time in my life, to a place like Yemen.

I wrote to the FCO to seek advice about getting a visa for myself and Mo. A Miss Clay wrote back some time later. The letter contained the usual rubbish about the girls being Yemeni and stated that they would need the permission of their husbands to be allowed to leave the country. She concluded: 'I am so sorry that I cannot be more helpful to you.'

Well, so was I, but it was nothing unexpected, now, was it!

I would do it alone. I got our visas – the next step was the tickets. I bought two return tickets and, being so sure that we would be successful, I got two singles for the girls. The moment I had those tickets in my hand I felt on top of the world. The fact that we had to travel to an unknown land, fraught with danger and peril, didn't faze me in the least. I had a mission: I was going to bring my girls home.

I wrote to the girls and told them I was on my way.

I was filled with trepidation and excitement all at the same time. Ann Sufi took Mo and me to the Rotunda in Birmingham, where we waited for our coach to Heathrow Airport.

Chapter Twenty-Four

'This is your captain speaking. We are making our descent into Sanaa, Yemen.' The voice over the system brought us back to life. Mo and I craned our necks to look out of the window. Nothing. As far as the eye could see, nothing but mud, rocks and mountains. How the hell would they land the plane? *Where* would they land the plane? A vast stretch of nothingness. No little patchwork meadows like those we had seen after taking off in England. No scattering of houses. Nothing!

We bumped to the ground and the captain informed us that we were now in Yemen. A building stuck on the tarmac was the Yemeni answer to Heathrow.

They managed to lose Mo's suitcase. It was in some other part of the world. Enviously, I wished the same applied to us and my daughters. I thought about conspiracies to delay us or make life awkward.

It took us three hours to get out of the 'airport' and into the streets of Sanaa. I was here, at last, in the same country as most of my children. It would all be downhill from now on. I sent Mo to find a taxi to take us to an hotel. We were driven through the streets of Sanaa. Barren lands greeted us in the bland scenery of mud and rock and then, as we got closer to the city, it changed to villages of working land and shops in every available position. They were not convenience stores like those at home. They were like shelters, garages. All had blue metal pull-down shutters guarding their entrances. Dry, withered trees bordered the dusty roads.

Soon we got to the hub of the city. This was more like it. Good wide roads and thousands of cars, all honking their horns at invisible obstacles. Occasionally a donkey and cart would stroll by, overtaking us as we were stuck in a traffic jam. The women were completely covered in black, some showing their eyes, many not. As vehicles crawled along the road, they and their children begged for money at the window. They looked pitiful, the women carrying disabled or very sick children to procure money from the people stuck in the cars. There was no escape from these creatures. Men in *futahs*, wraparound skirts, and typical headdress.

All the men had that huge bulge protruding from their cheeks – *qat*! As the car passed the men, they stared through the window, looking in directly at me, leering. I felt vulnerable and naked.

So this was Yemen. Muthana's Paradise. I hoped with all my heart that he would suffer greatly. A festering hole in his rear end – a festering hole to remind him of Yemen. Same thing!

Huge amounts of rubble blocking off parts of the road were causing the traffic jam. The pavement was lined with vendors selling everything from cigarettes to flower garlands made of sweet-smelling jasmine. The taxi pulled off the main road and took a narrow side road. Tall buildings centuries old still stood here, proud and majestic in the humble surroundings of poverty and decay.

132

Children, filthy and tattily dressed in rags, ran laughing through a maze of tiny streets, dodging the cars, squealing with delight. Goats chewed the thin, dry grass at the side of the road as our driver honked his horn with extreme impatience at their obstructive idle way of life. We left the tiny side road and joined a larger, quieter one.

This could have been England if the cars had driven on the other side of the road, the left-hand side. The road was clean and devoid of rubble. We approached the hotel and I let out a sigh of relief, glad we were on a brightly lit, well-maintained main road.

We checked into the hotel with no problem. I asked for tea to be brought up to my room, and a drink for Mo. We were both tired and needed a bath. Poor Mo could not even change his clothes since his case had been misdirected. When the porter brought us the tea I asked him where the British Embassy was and he gave me rough directions from the hotel. I was grateful that he spoke fairly good English. 'Your English is good!' I complimented him. 'Have you ever been there?'

Smiling, he told me: 'I was living in the Midlands for three years. A place called Birmingham. Do you know it?'

I admitted that I had heard of it. 'What part of Birmingham?'

'Balsall Heath.'

I nodded politely. He was probably a plant. Balsall Heath, indeed! I should have known.

I knew my task would be difficult. I had come here armed with a photograph I had managed to find of Mohammed, Abdul Khada's eldest son, a PO box number – Gowad's number at that – and the name of a village, Ashube. The British Consul would provide more help.

I ordered a taxi for the following morning. Before we dared to venture into the villages we must go to see Mr Colin Page at the Consulate. He would know where they were. Perhaps he'd even escort us in.

The Consulate was situated on a very wide main road, surrounded by a huge, tall brick wall, prettily adorned with barbed wire, a small glass window on one side and a sentry box on the other. The centrepiece was the good old Union Jack flapping limply in the hot air. We had been here only a few hours yet already the Embassy was a welcome sight. Alighting from the taxi, we approached the small window. 'We have come to see Mr Page. We are British.'

The small Arab behind the glass eyed me; I eyed his machine-gun. The huge, green Embassy doors looked imposing. A small door concealed in the centre opened and the man with the machine-gun motioned us inside. He wanted to search my bags. No problem. He searched Mo, too. Then, satisfied, he pointed to a flight of steps off to the left and a path on a higher level. We followed his directions and entered the Embassy. A smaller door was opened and a man who was obviously on his way out after finishing his business held the door open as we passed.

'I have come to see Mr Page,' I announced to another Arab behind a glass partition.

'Name, please?' he smiled.

'Ali, Miriam Ali.'

'OK. Take seat through there. I will tell him you are here.'

He indicated a small reception room. A coffee table and a few chairs were the only furniture. The walls, covered with pictures of the Queen and her family gave me the reassurance that I was on British territory. The air-conditioning took care of the intense heat. Mo and I sat down. I lit a cigarette. It had been so hot outside. I felt the perspiration dry on my skin in the cool air of the Embassy. I could have killed for a drink.

'Mrs Ali?'

A tall, thickset man with brown hair approached. He was carrying a huge file of papers. He spoke the real Queen's English, a plum-in-the-mouth type of person.

'Miss Ali,' I corrected. I hated being called Mrs.

'Right. Miss Ali. Colin Page. Hello. What can I do for you? You are a long way from home!'

'This is my son Mohammed. We have come to get my daughters, Zana and Nadia. I have their tickets with me. I would like your help. First I need to find them. I need to know where Ashube is. It might be too much to ask you to take us there, but if you could just tell us how to find it that will be a good start. Secondly, I will need to have their passports sorted.'

'Miss Ali, I think you have made a very big mistake. It is most unwise for you and your son to have come out to Yemen.'

I stood up, open-mouthed, stunned into silence.

'Look, the girls are married now. They are married to Yemenis and are Yemeni themselves by their father's birth. I am sorry, but there is nothing to be done to help them, nothing at all. Go home, Miss Ali.' Page shuffled the papers from his large file.

'What? They are coming home with me. I— '

'You will achieve nothing here. You certainly won't be able to use those tickets. I'm afraid you have wasted your time and your money. You should go back to the UK as soon as possible and forget this – this whole thing.' Page turned to leave the room.

'Are you serious? You mean to tell me that *you* will do nothing? You won't even direct us to Ashube?'

'Miss Ali . . . Miss Ali. There is nothing to be done. It will be too dangerous for you to travel to the village. I will have no part of it. As for your son, I would watch him very closely. You could go home alone!'

He went, leaving Mo and me in a terrible state of shock and crazy with anger. This was the British Embassy?

Storming out of the Consulate we stood at the side of the main road, confused and alone. We knew we would have to go to Taiz. It would be closer to the village, anyway. We asked the guard how to get to Taiz and he told us of a bus that made the journey at noon. We would just make it to the station. Without further ado we hailed a taxi to take us to the bus station and on to Taiz.

I wasn't expecting too much – I wasn't expecting much more than Digbeth Coach Station. There was an old clapped-out vehicle from the war era chugging patiently at the side of a wide and dusty road. It had the seating capacity for maybe thirty people and already there must have been twenty or so on board. An employee took my suitcase and hurled it, accurately but none too carefully, to another man perched precariously on the roof of the bus. The second man caught the case in midair and tied it to the roof with the few other bags and cages of live chickens. Mo and I took a double seat at the rear of the bus and waited some fifteen minutes for it to begin its journey. It was 12.10 when the bus shuddered and spluttered into motion. As we left Sanaa, my thoughts turned to Zana and Nadia. A bubble of excitement surged through my stomach. I began to try to visualise their homes and the land they occupied, expecting nothing and fearing the worst.

In less than an hour we hit the first of many border

controls. Very young-looking uniformed men, armed with machine-guns, flagged the bus to a halt. The driver and a guard spoke in loud hurried Arabic. I thought we were on our way when the bus started to roll again, but instead we were pulled to the side of the road. The old bus hissed as the ignition was turned off. The metal door shuddered open. Two of the soldiers climbed aboard the bus and surveyed the occupants. They made straight for Mo and me, who had by this time slid down in the over-stuffed seats.

'Bassabort!' the taller one ordered, extending his hand to receive the document. I handed over my passport, flinching as he snatched the tiny book from my fingers. Opening it, upside-down, he flicked through the pages. 'You English?' He raised his eyebrows questioningly at me.

'Yes.'

'Who he?' He tilted his head towards Mo.

'My son. Mohammed.'

'Why you come Yemen?' His partner closed in.

I wondered if I should say, 'To see your paradise on earth.' Instead I told him we were visiting family. This was nearer the truth. They talked in hurried Arabic, then the taller one threw my passport at me and turned his back on us. They casually walked back down the aisle of the bus and left. The bus chugged back into life and began to roll towards the next city, Taiz.

I thought it would be a matter of a couple of hours. We were captives on this vehicle for seven hours. Most of the land was barren and dry but the closer we got to Taiz, the more interesting the scenery became. Lush green pastures reached as far as the eye could see, the odd building or two the only hint of settlement. Goats, sheep, chickens and donkeys were grazing or roaming the land. The road was littered with the carcasses of dead dogs and the occasional sheep or goat – a testimony to the local driving standards, no doubt. The road climbed, up and up into a huge mountain range.

I clung to Mo's arm, he clung to mine. We had taken our seats on the right-hand side of the bus, so now, as it weaved its way through the twists and turns of the British- and French-built road, all we could see was the drop to the bottom of the valley some 3,000 feet below. The cars and buses coming in the opposite direction carved their own carriageway out of the road, seemingly driving directly into our path.

It was a scary journey which took us higher and higher over the mountain pass. We went through villages where the children carried large bundles on their heads or herded goats and sheep. Women squatted on their haunches in the middle of large grain fields, reaping the crop by hand, using a knife and baskets. A whole line of women dressed in black with huge straw hats were hacking down the grain in neat lines, methodically and relentlessly in the heat of the dry sun.

The higher the bus climbed, the cooler and more misty it became. The clouds touched the mountain road, hiding the perilous drop just a few feet away. There were very few guard-rails to prevent an out-of-control vehicle plummeting, occupants and all, to certain death and total destruction far below, where the scene would be hidden from view in the valley of mist. At last we reached the crest of the mountain and the bus ground its gears to cope with a new peril: the descent.

The brakes screeched and the stench of burning rubber filled the bus as the old vehicle had to cope with a near- vertical drop. Rocks and boulders strewn across the road provided added obstacles to be avoided, in addition to the oncoming traffic. As we descended the mist slowly cleared. The scene was awesome. A valley of greens and browns greeted us in a magical mixture of depth and volume. Tiny gardens of greenery perched precariously on the very edge of the cliffs. I wondered who looked after these gardens, as they were obviously grown for a purpose. How on earth did they manage to get to these awkward places to tend their crops? A scattering of houses broke the contours of the land far down in the heart of the valley. The little gardens must belong to those people. The road twisted, swinging in, away from the edge of the mountain. We were now on the south side of the mountain. It was fairly barren here, with a few cacti growing wild on the roadside. The road became wider. There were more houses on one side, carved deep into the side of the mountain rock. I could see no way of accessing these homes apart from a precarious climb up the mountain itself. The inhabitants of these houses would have to be extremely fit and agile. They would have to have feet like goats to grip into the sharp inclines and not fall.

Lower down, a camel roaming free at the roadside, munching on the vegetation, took no notice of the traffic creeping along the road in a long convoy. The houses became tattier, the poverty of the area more evident. Tents of rags and cardboard housed people and their families. Children, barefoot and scantily dressed, ran wild along the roadside, holding out bags of limes to sell to passers-by; dirty, snotty-nosed kids. The sharp lumps of shattered rock on the ground gave no hindrance to their tiny, dusty feet. Maybe the bus was particularly slow, but the kids ran hell for leather, easily outpacing the vehicle, no effort showing on their faces.

Now we were on virtually flat ground, a few dips and dives apart, and finally getting up a little speed. The scenery changed time and time again, from beautiful valleys, untouched by time since creation itself, to little villages crammed with merchants selling their wares from the side of the road, or from dug-out shops, full of hustle and bustle.

We were stopped several times by soldiers patrolling the roads. All the boys seemed to be so young. At every control point a truck would be parked to the side of the road, and on it would be an old Second World War Lewis mounted on a tripod and a huge circular searchlight. Just in case anyone got any funny ideas. By this time of day all the men had huge gobs of *qat* stored in their cheeks and spat green phlegm on to the roadside.

Again we were in the quiet countryside of Yemen, although this time there was no greenery. The road was good, wide and clear of rubble but the landscape on the whole was barren and arid. This was the area that was prone to earthquakes. Until recently, I later discovered, it had been farmland, growing corn, barley and sweetcorn. All the men had been out of the village, having gone to a neighbouring village to sell their wares, when suddenly the ground had started to shake and the whole area was disturbed. Gaping great holes had swallowed the main part of the settlement, taking with it the women and children, animals and stores. The men had come home to a great nothingness, barren and devoid of life. There was nothing to be done. It was all gone, as if it had never been there. The men of the village had no choice but to move on. This area had become a huge cemetery for their families and it would be going against the will of Allah to rebuild on this land, or to grow crops. It was deserted after the traditional mourning period of forty days, never to be inhabited again. All people knew this, and reflected on it as they passed the land, muttering '*Ma Shallah!*' – God protect – as they bowed their heads in remembrance, not out of respect for the dead – as tradition has it, the dead are forgotten 369 days after their death and it is *haram*, against Allah's will, to utter the names of these unfortunates again – but out of respect for Allah, in awe of his great power.

The day was drawing to a close. It was past 6.30. Sitting on my backside all this time was making my legs hungry for the circulation of blood. Mo slept fitfully beside me. I fantasised about a freshly brewed cup of tea.

And there it was, at last. Taiz.

Chapter Twenty-Five

Taiz. Our first sighting of the city was piles of rubble and a scattering of buildings.

White stone houses massed together marked the edge of the city. Mountains surrounded the whole area – in fact Taiz was built in the bowl of several mountains, nestling at their feet. Being a biggish place, the second city of Yemen, the roads were chaotic, with scrapyard-quality cars bibbing and tooting. Their drivers made up their own Highway Code as they went along their merry way, stopping in the fast lane of the dual carriageway, swinging into U-turns at random and cutting into the flow of the traffic struggling in the other direction. I closed my eyes in fear of a crash several times. Soon we came across a huge crater in the road. It must have been thirty feet in diameter and four foot deep in the centre. The bus driver knew it was there but had to swerve perilously close to it to avoid the oncoming traffic. So this was Taiz.

I spotted a hotel on the left-hand side of the road and made a mental note of its name. That was something to start with. We would stay there, regardless of cost or condition. Some five minutes later, the bus ground to a halt and the driver shouted. 'Taiz!'

'We are here, son. Come on, let's get out of this bloody bus!'

Mo woke and stretched. I stood up, a cramped standing position, and rubbed my legs, urging the circulation to return. We collected my bag and pulled it all the way back down the road to the hotel. Mo was impressed with my navigation skills, and thought my intuition perfect, finding a hotel so quickly. I didn't disillusion him by admitting that I had seen it from the bus while he slept. Better that he had faith in me, I convinced myself.

We checked into the hotel. The reception area was dim and dingy. I didn't care. At least the staff were friendly and co-operative. They welcomed us and showed us to a twin room. It was clean and tidy, although it was crying out for a lick of paint. The bathroom was gleaming and had a shower, toilet and a hole in the floor. At the time I thought it was an overflow of some sort but I soon found out that it was an alternative toilet for those who preferred to squat over this hole rather than perch on the porcelain.

I ordered tea immediately. The service was good: it arrived within minutes, fresh and steaming. I had to get used to the evaporated milk, but it was tea and most welcome.

There was nothing to be done tonight. It was now nearly nine. We were tired and travel-weary. A simple omelette each from room service bucked us up. Having something hot in our bellies and clean now, we soon slept.

The *imams* calling the faithful to prayer woke me up at first light. It was nearly five. Mo didn't stir. I sat and watched the dawn until the street below came alive with traders and kids running to school or to help in the *souk*, the local market. Soon the bibbing of the cars started; Mo tossed in his sleep, huffing at the noise. I rang room service and ordered a pot of tea for me and breakfast for Mo. It arrived a little after nine.

By ten, we had taken to the streets of Taiz to find out the whereabouts of Ashube and the girls. I was armed with a black and white photo of Abdul Khada's son, Mohammed, the name of the village of Ashube and the name of Gowad's agent, Naser Saleh. For hours, Mo and I walked the streets, going round and round in concentric circles, asking anyone and everyone if they recognised either the names or the man in the photo. Nothing. I would not give up. The dryness and dust from the roads bit deep into our skin and sun burned on relentlessly. People stared in surprise at a woman and a young boy roaming the streets, talking to anyone who stopped still long enough to be approached. I became more brazen as the day wore on, buttonholing anyone who slowed down. How could it be that the locals had never heard of Ashube?

Up and down, round and round we walked, stopping at each stall in the *souk* to ask. The traders smiled and shook their heads. They were selling spices of all kinds, sweets, vegetables, materials in bright gaudy colours, clothes that had gone out of fashion about a decade before, some of them fantastically over-elaborate, with buttons, sequins and bows, frills and flouncy laces. Did anyone buy this stuff? Pots and pans hung from hooks, side by side with shoes and shirts. A strange combination here – biscuits and tyres. One proud vendor's shop boasted electrical goods, baby clothes and underwear. There were a thousand stallholders to ask, all selling a variety of goods, and each one would do his best to sell me something, starting with his most expensive range of goods and moving down to a packet of sweets or simple toy. Their smiles faded to scowls as I refused to barter.

By seven that evening we were tired and frustrated. We returned to our room empty-handed. We bathed, ate and slept the sleep of the just. The *imam* could call all he liked the next morning. I didn't wake up until nine o'clock, much to my own disgust. Sleeping in was wasting time. I clambered out of bed, ordered tea and breakfast and rushed to the bathroom to wash before the food arrived. Mo was awake, and took care of the service charge while I bathed. By half past ten we were back on the streets of Taiz to resume the search for someone to point us in the right direction.

It was another fruitless day. We cried 'enough' after nine hours, tired, hungry and unsuccessful. How long was this going to take? I racked my brains to think of a quicker solution. Nothing came to mind. We would have to do it all again tomorrow, and would keep doing it until we had some joy.

The third day started off in just the same way. Mo and I wandered the streets and alleys, braving the stares of the locals, being followed by curious children. It was approaching noon when I stopped yet another passer-by. I took the now crumpled photo of Mohammed out of my pocket and asked the man if he knew where this man was. In remarkably good English he said that he was afraid he didn't, but the name of Naser Saleh was familiar to him. I should inquire at the Post Office, where he believed Naser Saleh to be known.

'Where is the Post Office?' I asked.

'Do you know of the Al Gnad hotel?'

'Well, yes – yes we do.'

'You will find the Post Office situated opposite this hotel. You will be able to see it from the main entrance of the hotel itself.' He smiled, wished us good luck and a pleasant stay in Yemen and continued on his way. I stood staring after him gobsmacked, watching him until he was out of sight. Mo pulled at my sleeve.

'Come on, Mom!' he urged. 'We might have found them!'

'Yes, yes.' The breakthrough was a little marred by discovering that the answer could have been under our noses all the time. I hadn't considered asking anyone whether there was a Post Office, a logical starting-point. And the damned place was right opposite the hotel we had set off from for the past three mornings! It was such a waste of time.

We rushed off to the Post Office. It was a large, fairly modern building set on the side of a hill. Inside it was wide and uncluttered, allowing people to queue in long lines at each counter to be served by men behind wire grids. Mo and I took the smallest queue and waited impatiently.

When at last it was our turn, I asked the assistant if he could speak English. Thankfully, he nodded. I slipped the photograph through the narrow gap under the grille and asked if he knew this person. He varied the distance between the photo and his eyes, adjusting his focus, frowning. Without waiting for his reply, I asked whether he knew Naser Saleh.

'Yes, I know him. He is here. Wait one moment!'

He slipped the photograph back to me and left his desk to disappear into a rear office, returning after a few moments with a little man in his fifties. They stood side by side and spoke quickly. The younger man nodded his head and came over. 'He speaks little English. I may help you?'

Gratefully, I agreed. The older man approached and slapped his chest. 'Naser Saleh.' Then he raised his hands in a questioning gesture.

'What do you want with him?' interpreted the clerk unnecessarily.

'I am looking for this man. Can you help?' I held out the photograph.

A withered hand took the proffered picture. He glanced at it, only a passing look. He eyed me suspiciously. 'Do you know who this is?' *He* was asking *me*?

'Yes. Mohammed, brother of Abdullah, son of Abdul Khada.'

'Why do you want this man?'

'So that he can take me to my daughters.'

I watched his face crease with suspicion. Still he had to be sure. He took a deep breath and, through the clerk, asked, 'Who are you?'

'I am Miriam Ali, mother of the two sisters in the village of Ashube. I am here to see them, and I *will* see them.' I wanted to dispel any thoughts he might have had to the contrary.

Naser Saleh snapped at the clerk in Arabic and walked off with his head bowed. Reaching the main doors, he turned to check that we were following. We were a short distance behind him. '*Yullah!*' he ordered. His meaning was obvious.

We followed Naser Saleh some fifty yards along the main road and up a small dirt track. The house looked ancient. We followed him deep into the dark dwelling. Was this the beginning of the end of our search? Within yards of the hotel where we'd spent the previous two nights?

The smell in the hall caught in our throats, making us gag. It filled our nostrils and lungs. The place was so dark. We passed a few rooms leading off this passage, through the kitchen, a horror of horrors where a woman was cooking eggs in a stained black pan. As she stirred the food, she hawked, clearing her tubes, caught the phlegm at the back of her throat, and discharged the mucus by spitting across the room, where it ran down the wall alongside the marks of her previous efforts. Hurrying through, gagging, as she began to clear her sinuses again, Mo and I followed Naser Saleh.

I remembered his name well. It was Naser Saleh, acting agent for Gowad, Muthana and Abdul Khada, who would have intercepted my mail and any letters written to me by the girls. I had complained about him to the Yemen authorities after Muthana had said the mail was monitored by him. He had been arrested and his three principals had had to pay a lot of money to bail him out of prison. Naser Saleh had not spent enough time in jail; his being out of the way would have opened a line of communication between me and my girls, had we but known.

We caught up with him in a small dark, smelly room. We stood around as Naser Saleh seated himself on the single small cushion in the room. He stared at us. Our eyes were becoming accustomed to the gloom. Another man walked into this hellish place. I strained my eyes to make out a short, plump figure.

It was him, Mohammed Abdul Khada. I recognised him immediately. He had not changed all that much. Never would I have thought I would be so pleased to see someone who was really the enemy. Naser Saleh spoke to Mohammed in Arabic. His eyes widened in shock and surprise as he finally recognised me.

'This make much trouble for me – all times!' Naser Saleh struggled with his poor English.

I sucked air through my teeth and his eyes darkened at

the insult. It felt good, but I would have to control myself. I had a long way to go yet.

Mohammed was completely flummoxed. It seemed to me that he didn't know whether to say 'hello' or 'oh, no!' or if he should question me or console Naser Saleh. Then he disappeared, leaving Mo and me standing there and Naser Saleh squatting on his cushion. The only sound to be heard was the woman in the kitchen hawking. Fifteen minutes later he called me. I motioned to Mo to stay where he was and pushed my way through a pair of stuffy hanging curtains which obscured a doorway. I found Mohammed, holding a telephone out to me. I took it. 'Hello?'

The line crackled, static ebbed and flowed, distorting the sound, but there was no mistaking the angry, frightened voice of one of my main adversaries, Abdul Khada.

'What are you doing there?' he demanded. Then, without waiting for an answer, he added, 'You better not have come to cause trouble!'

'I don't know what you're talking about. I've come all the way from England to see my daughters in this land of plenty and watch them enjoy the paradise you spoke so often about.'

Abdul Khada growled. 'You ought to know, Miriam. I have had a letter from Muthana. He has authorised me to take the girls to Marais in Aden if you cause any problems.'

'Well, if that happens I can visit with Laila and Ahmed at the same time. The location of their grandparents is no great secret to me. You have to realise that I have just come to visit my family. If you have nothing to hide you will have no objection to that. I am their mother. What has happened between Muthana and myself is irrelevant, certainly nothing to concern you. I have come a long way,

Abdul Khada. I need to see my daughters. Then I will go home, satisfied and happy – if all is well.'

Without waiting for his reply I hung up the phone, gulping great mouthfuls of air to try to calm myself. I turned to face Mohammed. He was paler than before. He kicked at the ground with his sandalled foot. 'You are very brave to come here. Braver still to want to go to the village.'

I held up my hand to silence him. I didn't want to know about danger. I knew the risk was great – I didn't need some well-meaning individual to point it out to me. I would forge on in comparative ignorance. It was safer for me that way. All I was armed with was hope, determination and my cloak of ignorance. I needed to keep all three intact.

'It's true, you know,' he muttered. 'Muthana sold your daughters to Gowad and my father, Abdul Khada. They paid thirteen hundred pounds each. I am so sorry. It should never have happened to them. It is the way of the village, it rarely happens in the cities. People can find work here in Taiz. Many come from villages of Mokbana, like myself. It's not same, like city. The old ones there have old ideas. They must barter for brides for their sons. The more children they have, the better. The women in the city won't go to the village for anything. Their life here is much better and richer husbands can be found. They have a good house and a social life. It's not like that in the village. The women work hard in the mountains. City women won't accept that way of life. Brides have to be found elsewhere.

'It has caused us a lot of trouble. I had a daughter, my eldest daughter. We all lived in the village. Me, my wife, two daughters and my young son. While I was working in Saudi, my father arranged the marriage of my daughter

150

to an elder in the village. He was over sixty years old, my daughter was nine. By the time I found out and got back to Yemen, it was too late. This elder had made my daughter his own. The union was complete. Oh, I had many arguments, I was very angry, but I could do nothing. It is not good to go against the wishes of your father or his father before him. All I could do was move my family to Taiz and keep them far away.'

Mohammed had tears in his eyes as he spoke, which he fought back in manly fashion. 'You must be careful in the village, Miriam. Please!'

Chapter Twenty-Six

Mo and I spent the night with Mohammed, his wife Bakela and their two children. In the morning, Mohammed hired a jeep and driver to take us to Zana's village of Hokail. 'It is a little nearer and a lot easier to get to,' he explained. We set off really early, leaving the city of Taiz behind us. The further we got from the city, the more barren and desolate the surroundings. An endless expanse of dry, rocky land and occasional mud huts at the roadside were the only scenery for miles and miles but the road was good. The desert reached as far as the eye could see until, way off on the horizon, a range of mountains came into view. In that range of mountains was our destination: Mokbana and its tiny neighbouring villages. A feeling of dread set in.

We took a turning off to the right, a smaller road but still fairly good. Suddenly the cushion of tarmac and concrete disappeared and we were on a road carved out of the soil, which made our journey bumpy and hazardous. We were thrown around inside the vehicle and had to hold on tight to keep our seats. In the open, dry land, the wind had nothing to restrain it. It whipped up sand and dry dirt into our faces, into our mouths and eyes, as we fought to hold on. We were thirsty but we could not afford to let go our grip on the side of the jeep to try to get a drink. The heat was unbearable. A thick heat haze distorted the view of the landscape.

We made slow progress. After two interminable hours we stopped at a row of tiny stone and mud houses. We were able to stretch our legs and, more welcome, to buy more water and swill the dirt from our mouths. We still had a couple of hours' drive in front of us. After a short break we hauled our bruised bodies back into the jeep and wedged ourselves securely for the last part of our journey. This time it was somewhat easier but by no means less bumpy. Rocks and open holes in the ground peppered our path. The jeep was forced to go slower, more cautiously. It took an age to reach a point where we could see any sign of life and even then it was only empty, discarded water bottles and abandoned plastic bags.

On and on we went, through the unchanging heart of the scrublands. At last we arrived. A beautiful scene appeared. One minute there were rocks and dry soil all around and the next a lush green village appeared. A tiny stream flowed through the heart of the village, irrigating the fruit trees and crops. This was it. The paradise! And every inch a paradise it was. The locals here were very dark, almost black, burned by years of hard toil under the sun. The jeep pulled up and the driver purchased more water and, this time, fruit. I assumed that this was for his journey back to Taiz. I fidgeted in my seat, waiting for confirmation that this was the end of our journey, hopefully scanning the area for Zana and Nadia. The driver motioned us to stay where we were, climbed aboard and away we went again. Behind us the beautiful village slipped further and further away. We drove on – and on and on.

Suddenly we stopped. Not just for an obstacle in our path, but a definite stop. The driver had switched off the engine. I thought perhaps he needed to answer a call of nature or something. I took the opportunity to light a cigarette and take in the surroundings: very large mountains, all around us.

The driver looked at us, a little puzzled. 'Hokail,' he stated flatly.

'Hokail? Where?' I could see no village, only mountains.

'Hokail,' he said again, this time pointing upward.

I followed his pointed finger. A huge mountain just sat there. Plain, bland, ordinary. Huge.

'That can't be right!' Mo put my thoughts into words. The driver was obviously trying to up his price by threatening to dump us in the middle of nowhere.

He got out of the jeep and went to the foot of the mountain. He took several steps backwards and began to shout up the mountain. After a few moments a woman appeared, quite a way up, and shouted back to him. They exchanged more shouts and she began to call to someone even higher up. A chain of voices continued, sounding further and further away each time until we could hear no more. The driver came back to the jeep and took out my case. He carried it to the spot where he had started yodelling.

'Hokail!' he said for the third time, emphatically.

We got out, straining our necks to see up the mountain. About ten minutes later half a dozen faces appeared, looking down at us. I wondered where Zana and Nadia could be. I sat on my case and lit another cigarette. Behind us the jeep spluttered into life, turned and started back to Taiz.

154

Mo tugged at my arm. A woman dressed from head to toe in black came tottering down the mountainside. We watched her slowly pick her way through the dry brushwood and loose stones. She was large, huge with child. Fancy sending her down to take us to Zana and Nadia! Not up that damned mountain, I hoped as I threw my cigarette end away.

The woman got closer. About ten feet away she stopped and straightened up to look at us. She wore purdah, I could see only her eyes.

My heart lurched. 'Zana! My God, it's Zana!'

The tears flowed down my face. My arms went out towards her. I wanted to hold her to me, tightly, and never let go but I was glued to the spot. Through a blur of tears, I watched as she ran closer. Then she was in my arms.

We cried. Oh God, how we cried! I held her tight and breathed in her smell. I had my Zana in my arms. We clung to each other, both talking nineteen to the dozen, neither listening. I thanked God that I had found her, I thanked him for letting me hold her again after all this time. There were only three things I wanted now. Nadia, home – and a box of tissues.

I doubt if we would ever have moved if Mo hadn't coughed. It broke the spell. Mo, in his patience, stood by, tears streaming down his cheeks. I looked over Zana's shaking shoulder and tried to focus my vision through a waterfall of tears. 'Say hello to your brother. He's missed you as much as the rest of us have.' I sniffed back my tears.

Zana backed off a little and looked at this tall, lean figure. Her bloodshot eyes brightened. She sniffed, wiping her tears with the back of her hand.

'No, never! Mo? Is that really you?'

Mo grinned through the tears streaking his dusty face. 'Hello sis. Long time no see!'

They embraced, laughing and crying together. Oh, that sounded so good.

'Come on. I'll get you out of the sun!' Zana grinned at us and started to scurry up the mountain. Mo and I followed but Zana went much too fast for me, despite being heavily pregnant.

'Zane, hold up will you? I ain't a bloody goat!' I pleaded. She looked back and gave me her hand to help me up the mountainside.

A woman passed us, going down the mountain. It seemed only a few minutes before she passed us again, this time going our way. On top of her head was my heavy suitcase. I had forgotten all about it. She rushed past us, working her way up and out of sight.

'How the hell can she do that?' I asked Zana.

She shrugged her shoulders, urging me up the mountain. I was breathless and petrified. Mo fared a lot better than me but even then he broke out in a sweat that was part hard labour and part fear. At last we reached a plateau. A house was there.

'This your house, Zana?' I panted, sitting thankfully on a nearby boulder.

'No. It's Abdul Noor's. Mom, how did you get here? Have you come to take us back? What's happening?'

My breath came in ragged gasps. I swallowed. My throat was dry and felt like I had swallowed glass. 'Let me rest. I've got to rest, then I'll explain.' It was such an effort to talk. 'Where's your house, then?'

Zana pointed up.

'Oh, no, please, no!' It looked like miles. 'We have to

156

go up there?' I closed my eyes and shook my head. I would never make it, not up there.

A woman came out of the house and offered us a drink. I later discovered her name was Amina and she was a friend of Zana's. I felt the cold fluid slide down my throat and down to my stomach. A slight pain shot through in my head. I sipped slowly at the drink until it went away. Zana paced up and down, obviously not at all strained; eager and not a little impatient to resume our ascent. Another climb! Oh, deep joy, I thought sarcastically, all those flat lands and my Zana gets lumbered with the Yemeni equivalent of Mount Everest. I wished I had brought a flag, to claim the peak for England.

The air became fresher and thinner the further up we went. Huge birds, ugly and dark, rode the currents that kept them airborne without the effort of flapping their wings. I didn't want to know what they were but had this depressing thought that they were waiting for me to fall. I shuddered and looked up rather than down into the valley.

Zana periodically stopped to monitor my progress, which wasn't much at all, really. I wished I hadn't worn sandals. I cursed the leather that only just covered my aching feet. Mo had no real problems after the initial climb, but he didn't smoke, wasn't wearing flimsy sandals, wasn't so unused to physical exertion.

The arduous climb seemed to take forever. Thankfully, finally, I had conquered this huge blot on the land-scape to join Mo and Zana on an adorable flat piece of ground.

I could have kissed it. I collapsed in a heap at the door of a small house and refused to budge. Another woman stood there, the one who had run up the mountain with my case on her head, Haola. She volunteered to run across to Nadia's village and fetch her.

Where did she get the stamina? Why weren't these women major competitors in the Olympics? I was glad of her athletic ability, though. She was going to bring Nadia to me. I willed Haola to have swift feet and run like a gazelle to my other daughter. I tried to imagine her running to Nadia and telling her that her mother had come. Nadia would outrun her easily on the way to me. Then I thought better of it. Zana had now told me that Nadia was pregnant again. We asked Haola not to tell Nadia anything, only to ask her to come straight away. Zana would prepare her for the news on arrival.

Haola set off at lightning speed. I remained slumped outside the door, waiting, but at the same time so pleased to have time with Zana. I couldn't be bothered to swat the flies off my exposed skin and they sucked my blood before my petrified eyes. I ached so much, I couldn't move a muscle. Swearing at them didn't prove effective, either. But I was in such high spirits that I didn't care. Tomorrow, however, I would care a lot.

Zana hauled me up and said I would be better off inside. I let her help me.

Abdul Khada's house sat on the top of a mountain, solitary and secluded, no other houses around. We entered through a doorway that seemed to have been carved from stone. Sheep, chickens and Ward's beloved goats all lived here. Ward was Abdul Khada's wife. The smell was overpowering. The livestock had the full run of the lower floor – after all, it was their home. Faeces littered the floor, joining puddles of urine.

Off to the left was a set of steps carved from stone, another feature that made me think that perhaps we were in a cave. Up the steps and a off to the left was Abdul Khada's room, which he shared with Ward when he was in Yemen. On the right was a blocked-off room, which I later found had been Mohammed's. Straight ahead was the grandad's room, which he hardly ever left, and over to the right was Zana's.

I tried not to show my horror at her living conditions. She had made a good job of what little she had. And boy, what little she had! It was a box about ten feet by seven with a very low ceiling. The only 'feature' of the room was a square window, adorned with bars and wooden shutters. It was so stiflingly hot that it was difficult to breathe. There was no air movement.

On the next floor was the extension that Abdul Khada had built on the roof. It was slightly cooler here.

The extension housed the 'kitchen' – a flat piece of roof with a *tanoor*, a clay oven, built on it. This was where Zana baked the chapatis they ate. The corn for this she ground by hand in the animals' room on the lower floor.

The bath was small, a bucket. You had to stand in it, filled with the water that Zana had transported up the mountain in a large container on her head. The same mountain that I had to climb on all fours. The bucket was usually used in another room, a small square with another square cut out of the floor, by the external wall. This was the toilet. The waste from this square would be taken, via gravity or whatever, to a sluice that ran to the outside of the house and thence to its ultimate repository down the side of the mountain.

Enough was enough. The tour of the house over, Zana took me to her tiny room to sit on her mattress on the floor.

It was a lot to cope with, emotionally. I was overjoyed

to see Zana, but at the same time I was mortified by her living conditions. But I had to grin and bear it for her sake. I watched her as she made tea. I burned with love for her and with utter hatred for those who had made her suffer so. My feelings swung from one emotion to another. I made the natural choice to wallow in her company and appreciate the reunion rather than let my anger at her condition or surroundings affect our joy. But I felt it deeply and it began to eat into my soul like a cancer.

I lit a cigarette for her, then one for myself. I took a deep draw. My throat was still a little raw from the effort of the climb, but I needed this cigarette. We had a lot to tell each other but we would wait for Nadia. Mo sat next to me, silent, brooding.

Haola came to the door and said something in Arabic to Zana. Zana replaced her yashmak and told us to wait there for a moment. She would fetch Nadia. I couldn't sit still. Mo felt the tension too. The pair of us paced back and forth in the tiny room.

The door swung open, and a figure completely covered in black entered. I couldn't even see the eyes but it was obviously a woman, heavily pregnant. It was Nadia. It had to be.

She lifted the yashmak and grinned, tears streaming down her face. 'Mommy!' she squealed and charged in to embrace me.

I met her halfway. My second daughter was at last in my arms. Tears of joy soaked our faces as we clung to each other. I wanted to squeeze her so tightly. Now I had both my daughters. The feeling, the relief, was marvellous.

A small boy clung fearfully to Nadia's skirts, looking up at the strange people before him, a look of bewilderment on his face. Nadia raised her head from my shoulder. She had seen Mo. She tore herself from my arms and hurled herself across the room into his welcoming arms. 'Mo!'

'Naggie Nose!'

The small boy held on to her skirts regardless and was hauled across the room with her as she and Mo bear-hugged each other. Tears everywhere, laughter and tears of joy.

'So, who is this?' I asked, knowing full well that this small boy was my first grandson.

'Haney,' Nadia said, laughing, 'come say hello to Nanna!'

He dug in his heels. She spoke in Arabic to him but he held on even tighter to her skirts. 'I think it's your red shirt and your uncovered hair, Mommy. He has never seen a woman uncovered before. He probably thinks you're from outer space!' Nadia's mirth couldn't be contained. I couldn't have been more pleased.

Zana told me later that since Nadia had come to Yemen she had hardly ever smiled, certainly never laughed aloud. She was quiet and withdrawn nearly all the time. It was good to see a shadow of her former self after so long.

Nadia was convinced, as was Zana, that I was here to take them home. My heart broke. I wished for nothing more. But I knew it was not possible. Damn Page for his arrogance.

Our reunion tasted so sweet, I would have loved to have savoured it a little longer. Already it was time to talk. We all looked at each other in silence. Finally, we sat down and settled ourselves for a family conference. It was taken for granted that I would speak first.

I went back in time; back to the shop, back to Muthana, his friends and that damned 'holiday of a lifetime'. They listened intently, interrupting occasionally. The most

161

important question from Zana was why had I not gone to the press. She told me she had been hinting at that all along.

How could I have gone to the press? I was terrified that the girls would be moved somewhere even more remote than this – although, now I'd seen it, I couldn't think of anywhere more remote than this. I would never have thought of looking up a mountain for my girls. There were no maps of the area; even the locals in Taiz didn't know where Ashube was.

I asked Zana to tell me her story before I went any further. We could put together the pieces of the picture a bit better when we both had both sides.

She told me about the day she arrived in the village. She had been introduced to Abdullah and was told to shake hands, which she did as a matter of courtesy. She was then told that this creature, six stone, five foot three, ill, puny and weak, was her husband. She told me she had written to me to warn Nadia of what was in store for her. But of course I had never got the letter.

When Nadia arrived in Yemen her fate was the same. She was introduced to Mohammed in the same way, although her 'husband' was not as sickly as Zana's. Neither would speak the names of their 'betrothed', preferring instead to refer to them as 'He', 'Him' or 'It'.

I watched Zana, her gesticulations, as she spoke in hurried gushes. Her hands were calloused and rough, nails bitten or broken to the quick on swollen fingers. Scars that I had never seen before marked her skin in deep and angry reminders of what she had suffered, reminders that would never leave her.

She had pulled down the yashmak, the veil that covered her face up to her eyes. Her face was older; not just

162

because I hadn't seen her for so long but because of the suffering, hardship, fear and illness. She'd had malaria three times. She told me how bad Ward had been to her because she would not conform to their rules, bend to their will; how she had to beg for food because Abdullah would leave her short of money when he went away to Saudi to work, for years at a time. How, on the rare occasions he did send money, his mother, Ward, would keep most if not all of it for herself.

She had written many letters to us, especially to her father, begging him to save them, let them come home. The only reply she'd had from him was to say that I had left him a broken man, taken everything he owned and left him to rot with broken bones. Even though she persisted in her attempts to change her father's mind she realised it wouldn't work. Both she and Nadia had found out that they had been bought. Bought from their father for £1,300 pounds each. Sold by him. There was never any marriage agreement, nor ceremony, nor consent. Abdul Khada had enjoyed telling her that. Zana hadn't had any letters from us for a long time. We knew why.

For over two hours we went over and over what had happened to us all since the girls had left for Yemen. I felt they were leaving things out, that there was a lot that they weren't telling us. I had to repeat what I had been doing to get them out.

'Two months after you left, I found out what your father had done. With the help of a social worker we started to write to the British Embassy, Yemeni Embassy, the Home Office and Foreign Office in London. The social worker and I went to visit Roy Hattersley, our MP. All the responses I got were negative and unhelpful but I persisted.

163

'There was also the trouble that Naser Saleh caused, with the help of your father, Gowad and Abdul Khada, but this has been sorted out, as you know. I also got in touch with this big children's charity in Geneva. Mr Cantwell, who is the president, has been helping a lot, but even he is limited. I have some of his letters with me, and some from the other places, too.'

I got the letters from my suitcase and gave a bundle to each of the girls. They sat quietly reading them. Zana swore, cursing the officialdom of the whole affair.

'The only thing to do is make a tape for Mr Cantwell. If they don't believe you want to come home we'll make a tape for them to listen to and play to the journalists. All we need is a cassette recorder.'

'Mommy, I'll do it.' Zana spat a chewed-off nail across the floor. 'This time it'll be my own words and I will tell the whole truth. I still have my recorder. I'll make a tape for you to take back with you.'

Nadia was confused. 'Why don't they believe you, Mommy?'

'Well, it's because of the tape they had you make for your father,' I explained. 'I knew as soon as I heard it that they had forced you to make it. Unfortunately, it was a good few years before I managed to get it from your father.'

'Yeah,' Mo interjected, 'I took it from his pocket one day. He went mad. He told me to choose between Mom and him. I chose Mom. What he did to yous was bad, man, really bad. He ain't no father of mine, and he ain't no father to yous either!' He scowled. 'You ain't seen what he did to Mom and the rest of us. I want to kill him – and Gowad and Abdul Khada too!'

'Mo, that's enough.' I waved a hand at him to hush him.

Nadia spoke softly. 'Mommy, Daddy said that you had just left him, with broken bones and ill. He said you took everything, Mo, Aish, Tina and all the furniture. He was left with nothing but his illness. He said you smashed his head, too. Now you won't let Mo and the girls see him.'

'Crap, man!' Mo was hopping mad. 'He did it all himself. Mom got this letter saying that a woman was coming to take Ashia and bring her here as a prostitute, then they were going to get Tina and me! He got thousands for his compensation – sixteen thousand, mega bucks. He spent it all on prostitutes in Balsall Heath. Got them presents and everything. That was just after Mom and us left.'

'How do you know that, Mo?' Nadia asked. Her dad's part in all this was hard for her to come to terms with.

'Cos Muriel Wellington saw him talking to these women, and he said it to us himself.'

Nadia's face reddened with shock.

'Look, Nadia. If you or any of my kids want to see your father, I will not stop you. Not now, not ever. I don't think I can ever consider forgiving him for what he has done to you, to all of us. I just want you both to be happy. I want you both to be free to choose your own way of life, not be forced to live your father's lie. You have written to me and begged me to get you out, and I want that too. I will never stop until I get that for you. Both of you.'

I meant every word of what I said.

Chapter Twenty-Seven

We sent Nadia home to tell her 'relatives' that she would be staying with Zana for a few days, to see her Mom and brother. She was really scared about this, but after a lot of cajoling from us she agreed to try and left to collect a few bits and pieces.

It became clear why she felt this way when she returned after a few hours, in full purdah, behind Gowad's father-in-law. He persisted in trying to lay down the law, not just with Nadia but with me, too.

This decrepit old man had lived in Birmingham almost all of his life, having gone there as a young man. He had settled and worked in Smethwick until his retirement when he decided it was time to draw his pension and spend the rest of his days in Yemen. When in England he used to brag about having sex with women, say how good the life was, how easy it was to live there. Now he squatted on his haunches in Zana's home, telling me what an awful place England was, belittling our way of life and culture. At one point he said that all the British women were whores and he had had sex with almost every woman he wanted, free or paid for. He boasted that he had forged documents to say he had a large family to support in Yemen and drew benefits for them from our Social Security. He had obtained a house from our over-burdened waiting lists for council houses and had rented it out to other Yemenis. He had committed adultery, fraud and theft. He spent his days now in Yemen, calling his brother Arabs to prayer from the minarets every four hours, not out of penitence for his sins but for his own prestige and honour, a legacy he had obviously passed on to Gowad. Such hypocrisy beggared belief.

During our heated argument, he made it quite clear that he would not allow any woman in this, his village, to go uncovered, to smoke or take initiative, such as inviting Nadia to stay with Zana. He pointed out that I had not sought his permission to stay in the Yemen and this had offended him greatly. I would have to ask him, in future, if I could go from one house to another, whom I could talk to, or who would be allowed to visit the house of Zana. How long did I intend to stay in Hokail, he wanted to know, so he could consider the application?

In no uncertain terms, and with a generous peppering of the English profanities with which he was familiar, I told him what I thought of him, and what he could do with his opinions and approvals. I added that I knew that Salama, his own daughter, was not going to return to the Yemen now that she had a life in Balsall Heath. She had left nine months ago, and if the Yemen was that great she would be itching to return. Instead, she and Gowad had made it clear to me a long time before that neither of them had the slightest intention of returning to Yemen to live on a long-term basis.

He was stunned into silence, which was the best possible outcome. He never brought up the subject of his 'position' again.

Nadia stayed with us for two days before terror finally got the better of her and she begged me to let her return to Gowad's house. I could not dismiss her great anxiety and, knowing that I would have to leave without my daughters, I thought it better to relent for fear of the retaliation of her 'family'. Mo was so concerned for Nadia that he insisted on going with her. I had to agree it would be better that he did.

Mo was making mental notes about the area in case there was a chance of escape. He was upset, angry and felt incredibly bitter that his sisters were living in such appalling conditions. Adrenaline surged through his thirteen-year-old body as he made discovery after discovery – the workload his sisters endured and the appalling way these new 'relatives' treated them. For most of the time he kept quiet but a deep resentment tormented him as he was helpless to resolve his sisters' problems. It was driving him crazy. Though withdrawn and sullen, he tried to put on a brave face for his sisters, playing cards with Nadia or football with Haney.

We stayed for ten days, partly with Zana, partly with Nadia. To get from Zana's to Nadia's home we would go the back way, around to the other side of Abdul Khada's house and up to a plateau, then across a vast stretch of barren, hilly land with sparse clumps of wild grasses and cacti. It took a good half-hour to cross this tough terrain, hot, dusty and full of boulders, but compared to climbing the mountain itself, it was by far the easier route.

Nadia's home was one of a small collection of similar houses. The closer we got to village the more refuse we encountered. Paper, plastic bags and bottles littered the ground. The flies increased in proportion to the volume of garbage, attacking, us relentlessly as we ineffectively

168

fanned at them. They were persistent and vicious, making direct attacks on our eyes to get at the moisture. I wanted to scream but I knew that if I did I would have a mouthful of squatters the moment I opened up.

Nadia lived in the tiniest of houses, constructed from the Yemeni version of what we know as wattle and daub – clay and reeds. It had fewer rooms and an even smaller space for washing than Zana's home. The bathroom was so small that even I could not stand up straight. The main room was not as big as either Ward's bedroom or the room in which her animals lived.

As the area was more built up, packed with more houses and people, the smell was concentrated to an almost unbearable level. This was obviously why the flies showed a preference for Ashube. I was petrified of them. The girls also had to cope with scorpions and snakes. Both had been bitten by one or the other. There was absolutely nothing to commend the area.

Sanitation was non-existent. Behind each little house was a dug-out which served as a resting-place for the waste from the toilet, a haven for millions of flies. I never once went to the toilet in all the time that I was in that village. The flies swarmed on anything and everything, whether it moved or not. Mo was eaten alive. You could hardly see an untouched area of skin, yet he would sit in the sun and fan the flies off the sleeping form of Haney. He and Haney got along famously now, never moving too far away from each other.

Zana's home was always teeming with visiting females, curious to meet me and Mo. They were so nice. They cried as they told me how awful they felt about what had happened. They all knew that Zana and Nadia were in the village against their will, having been tricked, and that they had been used to a place vastly different from Yemen. My girls were well liked in the villages and were given as much help as was possible in the circumstances when they needed it. The exception was Ward, who tried to ignore our presence. I met her only once. A friend of Zana had sent a pot of meat as a gift for us. She had given it to Ward to pass on. Ward had removed all the meat but for one tiny portion. A heated argument ensued between her and Zana, culminating in Zana throwing the whole pot at Ward as she swore and cursed in Arabic at her 'mother-in-law'.

Zana, Nadia, Mo and I spent long hours going over what had happened in Birmingham and Yemen. We covered everything. I had no illusions about what the girls had been through, although never once did they tell me how hard they had to work. Oh, they told me about working in the fields – they had little choice once I had seen Zana's hands – and although I felt an intense anger, it was certainly not the time to display it, or to voice my great fear for my beloved daughters.

Both Zana and Nadia insisted that I did more to help. Did they really think I wasn't doing enough, I wondered. It left me with a feeling of inadequacy. I'd tried almost everything. What else was there? Where should I go next for help? I asked them. There was a long, long, silence. They thought the only answer was to go to the press.

To do that I had to get back to England as soon as possible and put the wheels in motion. That was all there was to it. I had to go, and I had to go soon.

The day before I left, Zana took off to the mountains. She came back several hours later with a snuffy nose and red sore eyes – and her tape recorder. She handed me a

Miriam's son, Ahmed, and his cousin just after reunion in Taiz in 1988.

Left to right: Ashia, Miriam, Tina, with Mo at the back, Birmingham 1984.

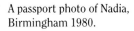

A passport photo of Nadia, Birmingham 1980.

Miriam and driver in Taiz in 1992. He's the one who assisted with our visas and took us to Campais.

The Sanaa to Taiz road - where the clouds kissed the mountaintops.

Sanaa to Taiz road (southside).

Miriam and Abdul, Sanaa 1992.

Driver, Jana, Miriam and Abdul, Sanaa 1992.

View of Sanaa from Chinese graveyard 1992.

1992. Campais.
The mountaintop just visible is Mokbana.

Taiz 1992.

Taiz 1992.

View of Taiz - with local children - from Mogillia mountain 1992.

North of Sanaa 1992.
Taiz 1992.

First sight of Taiz from the north.

Miriam (left) and Jana in purdah just before going to Aden 1992.

Miriam (left) and Jana, Sanaa 1992.

Miriam and Abdul, Sanaa 1992 (day of marriage).

Abdul and Jana, Taiz 1992.

Upmarket area of Taiz, Mogillia.

Jana and Miriam in Sanaa just before Jana left the Yemen.

Zana with Liam and Miriam in Birmingham in 1993. If only Nadia's children could enjoy this!

cassette. 'Mommy, hide that away and don't listen until you get home.'

I put it straight in my bag.

Zana had arranged a taxi for us, heaven knows how, and early next morning it arrived at the foot of the mountain. We had said a very difficult goodbye to Nadia the previous night. She was awfully strained, what with the pregnancy and the emotions of our impending departure. It was hard enough saying goodbye when I was still there, but this was the real McCoy. I was leaving and putting thousands of miles between me and my tormented daughters.

I had hoped that when we headed back to England I would be taking Zana and Nadia home. Going without them was breaking my heart. I had seen where they were living, how they were living, how they were. I would remember this always. Previously I'd had the illusion of paradise to ponder on; now I knew, oh so well, that this was no paradise. It doubled my resolve. Leaving my daughters behind in this hell-hole, I had to put my feelings into perspective. I had a burning ambition to achieve my goal and any displays of emotion would neutralise this, render me helpless. I had to be strong for them, they had to be strong for me.

I staggered back down the mountain behind a defiant Zana and a brooding Mo to the waiting car. 'Don't worry, Zana, I'll get this publicised and soon we'll have you home.'

'*Inshallah!*' Zana hugged us both briefly, as if too much physical contact bring her to breaking-point. We climbed aboard the taxi.

'I love you, Mommy. Tell everyone "hello." All our uncles and aunts, and my sisters, tell them I love them

171

and miss them.' She looked so sad, so forlorn, standing there in her black robes and yashmak.

'Come home and tell them yourself – soon. *Inshallah!*' I tried to smile, but a huge knot constricted my throat, restricting my breathing. I wanted to cry aloud and pull her into the car with us.

'*Ruher!*' she shouted to the driver. Go!

I watched from the rear window of the car as we bumped away. Despite her pregnancy, Zana shot off at a fair rate of knots and never once looked back. I knew she was crying, just as I was. I was grateful for the long journey ahead then. My mind was a turmoil of thoughts; I wouldn't have trusted myself to think clearly. I didn't take in the scenery as the miles of desolate desert rolled by. I stared out of the window, oblivious of Mo, oblivious of everything.

Back in Taiz, we booked in at the Al Gnad. Our flight was three days away. We had nothing to do, no interest in seeing Taiz or any other part of this hell-hole. I sat and smoked incessantly. Mo tried vainly to find entertainment on the television.

A knock came at the door quite late on our second day back in Taiz.

'Who is it?' I wasn't expecting anyone.

'Mohammed.'

I was surprised but asked Mo to open the door. Mohammed and Abdul Khada burst into the room. I was even more taken aback. 'Miriam Ali, I was surprised that you had come to Yemen, surprised that you had made it to the village, but nothing compares to the surprise I have to find you already preparing to leave!' He raised his eyebrows at me, waiting for an explanation of some sort.

I lit a cigarette and blew smoke in his face. 'Abdul Khada, you have a good life in England. I am not surprised that you left the life you had in the village for the lifestyle you enjoy in England. Why do you find it surprising that my daughters have that same need? After all, they had no desire to live in a village that is alien to them, no desire to marry, or bear children conceived during rape; no desire to have the skin stripped from their flesh, grinding corn for you and your like. No desire to have only flies as company or experience malaria as an alternative to flu. I cannot understand why you would ever think that I would allow my daughters to be treated in this manner, by you, Gowad, by these 'husbands' or by their own father. You were conned out of this money by Muthana and can't take the shame. The girls are mine. I *will* get them home, and soon. You'd better get used to that, Abdul Khada, and pass the message on to those who were conned with you!'

'Forget it Miriam, there is nothing you can do. Leave us alone. Just go home and forget it.'

Abdul Khada was getting so angry his face was fit to explode. I wished with all my heart that I could really speak out and tell him what I thought of him. For my daughters' sakes I shut my mouth and controlled my temper. I had said too much already.

It was so difficult. I had to summon every ounce of my will power. I wanted him to know my anger, the full force of it, but I also wanted to let him know that it was over, or nearly, hoping that that might keep him away from Zana, at least for a while. 'There is something I can do, Abdul Khada, and I have already done it. It's too late, and out of your hands.'

Abdul Khada, furious and red-faced, glared at me. I could read his thoughts. What has she done? Is she bluffing? He spun round, slamming out of the room.

Mohammed, ashamed, head bowed, followed. At the door he paused, turned to me. 'I think you will have to buy them back, Miriam.'

'Like you did with your daughter, Mohammed?'

His eyes moistened. He left quietly to follow his father out of the hotel. Through the window I could see Abdul Khada storming up the hill, Mohammed running after him.

Tomorrow we would leave for home. Only one more day to be suffered in Yemen, waiting impatiently, and then I would be able to fight.

Chapter Twenty-Eight

We arrived home tired, filthy and exhausted. The ten-hour trip had done nothing to settle our minds. Ashia and Tina greeted us eagerly, looking for Zana and Nadia close behind us. Their disappointment was strongly evident in their faces.

I thought about Zana and Nadia. If I felt this wrecked after three weeks in Yemen, how the bloody hell did my poor girls feel after six years? How the devil had they managed to survive in such filth and squalor? Why anyone would want to impose such suffering on two young girls, knowing what they were sending them to, was beyond me. And to do it with no moral scruples was beyond contempt.

We rested for the remainder of the day. The following morning I arranged to have a telephone installed. Zana's cassette was still in my suitcase. I decided to send it to Mr Cantwell of the Defence for Children foundation in Geneva, which I did on 2 May 1986, with a covering letter.

As soon as he heard the tape Mr Cantwell sought advice from the Home Office. Again, he insisted that the girls were not dual nationals, nor Yemeni. Douglas Hurd, the current Home Office Minister, said he would look into my case and talk to Geoffrey Howe, the Foreign Office Minister. In the meantime we should not publish the tape. Now that I had pricked the conscience of Douglas Hurd, Geoffrey Howe and associated ministers I felt quietly confident that things would move in my favour.

In August Mr Cantwell instructed Geraldine van Buren, a top barrister at Defence for Children in Geneva, to investigate the case. In her findings she argued that the girls were *not* dual nationals and that I, their mother, was their sole legal guardian. She put this to the Foreign Office in London, addressing a Miss Clay.

Miss Clay responded the following month, adamant that there would still be no assistance given whatsoever. She suggested that the girls would probably have become Yemeni citizens upon marrying Yemeni men! Why did they keep on referring to 'marriage'? These so-called 'marriages' were backed only by certificates forged by incompetent men who could not even make up their minds what the names of the participants were.

Miss Clay declined a request for a meeting with Geraldine, Mr Cantwell and myself, adding: 'The assistance we can offer to Nadia and Zana is, sadly, likely to be very limited.'

Mr Cantwell was furious. What was the function of the Foreign Office? 'You are the girls' sole legal guardian. Muthana had no rights to do what he did,' he wrote.

But he *had* done it and, so far, he had actually got away with it.

Ms van Buren's findings were a new straw to cling to but I didn't feel elated, knowing that no matter what I found out to add to my case, the Foreign Office would not be assisting me. I talked to Mr Cantwell again about forcing the government's hand by publishing the tape. So far our main consideration had been the girls themselves. If we published the tape, I was advised, the publicity might have an adverse affect on their safety. I had conflicting feelings about this, but I had faith in Mr Cantwell and chose to go along the path he recommended as his assistance had proved invaluable. We held off a little longer, hoping that something would turn up to save the girls. Mr Cantwell would investigate our options, I would hold on to my sanity by the skin of my teeth.

After a disastrous Christmas my New Year resolution was to keep on trying, never to give up. In this I had the full support of Mr Cantwell and my solicitors. We decided to make preparations for the girls' homecoming, to behave as if they could be given their freedom at any moment.

On 12 January 1987 I wrote to Mr Page in Yemen, inquiring about obtaining new British passports for my girls to travel should the opportunity arise.

On 8 February I received the application forms from Page, together with instructions on how to apply. I immediately sent them off to Zana and Nadia, disguised as birthday cards. Somehow they would have to get these forms completed and sent back to me. I felt awful asking them for photographs, knowing how difficult it would be.

In April I had the anticipated response from Zana. 'Mom, you know we're in a prison and you asked us to go to Taiz for the photos. If you had asked me to climb Mount Everest barefoot it would have been a lot easier. How on earth can we get to Taiz? Every time I read the line where you said, "You have to get the photos", it stabs me like a knife because we *can't*. We're stuck here in this Godforsaken village. I knew something would go wrong.

177

I had the feeling all the way and I hate myself. What we gonna do now? *Rot here?* Can't Geraldine van Buren or Cantwell do something? Phone him and explain to him that we haven't got any small recent photos. We have got a Kodak film and we took two each and I cut them like passport photos, but I've got that feeling that they won't be any good.'

Enclosed were two Kodak 'instant' photos of Zana and Nadia, which they had taken themselves and cut to the required size. I was truly amazed at their achievement and consistent willpower. But they were right. The photos were useless. Well, I would just have to bend the rules and use the old original 1980 passport photos. What choice did we have?

In May I sent all the documents to Page, by registered post, enclosing 600 ryals and the photographs for the application. I didn't hear a thing for ages. By August, I was totally cheesed off. I got on to the FCO to complain about the delay in getting the passports issued. The FCO contacted Page. He denied ever receiving the applications and money. The FCO came back to me. I still had the registered post receipt. Page's denial was challenged and my letter was found at the bottom of a dusty, unopened pile which had been lying around for some time. He subsequently admitted that he *had* received the applications and money but he excused himself by saying that he was waiting for the girls' birth certificates, without offering an explanation about the delay, or the confusion. I sent them off post haste.

All this time I was in close contact with my solicitors. Although I had been busy with the kerfuffle of the passports, at the end of the day it seemed that I was no closer to getting my girls out than I was to the moon.

178

Time rolled by with no news at all. September arrived and things were not much better.

Ashia had a boyfriend whom she'd been seeing for some time now, and he knew of the family's problem. It was he who suggested that we seek the advice of a local community adviser, Alf Dickens, who, for a fee, would act on our behalf. An appointment was made and we made our way to his office in Heathfield Road, Handsworth.

Phoenix Enterprise was run from Alf's parlour. He listened intently as I told him my story and immediately agreed to help me in any way he could, starting by waiving his fee. He told me about a friend of his who worked for the *Birmingham Post*. Alf rang the reporter, who came round. His name was Tom Quirke.

Although he was shown the letters and documents, Tom questioned me repeatedly over the next week as he found the story too incredible to believe. I wondered about the tape. Should I? Hell, it had been sixteen months since I had sent it to Cantwell. I worried about invisible hands moving my girls further into the desert, intimidated by the threat. However, I also remembered why the tape had been made and, on balance, decided that it was the only way. It would upset a lot of people, but we had to take the chance.

Tom decided that this was one of the biggest stories the *Post* had ever covered. He even went to interview Muthana, who told him that he was unhappy with the girls' behaviour and was keen for them to learn from the Yemeni traditional Muslim culture. 'I said that if they didn't like it they should write to me and they could come home.'

The story hit the headlines on 27 November and everything started to snowball from there. It generated a massive uproar and a lot of support. I was on cloud nine. One of the greatest things Alf ever did for me, and he did such a lot, was to arrange a huge press conference, at Tom's suggestion, in response to the media interest in his report.

I tried to remain in my chair, but when the tape was slipped into the machine and the first sounds of my Zana's voice filled the air with her still very evident Brummie accent I had to leave the room and let them get on with it. I took myself outside the office for a cigarette and quiet reflection while inside the tape played on to the journalists, who listened, utterly spellbound.

This is a verbatim transcript of the cassette made in Yemen by Zana during my visit.

Hello, Mr Cantwell. I am Zana speaking now. I have wrote you a letter, which I think you'll publish, and I have wrote a letter personally to you as well, and I'd thought I'd make a tape as well.

My mom came a couple of weeks ago but she didn't like it here, she didn't like the life here, and anyway me and my sister Nadia were so impatient, we wanted our mom to go back to England, 'cos she can't do anything about it here, she can't, she couldn't get us out. She went to the British Embassy when she got to Sanaa airport in the Yemen, and as she said, the man who works there, his name is Mr Page, she said he was very hostile to her. He didn't seem interested and he tried to scare my mom as well. He doesn't want her to come here, I don't know why. Anyway she will explain to you when she gets back.

When she got to us she said she couldn't do anything but she said as soon as she gets back she is going to tell you to publish it. I want to get out of here as soon as possible. Mr Cantwell, if only you could see how we're

180

living. It is terrible. I've been suffering for six years and there is nothing I could have done about it anyway 'cos I'm stuck in the village and I've got nobody to turn to, but when my mom told me about you, that you are trying to help us, I was very happy of the thought that somebody cares.

I . . . I . . . I've never heard anything about it. I dunno. It's just terrible. They're just keeping us here against our will and I dunno what for . . . I just wanna go home to my mother. Abdul Khada, the man who brought me here, he just told me that I was coming for a short holiday, and he'll take me back home and when I got here – they brought me up the big mountain, 'cos his house is on a high mountain – and when I got here, they told me that I was married! I nearly went in hysterics. They couldn't even hold me. I even tried to kill myself, Mr Cantwell! I took an overdose, but they choked me until I vomited them all out, the tablets. And I wrote a letter to my sister 'cos she came a couple of weeks after me, and I wrote her a letter. I tried to warn her . . . but she never got the letter. I wrote to her and I told her not to come. I'm enough! I couldn't stand it, her as well, but she didn't get the letter and she came and it happened to her as well and they separated us. And he took me to Campais. It was very far from here. We stayed there for six months and I went through hell, honest to God. I was so sick, he had to bring me back to the village, because I wanted to be with my sister. No doctors, no nothing. There is nobody I can turn to. If I'm sick or anything, I just have to put up with it and I have to work. Honest to God, Mr Cantwell, all they brought us here for is to work. That's all we've been doing is working!

If you'd have seen the boys that we were supposed to be married to, you wouldn't believe it, 'cos when I got here he was too small! He is younger than me and on our passport it says Miss, so how can we be married? And as I was told, by Abdul Khada's big son, his name is Mohammed Abdul Khada, he told me my passport's with him anyway, and my birth certificate, and my marriage certificate, well the false one anyway. It must be false, he said that they made it in England. How could they have made it in England, when we're Miss on the passport? Why didn't they let us have a marriage ceremony, or even *ask* us if we wanted to be married? I was only fifteen and my sister Nadia, she was only fourteen when she got here. We had to put up with it!

We had to live through hell and I hope and pray to God today that when my mom gets back and she lets you know everything, I hope that they come for us and just take us. I don't wanna stay here. I'm gonna go crazy, honestly. I'm gonna kill myself even, if I have to. I'd rather die than live here. Yes, Mr Cantwell, it is *that bad*! It is more worse that anyone would ever think. I don't think no girls have been through what we have been through . . . and they forced me to go to bed with him. I said *no*! They said, 'You'd better, because if you don't, we'll hold you down,' so . . . so I had to . . . what do you think about that, Mr Cantwell? [Zana is crying.]

Abdul Khada is in Saudi at the moment. He went to work there, and his son is . . . the one . . . I'm supposed to be married to. I hate him! I cannot accept him, I just *don't* want him, but it happened. [Her tone drops, confidential, bashful, ashamed.] You see . . .

182

I'm due to have a baby in about a month's time . . .
and my sister! [With defiance and anger in her voice
Zana continues.] She already has a baby son, he is two
years old. Well *they* do belong to us anyway, 'cos we
was *forced*! And now she is pregnant again. They are
in Saudi now, working. It's a shame about my sister,
Mr Cantwell, you should see how she is living, all on
her own. Gowad Abdul Magid, the man who bought
her, went to England. He has been there for five years,
since he left her here. He only stayed a year and he went
to England! And about eight or nine months ago he sent
for his wife and she went to England with him. She was
supposed to have only gone for three months, she has a
daughter and son and she left them with my sister Nadia
to look after them while she has a nice time in England.
My sister is suffering with them kids, they're terrible and
she has her own son and she is pregnant and she has to
do all the work herself. She keeps writing to them, to
tell Gowad Abdul Magid to send his wife back for her
children, but they won't answer her, they don't care.
She is stuck all on her own in that house, it's terrible.

My mom, she'll tell you, my mom, she couldn't
stand it! That's why she's going back so quick. I want
everything to be over and done with. [Zana breaks
down into tears.] When you publish it, Mr Cantwell,
if any of your people are gonna come in for questions
or anything, and they want us for questions, they *must*
take us out of the village. My mom will explain that
to you. I wanna get out of here, to Taiz or Sanaa, for
questioning, then I don't wanna come back again. I just
wanna go home! What are they holding me here for? I
don't wanna stay! I am British. I was born and bred in
England. My mom looked after us all our lives, even

my father! I don't even know him. I hate him! He was so wicked! [Zana loses all control as she speaks of her father.] He don't care! I used to write him letters, and tell him, 'Dad *please* let me come home!' but he doesn't answer me. [She is crying, now, talking through sobs.] I can't accept him as a father, ever, ever again! I'll never, ever forgive him all his life! I'll curse his grave. I just wanna go home to Mommy, that's all.

[There is a click as she presses the stop button, then another as she starts recording again, her voice stronger.]

I'm absolutely petrified from Abdul Khada! He hits me whenever he chooses, whenever he pleases. Even if he is in a bad temper, he just takes it out on me and hits me for nothing. I haven't done anything wrong to them. I've just been patient, that's all. All on my own! I haven't made any trouble for them. He used to force me to write nice letters to my mom and dad, that I'm happy here . . . I *had* to.

When your reporters get through, I hope, and they take us for questioning or anything, they're gonna try and make excuses. They're gonna say, 'Oh, listen, Zana's made a tape for her mom and dad, that she is happy!' and they will let them listen to it, you know, to make them believe that I said it. But I was forced to, Mr Cantwell! You *must* believe me. I read some of your letters, what you wrote to my mom, and I know that you are more impatient than she is. When she got here, and she saw how we lived, she nearly blew her head off! So I told her, 'Mom, go home, take it easy. Send the letters and the tape to Mr Cantwell from us and then he'll do everything, smoothly. Take time Mom, don't worry about us, and then we'll get out of here.' She

184

said OK, but she is worrying, Mr Cantwell. I feel so sick, because she is worrying so much. That's why I hate them, because they made my mother suffer.

He hits me sometimes, when he is here. And I've got nobody to turn to. He is going to make excuses to the government. He's gonna say, 'I buy her jewellery and gold and I give her clothes and everything.' Mr Cantwell, my mother *is* my gold! I only want my mom. I don't even wear their gold. I don't want it. I don't want nothing. It's just hard work and that's all we have been through, hard work in the village. I had blisters on my hands and feet from working in the hot weather. I just don't know how to explain it. It's just terrible I get a headache just thinking about it. And now my mom, she has to leave us again. My heart is going to rip to pieces when she goes. I thought we were gonna go with her. And she said that it didn't turn out right. [Zana is crying again.]

I have faith in you, Mr Cantwell. And I have faith in God! I'll be patient. My father should be chucked out of England for making that false marriage certificate. My mom, she's not married to him, they should ask for her consent anyway, but they never! God knows! Only God knows what they done! My mom said she is going to get a telephone fixed in when she gets home and she'll explain to you on the phone. I just hope everything works out.

Abdul Khada, when he found out that my mom come here, I think he got scared. He even had the cheek to tell the people to come up and listen if we're going to say anything or if my mom is going to do anything and now they say he's coming back to his house here 'cos he is so scared. He thinks my mom is going to take us

185

away. They're all scared, even my father. He hasn't had anything to do with us since we have been here. He just sold us, Mr Cantwell. For money – they *did* give him money. As we were told he was paid thirteen hundred pounds for us, in England. And my mom? She never even saw that money. She didn't know anything about it. And when my mom tried to get us out of here before, all these years she's been trying they get to Taiz and they pay the police money. They paid them twice, which is true. They paid them two thousand ryals the first time to stop them from doing anything and they paid them two thousand ryals the next time, because they get to Taiz . . . the people, who tried to get us, get through to us, because we are far from Taiz – it's over two hours' drive in a car, we are in the village, and they get paid off, the police. They pay the police money and they keep quiet, they don't do anything after 'cos they're so hungry, all they want is money, the police here. It's a terrible government. My mom, she will tell you when they are going to come for us she don't want the police to get involved 'cos they are just gonna get paid off again, like they always are. They are not to get involved at all. She will tell you anyway!

As I was told, when we were in England and they was getting everything arranged behind our backs, about the marriage. There is a man in England, his name is Mohammed Abdul Karim, my mom has to find out where he is anyway, because he is the one who did everything, he knows everything as I was told, about the marriage certificate, how it was made and everything. I've seen it, even myself, the marriage certificate. Abdul Khada showed me when I was here. It's like . . . er . . . it's a piece of paper and it's thick, like a card, and it's got all Arab writing on it – I didn't understand what it said, though – in ink pen! It's all Arab writing and it's been stamped. I don't know where it was stamped, I think it was stamped by Mohammed Abdul Karim, I think. False! He is not supposed to and there was two witnesses as well, with my father. One of them, as I was told, died, and the other one – I don't know about him. And my father and Abdul Khada, they were the only ones involved.

I don't know, I just don't know what is happening and I don't know how they done it. I don't know how they got away with it. Just paying money, I think that's how they got away with it, because they was gonna come once, the police! The agent man in Taiz, who used to hide my mom's letters. He got took in prison when my mom phoned or wrote a letter, I think, to say my daughters don't get my letters. He got chucked in prison and he paid money to get out. Well, *him*, he is in Taiz, he lives in Taiz, he is the agent. He is the one who was supposed to give us our letters, but he didn't. My mom, she said she wrote two letters recently, before she got here, we got them, but when we wrote to her, she never got ours! They held them. They never sent them to her. They got to Abdul Khada's hands, but I don't know how! I think that man in Taiz, he took my letter and he sent it to Abdul Khada and he opened it and he read it. He had the cheek. He never sent my letter just to my mom and she was worried and that is what we are going through, Mr Cantwell!

We can't trust anybody any more, even if we want to write a letter we can't. We just have to suffer. I just don't know how they are ever going to get away with that. Mr Cantwell, don't let them. They should

187

be punished, they should be thrown in prison even for doing that. Forcing us into marriage, forcing us to go to bed, keeping us here against our will, not giving our letters to our mother, even hitting us.

When my mom arrived here she got to Taiz. Abdul Khada's son, Mohammed, he lives in Taiz. She went to his house before she got to us in the village, he had to get her a car, and he phoned his father up in Saudi and he said that he wanted to talk to my mom. She answered him and he said, 'Hello! I hope you have not come to cause any trouble, because if you have, I've got the girls' father's consent to take them to Marais.' That's *his* country, my father's country, it's near to Aden. He said: 'I've got his consent. I'll just take the girls to Marais and wipe my hands clean.' He was trying to threaten my mom.

I told her, 'Don't worry Mom, he can't take us there, he can't do nothing!' They are only trying to scare my mom. They said that they got a sort of letter off of my dad, the government here, I think anyway, to say that we are going to be taken to Marais if there is going to be any trouble caused. So watch out, Mr Cantwell. That's what I'm scared of, because when they get through, your reporters or any reporters, or any publishers or anything, they are gonna try and take us to Marais. I know they are! They will try, anyway.

If only you knew how crafty they are. They're Arabs! They are very sly, they just want their own way and they don't want to lose, but they have to lose this time, Mr Cantwell. Please believe me! You *must* make them ashamed of what they have done. They *must* be! They *should* be! I know God is gonna punish them anyway, on Judgement Day, but I want them to be punished today! I want them to know what they have done wrong. I just wanna go home. I just wanna go to England. I wanna go to my mother and live happy. Honestly, really, I'll kill myself if I have to . . . if they don't take me and my sister. My sister is suffering even more.

I don't know what else to say. They just keep trying to threaten my mother. It's a shame for my mom, she has been through a lot, you know. I just hate to think what she has been through, even us!

So, Mr Cantwell, it's all up to you now. God be with you. Be careful because they are very, very crafty, the people. Goodbye for now from Zana. I hope everything will work out OK and I get back to my country. Goodbye. *Please help us!* Please, *Please*, I beg you! We are suffering. I've gotta get out of here! Goodbye and good luck . . . for all of us.

Chapter Twenty-Nine

It was a Saturday afternoon, the day after the press conference. I was in Alf's office. I was there because he had told me that a journalist was coming to interview me. We were expecting Eileen MacDonald from the *Observer*.

She arrived, fresh-faced and young. I was impressed. Speaking softly, she introduced herself as she took off her coat and handed it to Alf. Sitting down, she began to ask questions and took notes in shorthand as I began the story from the beginning – yet again.

Tom Quirke and Eileen, along with an *Observer* photographer, John Riordan, had already been to interview Muthana. After Eileen and Alf had left, Tom placed a micro-cassette recorder on the table. 'Muthana was obliging!' he sighed. Alone in the office we sat, listening intently.

M: Yes – what do you want this time?

EM: My name is Eileen MacDonald. I'm from the *Observer* newspaper. It's obviously about this story concerning—

M: I don't know where you get these bits and pieces from, honest to God. The missus went over to Yemen to bring them back. They won't come back. It is a load of rubbish. I don't know who made that tape. Honest to God, that's the truth. If you want to give us money or somebody else by now money that's up to you. It's nothing to do with me. Since I've been there they don't want to come back. They say that I have tapes and everything. They say they're happy.

EM: Well, did you actually sell your daughters?

M: Why should I sell them? Piss off! Did I sell my daughters? I worship my daughters, I worship them . . . [Muthana goes into a screaming rage] . . . You prove it! You prove I sold my daughters, and I cut my throat!

[Eileen tries to apologise for her remark as Muthana makes dramatic slicing motions at his throat. John captures this moment on film.]

M(hissing): I'm going to get my solicitor.

EM: What's the name of your solicitor?

M: (parrying the question): I'm going to see my solicitor.

[Tom asks if he can take a photograph.]

M: Not yet. What for?

EM: Can we just talk about it? It seems we've got the wrong end of the stick. Could you explain what's happened?

M: (sounding confused): Look, stand there. You can take a photo outside.

[Tom agrees but Eileen pushes for the interview.]

EM: Can we sit down and talk about it?

M: I'll talk to him over there!

TQ: You have talked to me, yes.

M: I did a photograph. I was a witness. There's nothing to talk— I'm not worried.

TQ: I don't understand that. These people have come from London, you see.

M: Yes, but don't give no story to nobody. You have to get paid to get a story. What do you want to know?

EM: Can you just tell me what's happened about your daughters?

M: My daughters went out for a holiday.

EM: Are you from Yemen?

M: I'm from Yemen, yes. I've been here thirty-two years.

EM: They went for a holiday and that was about 1980, yes?

M: They met somebody there and they got involved and they got married. They got kids. The missus say why you, er, she give her consent. She filled a form when they were there. She fill a form, she give her consent for them to go there. I think you can have them. She give her consent.

EM: She gave her consent. Right. So who actually took the girls to the Yemen?

M: Friends, for a holiday. They know them otherwise they would never go with anybody stranger. They went with friends who we have known over thirty years.

EM: What is the marriage age in the Yemen?

M: From thirteen onwards.

EM: From thirteen?

M: They were seventeen or eighteen when they got married. Not fourteen.

TQ: According to the birth certificate, Nadia was fourteen years old. We've seen the birth certificate, she was fourteen years old. In 1980, when she left this country, Nadia was fourteen years old.

M: In 1964 she was born.

TQ: I've seen the birth certificate. Well, we won't argue this point. She was fourteen.

M: Yes, I know the birth certificate. 1964 she was born so how old is she now? How old in 1980?

TQ: OK. Sixteen, fair enough.

M: Sixteen? But when she got married there, she didn't get married until about one and a half years later, nearly two years.

EM: Was she actually formally married in a ceremony?

M: Doesn't matter. Muslim. You have to sit, six to eight witnesses, and write what God says in Hindi. That's how we are married all our lives. Because we do go to church like here. Like here. No, we sit down at a table and we sign the papers. If you want to know about Muslims, ask somebody else about how they got married, not me.

EM: There is an article in the *Birmingham Post* saying that you weren't pleased with the girls' behaviour in this country. Were they misbehaving?

M: I don't want to get mixed up with that, what people say. I don't want to be in a court of constitution.

EM: So you were worried about it?

M: Everybody worried about their child.

[Tom finding Muthana's reference to 'child' intriguing, asks him which child he is referring to. Muthana begins to back away and, Tom, sensing this, tries to reassure Muthana so that he carries on talking. Eileen, seeing a problem arising, tries to get around to Muthana's side of the debate.]

EM: So, you were worried about how they were going to be brought up in this country?

M: Not because I was worried about how they were like. I didn't want them to get mixed up with any-body. [He swears uncontrollably for a few moments] I did not want them to grow up in Birmingham where they would marry a black or they would become prostitutes, like their mother. In Yemen, they are good. They are Muslim. No one does anything bad to them. What they say is untrue, they are happy. Everyone says they are not, but they are. I have letters that say they are happy.

EM: Are you saying that their mother was a prostitute?

M: That's what she is doing now.

EM: So, you got a holiday for them. How long was the holiday meant to be for?

M: Ten days.

EM: You paid for them. Did you know where they were going to be staying when they were there?

M: In the Lebanon with my friends.

EM: Was that friends of your family?

M: It was a long time ago, I can't tell you that.

EM: So when they didn't come back, how long was it till you heard that they had been married or that they wanted to stay?

M: Nearly two years.

EM: Nearly two years? You weren't worried about them, especially with what you were saying?

[Muthana rants and raves. The only intelligible words are 'no one', then, 'I'm going to make coffee!' He reappears.]

M: That's it! I don't want to say any more.

EM: There's just one more thing. This friend of yours, Gowad, now he says that he took Nadia, the younger girl, and it was an arranged marriage. Everything was arranged. The girl knew she was going to get married?

M: I can't help you!

EM: When did they know they were going to get married?

194

M: After they meet somebody. They're bound to meet somebody!

EM: When the girls went away, did you think they were going on a holiday?

M: It was a holiday!

EM: It was a holiday? It was a holiday as long as they wanted?

M: Ten days, as I told you!

EM: It just seems coincidence that Gowad is a friend of yours and Nadia is married to his son. Is that just a coincidence?

M: It is a coincidence. It's a mix-up with his son.

EM: Have you had any letters from the girls saying they're unhappy?

M: Unhappy?

EM: What do the letters say?

M: Look, I'm making a cup of tea and I'll sort them out. I've got some letters but I don't know what they are.

EM: Are they happy letters, or are they sad?

M: I showed him some letters yesterday.

EM: Was there money exchanged? Any bribery?

M: Never!

EM: It's normal isn't it, for you to accept some dowry?

M: Never. I've known Gowad about sixteen years!

EM: Yes, but people say that you received thirteen hundred each for the marriage.

M: Never. It isn't true that I received money. I never had a penny. I lost some money! [Muthana goes crazy, cursing Gowad in fits and starts, implying that he, in fact, gave money to Gowad.]

EM: How much money did you give him?

M: Fifty pounds. [His voice fades as he goes back into the house. Tom's voice can be heard as he shouts, apparently through the door, 'Is that it? Sorry to have troubled you on a Saturday morning. Thanks, Mr Muhsen. Bye bye. Nice to see you again. Sorry to interrupt your Saturday morning.']

The part which intrigued me most was the reference Muthana made to a letter from the girls, which he had shown to Tom. I asked, then, if he remembered what it said. Tom said it read: 'Daddy, if you love us please let us come home.'

That Sunday, 30 November, the *Observer* ran a story headlined BRITISH GIRLS SOLD AS YEMEN BRIDES. Now Muthana was pursued relentlessly by the media. The following Wednesday, 3 December, Tom Quirke again witnessed Muthana's hypocrisy.

'I showed my girls photographs of the two boys. We [meaning himself, Gowad and Abdul Khada] hoped that when they got to Yemen the girls would get on well with the boys and want to marry them. In the Yemen men and women are not allowed to walk down the street together if they are not married, let alone touch each other, but I said if the girls didn't want to marry the boys, then that was that and they would have to give the certificates back to me.'

This, he admitted, was unbeknown to me and my daughters. The fact that he was more interested in getting the paperwork back, rather than considering the wellbeing of his own kin, was alarming. But he had admitted that he *had* sent them on holiday, after making sure that all papers were in order, just in case the girls liked the boys enough to marry them. What kind of father was he?

During the week many papers carried Muthana's racist, derogatory comments, which he had repeatedly made to different journalists. He was summoned before the Race Relations Board. I really wish I could have been a fly on the wall, to find out what happened to him.

The following Sunday the *Observer* ran another story, this time exposing that there were many more British 'child brides' in Yemen who had simply disappeared than anyone could dare estimate.

I had a call from Geraldine van Buren. She was concerned about all the publicity and, more importantly, the type of publicity, we were getting. She reiterated that the point of holding back the tape was to ensure the safety of my daughters in Yemen, and added reflectively, 'Perhaps you should consider that when I harangued the Foreign Office about British girls duped into marriage, their response was "Which ones?".'

Chapter Thirty

The media coverage had generated so much interest and public sympathy that it seemed a little out of control, with headlines about 'sex slave sisters' appearing in one of the more lurid tabloids. That upset all of us. Mo was having an awful time at school being teased by his classmates. Cruelly, they mocked him about his sisters' rape. He defended their honour admirably – though bruised and battered, he assured me that these others were far worse off than himself.

Ever since we'd returned from the mountains we had been plagued by the memory of the horrors the girls endured daily – and the smell, the filth and flies. What we experienced was merely the tip of the iceberg. There was a lot that the girls had not told me. My presence had made the girls too busy or embarrassed to talk about their normal daily routine, but I had seen the other women working. So my imagination worked overtime, tormenting me with ideas about what was going on.

A national paper had telephoned with an offer to pay my air fare to the Yemen and the fares for my girls to come back with me. Elated by this, I decided it was time to apply for a visa. It was a boring Sunday. I hate Sundays. All the offices were closed, nothing would be moving. Ann Sufi had come round early for a cuppa, to keep me company.

We strolled to the local newsagent's to buy a Sunday paper. Photographs of my family were plastered all over the front pages of one of them. We bought a copy each and raced back to my house. The front page of the paper was truly amazing and there was further coverage in the centre pages. Pictures of Zana and Nadia with her baby Tina were spread all over.

I cried long and hard when I saw the photographs. I hadn't seen them before and found them emotionally distressing. Zana looked distressed enough herself, but Nadia – my God! She looked empty. Her eyes stared vacantly into the open barren plains of the path between the villages.

For the first time I saw a picture of her new daughter, Tina, so named after Nadia's own sister. Both of the girls were out of the long purdah coats and veils. This meant that all the men in the villages must have been away working, probably in Saudi. When this happened the only males left in the villages were either very old – possibly blind from cataracts, as I witnessed myself – or very young. It was the only time when the girls, and quite a lot of the other women, could relax by wearing a *shalwa* and chemise, a dress and trousers set.

I was to be haunted by the expressions on my girls faces for so long. The more I read through the story the more confused I became. My emotions were all over the place. Alarm, hope, anger, cynicism, disbelief, anxiety – a touch of confidence. In and out of each emotion. I felt like I was in a maze.

I studied the pictures of my daughters and grandchild, I could only feel grief silently, totally absorbed in the story, seeing my daughters in those surroundings, the anguish etched on their faces. My vision blurred as I cried, at first quietly, then in racking sobs. Ann tried to comfort me, but I could find no solace in her words of reassurance. I wanted my babies back. That's all I'd ever asked. 'Look at them, Ann. They're so sad! And look – it's Nadia's new baby. What way is that to see my grandchild for the first time? Look at them!'

It took me a long time to compose myself. For quite a while I didn't see why I should even try. The feelings of helplessness and utter anguish had taken away any desire to congratulate the paper on a good cover. I didn't want a bloody story. I wanted my kids. Now.

Ann took me to her house. I can remember nothing more of that day or the next – or even the day after. A few days later, in a desperate hurry, Ann drove me to London, where I had made my visa application for Yemen.

The press were hot on our trail and, in fact, reached our destination well before we did. London was in the swing of the sales and the roads were chaos. By the time we got to the Embassy, the media had the entrance blocked off.

Mutual desperation led to my visa being issued in a nearby pub, where we were met by a staff member of the Consulate Division of the Yemen Embassy, in return for luring the press away from their doors.

Chapter Thirty-One

It was a crappy Christmas Eve. I went round to Ann's to see if she had any news. The reporters had been ringing her, too, since the story broke.

It was only then that Ann told me. On Wednesday, for the first time ever, Zana had rung. I could have kicked myself for being out. Ashia had been alone at home at the time of the phone call from Yemen. She was shocked to hear her sister's voice after all this time, but she insisted on asking Zana a few carefully chosen questions to make sure it was actually her speaking. Zana passed with flying colours, not minding the cost or length of the call, just enjoying talking to the kid sister who had always idolised her.

Ashia was so overjoyed, so full of emotion, that soon she'd had Zana crying too. 'We thought we'd see you soon, Aish. They keep telling us we'll be home in a week!'

Ashia told her, in between sobs, that I was going to Yemen again, soon. Zana was impatient to see me again, so that they could come home with me.

Reporters had been ringing and Ashia, overwhelmed, had told them all about the call. When pressed, she had given them a contact number in Yemen. Zana and Nadia were staying with Colonel Abdul Walli in Taiz during the day. He was Commander-in-Chief of the police at Mokbana, although he was based in Taiz. Zana had told Ashia that the Yemeni government had provided her and Nadia with a luxury apartment, right there in the city of Taiz. In the day, they could be reached at his phone number. At night they would go to their luxury apartment.

Angry, impatiently, I wished for morning when I could ring Zana and Nadia and actually speak to them on the phone in Yemen for the first time.

It was Christmas Day.

I spent the whole day pondering over that call from Zana. The fact that the girls had been moved from the wilderness into Taiz following international interest must mean that finally some Doubting Thomas in the Foreign Office had stirred himself. The news coverage had put us all in the strangest mixture of moods, feelings that swung constantly. But the one that kept surfacing was hope. We all had high hopes that officialdom would come through for us, to end the farce that had held my girls prisoner in Yemen.

We had hoped to have them home to celebrate Christmas all together. In anticipation of their imminent freedom we had bought a tree – only a green artificial one, but the first tree we had put up for many years.

I rang the number Zana left many, many times. Each attempt was greeted by the engaged tone. I had spent the last few days zapping up and down the motorway, going to and from London for various reasons, one of which was the offer from a newspaper to pay my fare to Yemen.

On this particular day, I had gone to London for a meeting, ostensibly to collect my ticket. But the offer soon turned into a fiasco as the terms and conditions emerged. Exclusive rights were one thing, but when the editor produced a micro-camera, asking me to take pictures of buildings and anyone toting a gun, emphasising 'politically sensitive shots' as a priority, the meeting erupted into a seriously nasty slanging-match.

I spent Christmas Day in London, in the *Observer* offices, sorting through all the mail that had seen sent by the sympathetic British public. In the end it was the *Observer* who paid for my ticket – with no apparent strings attached: that is to say, no exclusive rights and no camera. In their office I tried again to contact my daughters. After an unsuccessful rally of calls to Yemen, I finally got through to Zana. Nadia would not speak, for fear of being punished by Mohammed or the government, and Zana herself spoke in a low and frightened voice that caused me great concern.

'Our dad has just rung. An hour and a half he was on the phone. It's the first we have heard from him in all this time and now he just says we have to wait until all the press coverage dies down before we can come home. He said that he would kill himself if things didn't work out properly because he would die of the shame. He begged us to stay in Taiz until the press have forgotten about the story. I just said he would be lucky! Then he said he would kill himself if we came home. I told him, good – do it!'

'Why are you in Taiz, Zana?'

'They have moved us into Taiz, Mom . . .' Zana hesitated. 'But they have made us leave the kids in the village. Nadia and I are frantic. They say now that we can't come home without "*them*"!' She spat down the phone in her annoyance at the insistence of the Yemen officials that they must bring their captors home with them. 'Otherwise we have to leave the kids behind. Nadia won't do that. I don't think this is right, Mom. And they keep on at us to sign things that we can't read, 'cos they're in Arab.' The line crackled and hissed at me.

'Don't sign anything, Zana! For God's sake. Don't sign anything! Give me Nadia!' I commanded.

'She won't come to the phone, Mom. She's shy and she's scared, too. She's with Abdul Walli now, keeping him busy while I talk to you.'

'Well, you tell her, then, that she is not to sign anything, and don't you sign anything. Nothing at all. Either of you. Do you hear me?'

Zana burst out crying. 'Mom, it's too late. We already have!'

'Oh, Christ!' I sobbed down the phone. 'What did you sign?'

'I told you, Mom, I couldn't read it!'

'Then WHY DID YOU SIGN IT?' I bellowed at her.

Zana stammered down the phone. I could hardly hear her. ''C-c-cos they said if I did sign, I-I-I could g-go home and b-be with yous!' She was crying her heart out. I felt faint.

'What do they want now, Zana?' I tried to soothe my daughter but I broke down, sobbing hysterically.

'They want *them* to come too!' she said. That was the last thing I heard.

I had blacked out for quite some time before I began to fight the fog in my brain. All I could think of was to ring the British Embassy in Sanaa. They would send someone to see the girls in Taiz as soon as possible, to find out what had happened.

Now I could not bear to be alone. Well, not just alone – I didn't like not having any of my family around. If I was at home and they all decided to go out, that was fine, so long as I knew that they were safe. Ever since Muthana's threats to Ashia, Tina and Mo, I hated being too far away from them unless it was absolutely unavoidable. I knew friends would take care of them, but I relished that role myself, so being away meant both missing the kids and worrying for them.

I could not stand the games my mind was playing any longer so I rang Mo, who was staying with Muriel Wellington, a good friend. He needed me right now, I needed him, too, and although Muriel was doing a great job, and would have cared for Mo for a year if necessary, he wanted to go home. And so did I. I told him to meet me at home that evening.

I took a taxi from London to my house in Birmingham. It was terribly expensive, but even so, I'd rather than face the English transport system, with its congestion of shoppers going home after a day at the sales.

All my remaining family were congregated at home that evening. It was a good feeling to be on my own territory and part of my own family again, even though the mood was sullen and oppressive.

The ceiling of the front room was alive with sparkling decorations in all colours and shapes, bells, snowflakes, stars. It was all very pretty. The tree twinkled with tiny lights and colourful delicate baubles, topped off with a good draping of tinsel in all colours of the rainbow. The girls and Mo had done a great job. Hope justified a small celebration for the festive season.

Tina and Ashia were cleaning the house yet again. I took a deep breath and called to them as they started to disappear up the stairs. 'Has there been any news? From Zana and Nadia or anyone?'

The girls turned back and slightly shook their heads. I had no choice but to wait it out. I didn't mention that I had spoken to Zana: they would want to know what had been said and I really didn't want to tell them that the latest development, judging by what Zana had told me, could have a devastating effect on our fight for their freedom.

At that moment, I hated the telephone. The damned thing just would not ring. I suffered from an overwhelming desire to pick it up and dial numbers that could be of help, but knowing that this would prevent a call from being received I kept away from it. The girls and Mo kept away from it, too. I would leap down their throats if I caught them on it, chatting to friends. 'What if someone is trying to ring me about the girls? How can they talk to me if you lot are yakking on the phone, keeping it busy!' I would scream at them, feeling angry but guilty at the same time.

I waited and waited and waited. I clenched my fists so tight they itched. It was a habit I could not break now, even if Zana and Nadia had been sitting in the front room in the flesh. I went upstairs to do some washing in the bathtub. I had to do something to keep busy, keep me away from the phone.

I had spent three hours washing clothes and sheets as time slipped by with still no news. All I could think about was the girls and their mysterious move to Taiz. I would have known what was going on had it not been for the ridiculous saga at the offices of that newspaper. I should have been issued with my tickets and gone straight out after getting my visa that Tuesday. Now I had to wait again.

Always waiting.

My blood began to simmer as I confronted the issues

that had built up the tension within me. I was so close to getting the girls home, yet so far away at the same time. As the clock ticked away the minutes, then the hours, my blood began to boil. An unexploded volcano inside me rumbled and flared into flames of pure anger, resentment and hate. I fought to regain control, scrubbing the clothes and sheets into a mountain of lather and soap bubbles which built up the side of the bath as my temper built up inside me, just waiting to be set free, unleashed to take in victims. I wanted Gowad to knock on my door, or Muthana. Abdul Khada. Either one, or all of them. I would destroy them!

As the dormant volcano built up its molten lava into an ugly, red-hot sea of destruction, I imagined the redness to be blood. The blood of justice. The blood of Muthana and Gowad and Abdul Khada . . . A voice inside my head spoke harshly to me. Not now. Fight it off. Damn it! Fight!

I felt weak. Weak and sick inside. I rinsed out the sheets, washing away the imaginary blood and lava. As the water swirled down the plug-hole in the bath most of my inner strength went with it. I was drained too. My eyes ached. They felt fit to burst. I had managed to regain control of my temper, my fury, but inside the volcano waited. I had tricked it with imaginary revenge. Tricked it into submission. I had held on and ridden a storm, but I didn't know how much longer I could hold on.

The volcano still simmered, waiting impatiently to be set free and explode out of my ragged system, shooting my nerves to shreds, possibly causing irreparable damage; once and for all placing me in that dark tunnel, maybe with no escape this time. I shuddered at the thought and firmly put such notions out of my mind while I still felt that I had some control over myself.

I knew there would be no news until the New Year had come. I finished the washing and stomped down the stairs to hang it next to the lighted open oven to dry out.

Ashia was on the telephone, talking to her boyfriend, giggling.

I dropped the washing on the floor and launched into an immediate attack. 'How long have you been on the phone?'

Ashia stopped talking and looked across the kitchen at me, confused and bewildered. '*How long?*' I screamed. The volcano inside flared up again.

Ashia put her hand over the receiver and sighed. 'Not long, Mom, just a few minutes,' she spoke softly.

'How long, Ashia?'

'Half an hour, maybe.' She didn't understand. How could she?

'You could have stopped me getting a call. An important call!'

'I waited for ages, Mom. No one is going to ring now!'

'How would you know if you are hogging the phone, talking to friends, when it could have been the Foreign Office or the Embassy in Sanaa, or Mr Cantwell?'

'Mom, it's Christmas. Even if they were still at work, they would be too . . . festive to ring you!'

'Don't tell me that! I know it's Christmas. Christmas! A load of crap. Now everyone will be on holiday and I can't contact anyone because they are on holiday. I hate holidays! I hate Christmas!'

I boiled over, my rage unleashed and out of control. I just grabbed a broom and tore down all the decorations, sweeping them from the ceiling in frantic swipes.

Ashia, Tina and Mo protested. 'Mom, for God's sake stop! Please!' Tina cried.

'Stop? I'll give you stop!' I screeched and flung down the broom to tackle the tree. I grabbed it by its base and swung it around like a hammer-thrower in a serious competition. Little baubles flew around the room, smashing against the walls of the lounge, but the tree would not break. I hammered it into the floor. Glitter and paper flew in all directions, but the tree still remained intact.

'It's our Christmas too, Mom!' Ashia cried. 'Spoil it for all of us, why don't you?'

I was growling at the tree now, furious that it didn't yield to my strength. Finally, with a dull snap, it bent in the middle. Not a clean break, the obvious break that I seemed intent on, but it was good enough. I opened the back door and slung the offending tree out of the house into the yard. I spun on my heel and confronted Ashia. 'We don't celebrate Christmas in this house. Not until I have my kids back!'

'You still have three kids, Mom. Not that you would notice. You won't forget Zana and Nadia and we won't forget them, but you forgot us, didn't you?' Ashia was in floods of tears, but they were tears of temper, frustration. I had never seen her in this mood before. I was too angry to console her, still too angry to control myself, lost in the momentum of my fury.

I picked up an ashtray and hurled it across the room, narrowly missing the face of Ashia's friend, who was waiting in the front room for Ashia to finish her call.

The kids stomped out of the house, leaving me writhing on the floor, cursing and screeching amid a litter of tinsel, baubles, broken branches and stars. It wasn't enough. I started on the kitchen and systematically broke every cup, saucer, plate and mug I could lay my hands on. China flew in all directions, chipping off the formica work surfaces. I hurled the iron across the kitchen, embedding it into the far wall. Vases and ornaments flew with wild abandon to shatter into a thousand pieces.

Pulverised!

I didn't stop until I had completely destroyed the kitchen and all its contents. But it still wasn't enough.

I moved into the lounge again, tripping over the torn decorations and broken baubles to set about wrecking the furniture and the entire contents of the display cabinet.

My head pounded in pain as I smashed the tiny china animals. I wished to God that I could pull the paper from the walls, then tear down the walls themselves. Raze the whole house to the ground. A pile of rubble and masonry, broken glass.

At last I fell to my knees exhausted, and cried aloud for God's help, asking him to give me my girls before I lost my sanity, give me the strength to fight on. Give me retribution from Muthana, Gowad and Abdul Khada.

My face wet with tears, I crawled on all fours out of the lounge, over the glass, china and broken baubles, leaving a trail of blood behind me, into the kitchen. I pulled down a tea towel from its resting-place on the cupboard and wiped my face, finally blowing my nose on it before throwing it in the dustbin. With all this destruction around me a tea towel was of very little significance now.

Before the towel hit the bottom of the bin, guilt set into my aching bones. I thought about Zana and Nadia, then about Ashia, Tina and Mo.

I had pushed them away! They were right. All this time they had said nothing. They had watched silently, tended to their own needs with little help from me. They understood me, but I was too blind to understand them too. That would have to change, and change before it was too late, if it wasn't too late already.

I was so very sorry afterwards. I was totally out of order.

I knew why. In my heart of hearts I knew something was brewing. I *knew* something was going to go wrong when I went to Yemen. I had to control myself. I was too close to lose it all now. I had to be stronger than this. Much stronger. Calmer now, I tried the phone number that would get me through to the Embassy in Sanaa in the Yemen.

It rang out. Straight through, first time.

I kicked at the debris on the floor as I listened to the beeps of the phone. At last someone answered. He was an official working at the Embassy for the emergency service over the holiday. He dug out my file.

'Well, now, the girls have gone back to the villages, apparently.'

I started to protest but he shut me up, adding: 'And it seems that on their return the girls and their husbands will be given a nice big house in Taiz!'

I told him of my previous conversation with Zana.

'Yes quite. Of course the husbands will have to be interviewed by the British Embassy for their visas, then they can *all* come home. I would say it could take up to four weeks.'

211

What could I say? I thanked the man for his time and replaced the receiver in its cradle. While I thought about all this, I started to clean up the results of my fury. I remember thinking that if the boys had to come with Zana and Nadia, it would be my daughters' choice what action they would take once they were here.

I finished cleaning about four the following morning and fell exhausted into bed. I slept until noon. The kids had skulked back into the house and Mo made tea for me.

After an hour of silence I apologised to the whole family and explained what had happened to Zana and Nadia. I wasn't trying to excuse my awful behaviour. I hoped that if I explained to them about the nervous wreck I had become, and how scared for their sisters I was, that they might forgive my destructive tantrum, or at least understand it. Again I had asked them to understand me, when I had not shown that I understood them, too. We spent the next couple of hours mending bridges.

Much later in the evening I rang Zana. She told me that they had not been to the village at all. The kids were still in the village. However, someone would bring them out today some time. 'You have to come, Mom! Even if it's just for a little while. You will come, won't you?'

I said of course I would.

'We have done what we have been told, and "accepted our 'husbands'". It's so nice to be in a house again, a proper house in a town, and seeing people and people being nice to us,' she added reflectively.

I wondered how they could have been deemed to 'accept', when that acceptance itself was a forced issue, given under duress. I didn't see any logic in this move but its value as a face-saver was potent. I could sense that this was a grave mistake. We were being manipulated, perhaps by these 'nice people' Zana had spoken of.

Things were moving, but in what direction?

Chapter Thirty-Two

It was 'Auld Lang Syne' with a difference. Spending New Year's Eve on an aeroplane with the crew and a bunch of strangers turned out to be far more pleasant than I had thought possible. The stewardesses tried their best, well beyond the call of duty, to make our New Year celebration as joyful as possible, breaking out bottles of champagne at just the right time to enable us to mark the end of the old year and the start of the new.

So the New Year was toasted with champagne in plastic cups. I drank to 1988 and a new beginning for my girls. As I sipped, I swallowed back my tears at the same time. Would life ever be normal, for myself and the girls, and for the family I had once again left behind me?

Early on New Year's Day 1988 we disembarked at Sanaa Airport. Much to my surprise, I was met by James Halley of the British Embassy Consular Department. He took me to the Ramada Hotel, explaining that I would have to have the permission of the Ministry to travel to Taiz and was not to contact my girls before this permission had been obtained. In the meantime, I would wait in this hotel.

The Ramada was very sumptuous. I felt out of place. I hadn't come here to languish in luxury. I just wanted my daughters. I felt guilty being surrounded with affluence, while Zana and Nadia suffered misery and poverty in human and animal excrement. I mentioned this to James. I didn't expect him to react at all but what he said then boosted my adrenaline. Hope surged through me.

'But they have both left the village, Miriam. They have apartments in Taiz. The Governor of Taiz, Colonel Al-Usifi, had them taken out of the village and brought to the city. He is apparently preparing for them all to leave Yemen with you when you go. Didn't you know?'

How could I know, exactly? I had been told that they were out of the village but the rest was certainly news to me. I was becoming optimistic.

James – Jim, as he preferred to be called – explained that we had an appointment to see the Minister of Foreign Affairs the next day, then he himself would take me to the city of Taiz to meet up with the girls. I should have a good night's rest and he would pick me up, a little after ten o'clock, to go to the Ministry. We would leave immediately afterwards for Taiz.

Chapter Thirty-Three

Jim arrived at ten and we drove in his jeep to the Ministry of Foreign Affairs to let them see that I was in Yemen being a good girl, doing as requested but still wanting to see my daughters. When we arrived, Jim said he would go in alone first and see what the score was.

Three and a half hours later, he returned to the car. The interior was like a smoke-filled oven. I had chain-smoked with the windows closed, not following the passage of time. My palms were bleeding – that nervous affliction of mine that I just can't control.

Jim was angry and frustrated. After all this time, the Ministry had told him to come back tomorrow, even though this meeting had been called by them. He urged me to keep calm and abide by their rules, no matter how angry I was.

I thought about this long and hard before I finally concurred. As Jim drove me back to the palatial splendour of the Hadda Ramada, I tried to keep calm. The stinging in my hands got worse as I continued to remove the skin from my palms. The sweat on my hand was seeping into the open sores, stinging like crazy. I went to the bathroom and bathed my hands. They looked like they belonged to a leper. 'Nervous eczema', the doctor had called it. 'Yemenitis' was more like it. I decided that next time I was in town, I would buy gloves to stop me scratching the skin off of my palms. Scratch mitts.

Next morning, having been up since dawn calculating that each strip of wallpaper in my room boasted a total of 1,647 flowers, I waited for Jim. I had to do something like this to keep my thoughts under some control. Counting to ten was totally insufficient. I was near crazy with anger and worry. I was sure that this was an attempt to stop me from taking preventative action. Delaying tactics by the authorities. The burning question for me was what had Zana and Nadia signed?

Jim arrived. He insisted on coffee before we set off again to see the officials at the Ministry. He'd seen my mood and wanted me to relax a little.

At last we had some success, thanks to Jim's influence and insistence. He virtually forced them to see us. They greeted me with indifference and made me wait for an hour while they made futile excuses to prevent me from seeing the girls. But Jim had had enough nonsense and told them off for wasting time. With the threat of similar treatment by the British Embassy if they didn't move themselves to consider, they obviously saw the error of their ways.

We nipped into the British Embassy and Jim arranged for us to fly down to Taiz in a Dash Seven, a small aircraft, and for this Colonel Abdul Walli to meet us in the Al Ikhwa Hotel in Taiz, a little after five that afternoon.

The weather was unusually overcast and misty. Jim assured me that we would be able to get to Taiz safely. Climbing aboard the small plane was easy enough. It only seated about fifty people, I think. Jim took a window seat and I took an aisle seat next to him.

'I have never flown to Taiz from Sanaa before. Looks like this plane is the original Wright Brothers invention!' Jim muttered nervously.

By the time the plane landed half an hour later, he was as white as a ghost. 'Did you see that!' he yelped. 'The bloody plane just dived down for a landing! It was going along, the runway appeared and the plane stopped dead in the air!' He was exaggerating.

'The pilot probably has a gob full of *qat*, Jim!' I half-joked. I thought he was going to pass out on me.

'Never again! I swear, never again! Next time I drive down,' he promised himself.

The airstrip at Taiz consisted of a tarmac runway, a concrete lounge and a hut with armed guards. It took us an hour after landing to get outside the airport, such was their 'efficiency'.

Within another hour we were climbing the steep hill to the hotel. Goats and sheep were ambling along the roadside, chewing on discarded rubbish and food rejected from the hotels.

The Mareb Hotel stood majestically on one side of the road, the Al Ikhwa was plonked down on the other. Grey breeze-blocks were the only materials used to raise this concrete lump out of the ground. The forecourt was a concrete slab gripping into the sharp incline in front of the main entrance and concrete steps marked the approach to the main doors. The lobby was huge and crammed full of sofas and coffee tables to one side, and an old semi-circular desk, standing over four foot high and housing the main switchboard, all hotel keys and mail room, on the other.

Jim ordered tea for two. Half an hour later Colonel Abdul Walli arrived. He was dressed in a white *dishdash* – a nightshirt kind of dress that came down to his ankles, a *jambia* – a curved sword over a foot long attached to a belt strapped to his waist, a red and white chequered scarf and a grey jacket. He was a little on the plump side, but taller than the average Yemeni and very attractive with his black waxy moustache and full beard.

Jim stood up and greeted him, then introduced me. I was weary of all Yemenis, especially those from Mokbana or, to be more accurate, the Shamiri tribes of the mountains in the north. The Shamiri are gypsies, living off of the barren land with little or no assistance from outside. Forced into the hills long, long ago because of their notorious ways, they are untouched by progress and civilisation, living under their own primitive laws, uninfluenced by state law and order. Wild. They are a source of shame for the rest of the Yemen. Some Yemenis say that even Allah does not venture to their land and that the peoples are still influenced by a voodoo-like culture. The Djinn – invisible people – inhabit this land even today, according to the lore of the country, and spells and curses can literally frighten the locals to death.

Colonel Abdul Walli spoke in fairly basic English. He was a strict Muslim, a true believer in the Islamic faith, who practised the teachings of Islam and submitted to the will of Allah.

I found myself drawing hope from this. I thought back to Birmingham, of Sufi, Ann's husband. He, a Muslim and a true believer, was a good man, one whom I could respect and trust. If Colonel Abdul Walli was of the same belief, faith and the same principles as Sufi, could I trust and respect him too? I said goodbye to Jim, taking comfort in his promise of constant contact.

Colonel Abdul Walli took me to his house. After climbing a huge incline that formed the side of the Mogillia

ntain, we reached a large whitewashed house, sur-
ounded by a blue metal fence and gate. He parked the
jeep and I followed him inside.

Zana and Nadia greeted me warmly, but calmly. This
time, there was no sudden rush into each other's arms, the
tears were few, and only Nadia and I suffered from that
throat-constricting emotion. Zana appeared emotionally
strong and determined. My hope surged even higher.

For the first time I saw my new grandchildren, Marcus,
Zana's son, and Tina, Nadia's daughter. They were beautiful, full of innocence and mirth. Haney was also there. He
seemed a lot bigger now, clinging to Nadia's skirts, eyeing
me warily, but I could see that he remembered me. I think
I even caught him looking behind me for Mo. I gave them
the toys that I had brought all the way from England.

They had never owned a toy in their lives. No grandchild
of mine was going to go without this simplest of pleasures.
Ladies first. I gave Tina a doll. She shied away from me,
so I gave it to Nadia to pass over to her. Initially, she
wouldn't touch it, but after a few moments, she held on to
the doll, lifting the skirts, laughing. Haney had a lorry with
cars on the tail-lift. He took to it immediately. Grinning
from ear to ear, he fell to the floor and dismantled it, then
reassembled the parts. For Marcus, a merry-go-round. He
took it and cuddled it tightly. Zana showed him how to
operate it. He flew across the room, a little startled, as
the tiny trains tooted round, peeking from behind a chair
as Zana laughed fully for the first time in ages. He soon
came bouncing back, claiming his gift and going to the
corner to play with his new treasure.

'Sit down, Mom, you must be tired by now,' Zana said.
I sat on a recliner.

'Gosh! What a comfortable chair!' That surprised me.

Zana had a fit of giggles. It was all worthwhile. I was elated, my spirits soaring into the clouds. I could see the twinkle in their eyes, which for so long had appeared lifeless and sunken. After all those years of fighting to hear my daughters laugh again I thanked God for his mercy to them and myself.

Adbul Walli was watching silently from the corner of the room. I had nearly forgotten he was there. I swear to God that man had tears in his eyes. He quickly excused himself, muttering something as he left. I couldn't catch his words to distinguish whether he spoke in Arabic or English, but I asked God to bless him and his family, for his respect of my family.

Then I saw them. Two figures lurking in the shadows of a recess across the lounge. There was something vaguely familiar about the larger man. Yes. The eyes. It must be them, Mohammed Gowad Majid Al Shamiri and Abdullah Abdul Khada Saleh. My instinct was to attack them, for stealing my girls' innocence by force, for the beatings they had administered and abetted, for the suffering, the filth and squalor to which they had subjected them, for impregnating them, asserting their 'rights' in a loveless union that should never have happened.

But common sense prevailed. It was not the right time for anger and revenge. I didn't want to see them, perhaps because they, too, were victims, forced by their own fathers to aid and abet an ungodly marriage. But I couldn't afford them sympathy just now. Not until I had found out why, found out who had pulled the strings besides their fathers. I wanted them out of my sight, out of my mind.

They scowled at me from across the room. I met their stare, and glared back displaying all my pent-up

221

feelings. Their heads dropped in shame. They slunk out of the room.

'Where are they going?' I asked anyone who would answer. 'To phone Muthana, Gowad and Abdul Khada?'

Zana answered. 'They have done that every day, Mom, especially with Gowad and Dad. Mohammed speaks to his father all the time. I think he's scared out of his wits!'

I didn't deign to comment on that. Nadia chipped in that, most likely, they would be chatting with Abdul Walli and chewing *qat*. I hoped, again, that Abdul Walli would perform miracles. I didn't want to waste my breath discussing those two, or their fathers. I had my daughters to myself for the first time in ages, with no outside interference, no people watching us like hawks, preying on our every word.

We all relaxed visibly after the three men had gone. I told the girls about Jim and the latest from the various official bodies, and they brought me up to date from their side. The document that both of them had signed was a statement publicly accepting the boys as their husbands.

My high spirits dropped like a stone from a great height.

'Abdul Walli compiled it by order, Mom. It was when they took us from the village and left the kids behind. We were frantic. He sent in Army guards to tell us that the Governor wanted to see us and we had to go immediately. When we got here, Abdul Walli told us that they [Mohammed and Abdullah] had been ordered to return to Taiz from Saudi, where they were working. They had to be here for when you came and wouldn't dare argue with Colonel Al-Usifi. Abdul Walli said if we signed that, he could arrange for the kids to be fetched into Taiz. He wrote it first in Arabic and we had to translate and copy it in English. He ripped up his original and we got it out of the bin to give to yous. I tried to write at the bottom that I had to say this, 'cos if I didn't, they wouldn't bring the kids out. Abdul Walli caught me and stopped me from finishing it. I refused to write another one, so he had to accept this. It just proves that we was forced against our will. We did it for the kids. They actually said if we wrote that we could all go home.'

She handed me a tatty piece of paper.

23rd/12/1987

TO WHOM IT MAY CONCERN.

I am Zana Muhsen. About what happened. I am writing this letter and I am very well, and all the problems that I used to complain about, the big reason was the village where I was at. And I am living with my husband in the city now. Under proper regulations for marriage.

My husband's name is Abdullah Abdul Khada. And I am happy in the city since I left the village. And there is nothing I complain about after today.

Yours sincerely. Zana Muhsen.

P.S. I have said this because if I do

The fact that this had been copied from Arabic script and on ordinary note paper made me nervous beyond words. And it confused me. Was this Abdul Walli to be trusted or not? Was this worth the paper it was written on? He had been instrumental in causing my girls to publicly accept what we had been condemning as illegal all these years. If a mere introduction could be deemed a legally binding marriage agreement in Yemen, could this rough, disjointed, almost spontaneously written note be a legal document? Especially when the translation had been done by intermediate level Arabic learners? Why had the original note been ripped up? Why? And look at the date. It was the day after my original 1987 visa application would have been issued. They probably thought that I would travel on 22 December, that same day, and had arranged a little insurance for themselves. This would account for the delay on the previous Thursday, when they told me to 'come back Tuesday, with five hundred dollars' despite Alazeeb's assurances of assistance. I had some answers, but there was still a lot of the jigsaw missing.

'They had my marriage certificate, too! Abdul Walli took a photocopy on his machine in his office and did something with the copy,' Nadia added. 'It was probably for the boys' visas to go to England.'

I wasn't so sure.

Abdul Walli's wife came in with a tray of tea and little sweets. She greeted me warmly, as best she could with her only English word: 'Hello!' She was a tiny woman, young and pretty. I later found out that she was only sixteen when she had married about two years before. His other wife was in the village, busy mothering eight children!

We had tea and soon afterwards Abdul Walli joined us, to ask Zana and Nadia whether they wanted to stay in his home for the night or go to their 'luxurious apartment'. They decided on the latter.

The apartment was situated in a block just off one of the main roads running through Taiz, Jamal Street. To the left of the block was a tiny dug-out shop. Down a dirt track, two flights of stone steps took us into the block. A dark tunnel, green with slime, led to the heavy, blue-painted wooden door to their flat. Inside there was a long, wide hallway with a stone floor; off to the left, a shower and toilet – or, to be precise, a hole in the floor. Next to it was a small sitting room, about ten feet by six, with flat, rectangular cushions on the floor. There were two bedrooms. The larger one contained a single bed, the smaller two double mattresses on the floor. There was a tiny kitchen with a sink, a two-ring butane gas cooker and a small cupboard. There were no facilities to prepare food.

I worried about cockroaches getting into the food, or coming anywhere within a mile of me, but the girls laughed – I had missed the cockroach season.

Abdullah and Mohammed made an appearance. They stayed in the background, watching as the girls gave me a tour of the flat. When we dragged the two mattresses from the small room into the larger one Mohammed protested to Nadia in Arabic.

'Tell him to sod off, Nard. I'm here now and they ain't gonna come anywhere near you while I'm here!'

He glared at me and turned on Nadia, his speech more urgent, his anger more evident. She looked concerned; then, suddenly, she grinned and threw him a mouthful of Arabic. With faces like thunder, he and Abdullah stormed out of the flat.

I hoped they wouldn't be back, but Nadia told me that just outside the front door was another which led to a room belonging to them. I hadn't noticed it. Even if I had I don't suppose I'd have connected the two. It seemed a little odd that the flat should have an additional external room. Mohammed returned soon afterwards, spending most of his time in the sitting room, sleeping on the oblong cushions. Somehow, the timid and quiet Abdullah had managed to secure the external room for himself. He kept well out of my way, too.

The girls had no money at all and there was nothing in the place. I had to buy food for a week. I didn't mind, but it just proved what sort of providers these boys were to their 'wives' and children. All I could eat was fruit and vegetables, I would not dare chance anything else. We had a plate of chips, English-style. The girls tucked into the simple meal with gusto while the kids really enjoyed their first taste of Brummie cooking. Neither of the boys permitted this Western food to be cooked in their homes.

We had also purchased a substantial amount of shampoo and soap. None of them had had a proper bath, shower, or even wash for years. They went straight into the shower after dinner. We sat the kids in the shower tray and let the water cascade over their heads. They screamed with delight as they slapped at the water. The whole room was flooded by the time we had finished.

Then it was the turn of the girls. Zana took ages. Then, while Nadia was in the shower, I started to brush Zana's hair. It was a mess. I had scissors, so I trimmed the straggly edges. She looked completely different. I was disappointed to see her putting on the Yemeni clothes that she had discarded before her shower. I went to my suitcase and pulled out an assortment of jeans and shirts. She was about my size but, unfortunately, she'd never been one for wearing jeans and she hadn't changed in that respect. We decided to look for something for her the next day.

Nadia came out of the shower and I began to brush her knotted hair. I gently untangled the strands. It was so long now, almost down to her knees.

The whole of her head was running alive with lice.

'Oh, my God!'

Nits coated each strand of her once beautiful hair. I screamed, pulling away from her head.

'What, Mom? What is it? What's the matter?'

226

'You've got lice. That's the matter!' My voice was small and shaky, like a child's.

'I know, Mom. So have the kids. All the people in the village have. What can we do? There is nothing in the village to remedy it, so we have to suffer.'

'Oh, come 'ere, I'll finish your hair!' Zana grabbed the brush and completed the job I had started.

'Do you have them, Zana?' I asked.

'Nah, I don't get near anyone!'

I scratched my head all night, dreaming that the lice were marching towards me to invade my hair. I don't know how many times I woke up during the night, feeling them climbing over my legs and arms. All in the mind. Ugh!

Chapter Thirty-Four

Next morning we had breakfast and I showered twice, purging my body and my mind. I tried all morning to get the girls to discard those black clothes of the villages before Jim came to pick us up. They didn't want to do it, feeling that they should respect the Governor, whom we were due to meet, to gain his favour if possible. It also enabled them to hide from all the curious stares they would get. I watched them as they put on layer after layer of black garb.

Jim arrived and in silence we took a taxi to the Governor's offices, where we were shown to a large room belonging to Colonel Al-Usifi, Governor of Taiz. It was furnished with a huge desk and a three-piece suite in black leather, with a beautiful, ornate coffee table on top of an enormous Chinese silk rug.

I resisted the urge to scratch at my head, which was running wild with imaginary lice. The room filled up with men; men I didn't know, didn't want to know. I took a seat next to the desk, Jim flopped down on one of the settees. Zana and Nadia remained standing, watching the kids playing with their new toys on the floor. Mohammed puffed out his chest, as if to say, 'All

228

this – for me?' Abdullah looked as if he were about to faint from fear as the room packed out to standing room only. All men: some in uniforms, more in *futahs* or *dishdash*.

A small man in a dark grey suit entered. It was Colonel Al-Usifi. He introduced himself. As I shook his hand, I hoped that the lice from Nadia's head would fly through the air and infest him in front of everyone. Divine retribution, Moses-style. A army of lice marching across the Chinese rug, to plague his balding head. I stifled a nervous giggle.

Mohammed and Abdullah took a standing position each side of the Colonel as he seated himself on a large leather armchair. I looked across to Colonel Abdul Walli. He stood there in uniform, his arms at his side, almost to attention. He didn't return my gaze.

Colonel Al-Usifi introduced his interpreter, Basher. Through Basher, he wanted my side of the story.

'Well, in 1980, the girls came out here for a holiday . . .' I went through the whole thing, giving as much detail as I could. When I had finished he gave his impression of the matter.

'I am sure you understand by now, Miriam, as you are married to a Yemeni and the girls also are married to Yemenis, that they can only leave with their husbands' permission, or leave in the company of the husbands.' Al-Usifi pursed his lips, then smirked at me.

The room filled with murmurs of approval from his sycophantic subordinates.

I breathed deeply to control my anger. 'Colonel Al-Usifi, the girls have been married illegally, and you know that. As for me, I am not married and have never been married to Muthana Muhsen, their father, or to anyone

229

else. I am their sole legal custodial parent. I am British and so are my children.'

As Basher translated the whole room was silent, so silent that the proverbial pin could have been heard to drop.

'But you have several children by this man. He is Muslim and this is *haram* [against God/forbidden] in Islam, to have children outside of marriage, as it is to indulge in human habits of married couples. I am sure you are, shall we say, mistaken.' The Colonel's eyes were popping out of his head.

'You ask Muthana to produce a marriage certificate for this, and it will be as forged as the ones announcing my daughters' marriages to these boys. I have never been married, I can assure you.'

The office rumbled with disbelief. Colonel Al-Usifi chose to avoid further discussion with me and turned his attention instead to Zana and Nadia. His first words to Zana were to shout at her to keep Marcus quiet. It was all I was privy to as the rest of the conversation was conducted in Arabic, with Basher obviously now redundant. When I was allowed to participate in the conversation, all that had been achieved was stalemate.

They came up with a lot of rules that had to apply in a situation like this. Where these rules came from, I don't know. How could they have had them before? This situation was unheard of.

They went on and on at Zana and Nadia, apparently saying that they would have to leave the children if they chose to leave the Yemen and their husbands – whom they were never married to: another *haram* in the eyes of Islam.

The final pronouncement by the Colonel was that they could all leave if the boys went with them, in accordance with their recent public acceptance of these boys as their 'husbands'.

Having little choice, the girls agreed for the sake of keeping their kids. The boys agreed that they would like to go too. And that was it.

Colonel Al-Usifi wiped the perspiration from his brow and requested that perhaps Mr Halley would arrange for the British Embassy to process the visa applications for the boys to go to England with my daughters and their children. Mr Halley agreed that he would try.

We left for a smaller office in the back of the building, where Jim was to help the boys complete their application forms. Mohammed proudly announced that he had saved £12,000 working as a waiter in Saudi for over seven years. All heads turned his way; mouths dropped open in disbelief, especially Nadia's. A darkness crossed her eyes. She sucked air through her teeth.

Jim tried to penetrate the atmosphere by saying that it looked hopeful. It worked like magic.

He took the applications to the Embassy to set the wheels in motion. He was now very worried because he had found two previous application forms, dated 1980, for Abdullah and Mohammed to come to England. The Embassy had been approached by Gowad and Abdul Khada stating that their sons were now married to British citizens, namely Zana' and Nadia, and therefore they would like their sons to be issued with passports, but in the meantime visas would suffice. The Embassy had replied that, if this were the case, the girls would have to attend in person, in Sanaa, to 'back up' this application. Gowad and Abdul Khada knew that they could not do this because both marriages were bogus, held together with red tape in a poor Middle Eastern country.

Applications dated 1980. The girls had been out there maybe three months! I worried about this because Jim had expressed concern over a statement he'd received from London while he was trying so desperately to arrange these visas.

Roy Hattersley, the Labour MP for Sparkbrook, Birmingham, was Shadow Foreign Office Minister and deputy leader of the Labour Party under Neil Kinnock. He had issued a press release in January 1988.

'The campaign, which has now gone on for many weeks, has been based on the statement that the two girls were married against their will. I believe that statement to be true.

'In that case, the marriages are not genuine by either the standards acceptable to British law or Muslim religion. As someone who has fought for the admission of many genuine husbands into this country, I am not prepared to support an arrangement which shows every sign of being a stratagem arranged by the Foreign Office and the Yemeni government to sweep the whole matter under the carpet.'

Hattersley told Geoffrey Howe, Mrs Thatcher's Foreign Minister, that the FCO should stop doing deals and just get the girls home.

Jim considered suing Hattersley for defamation. He was also very concerned that the Yemeni government would get to hear of the statement. I wondered why. It stood to reason that, if a shamefaced Yemen insisted on public acceptances of marriages that didn't exist, by girls forced to co-habit, they just had to be illegal in the first place, and could only be deemed as such. Why else would they be forced to accept something that was so controversially *haram*?

Left to my own devices, I wandered around, casually being nosy. Mooching. I picked up a document with Arab script. It looked formal enough to be used as possible ammunition. 'What's this?' I asked the girls.

'It's a copy of my marriage document. Where did you get it, Mom?' Nadia took it from me and held it closer to her eyes for better scrutiny.

'It was on the copier, but it isn't going back. I'm having it.' I plucked Nadia's certificate from her fingers. I put the paper in my bag, along with the torn statement that Abdul Walli had made the girls copy, and Zana's public acceptance document. 'Come on. Let's get out of here.'

I felt like a spy, sounding so melodramatic. We crept out of the house MI5 style but in a fit of giggles, feeling confident and triumphant.

We decided that our next mission was to go shopping. Our purpose was to find Pryalderm, a medical shampoo and lotion for the annihilation of head lice, and combs. It took us ages to find a shop which stocked these. I bought up their entire stock of six bottles and both combs and we went back to the flat. Nadia and the kids were given the full treatment. On the roof of the flat I smothered all of our heads with this lotion. It became our daily routine until eventually there was no trace of the horrible little bugs. We treated Nadia's hair to a good conditioner and I cut off the last twelve inches from its length.

In a week, her hair was back to the condition I remembered so well, a glossy raven black that glinted in shades of blue in the sun. She even took to sorting through my clothes, pinching jeans and a red checked shirt. She stuck a flower behind her ear, a deep red carnation. *This* was my Nadia. She was bubbling with happiness at being with me and full of thoughts about going home. She

233

smiled from the time she woke up to the time she slept again.

There was one particular point of concern. She was still very sore from having given birth to Tina twenty-two months before. It still hurt her where she had been cut with a rusty, dirty razor blade. It was the same blade which had been used to circumcise countless baby boys – and girls – in the village and would doubtless be used again and again. It had never been sterilised, and nor had its victim, before, during or after use. It would simply be returned to its jar until needed again, only discarded when absolutely useless.

A trip to a doctor was in order. Through the British Embassy, we found a good clinic. Zana was fine – underweight, but nothing serious. Nadia had a deep and nasty infection where she had been cut. It had been a large, ragged incision, six inches long, and deep. The fact that she hadn't been sterilised before or after the cut had caused the infection to set in.

It had healed to a certain extent but the skin had not been joined surgically and whenever she walked the movement of her legs pulled the skin in opposite directions, tearing the wound open again.

The doctor gave her creams, lotions and tablets to fight the infection, and told her that she should not bear any more children.

Chapter Thirty-Five

There was an authoritative knock on the door. An armed guard stood there with an official, who told us we must go and see Abdul Walli as soon as possible. They left as suddenly as they'd arrived – didn't offer us a lift, mind. I wondered if Abdul Walli had discovered that Nadia's marriage certificate was missing. Before we left for his house, I hid all my precious documents somewhere very safe. Just in case. We all dashed round to his house in a taxi.

'There is a meeting with Colonel Al-Usifi in one hour, in his office.' He refused to explain why.

I started to get suspicious then, anticipating my own arrest for espionage. I wondered whether it had been worth taking the documents and whether I should ring Jim and beg for diplomatic intervention. I didn't really fancy my chances.

'Mr Halley has already left Sanaa. He should be there with the Governor by now,' Abdul Walli smiled.

It had been several weeks since our last meeting. The girls and I had pottered about the flat most of the time, going to Abdul Walli's home in the afternoons to use his phone whenever necessary. He had no objections.

In fact, it was at his own insistence that we used his phone.

We met Jim at Al-Usifi's office. I carefully measured his reaction on catching sight of me. Something was definitely amiss. He asked us to wait until the Colonel called us into his office, dismissing any further formal conversation between us.

I shuddered and chain-smoked for the next half-hour, hoping that I had my lawyer's number with me. I tried not to look guilty. The meeting was fairly informal, and this time there were no additional men around.

The essence of the meeting was that Colonel Al-Usifi had had time to think about the matter since our last encounter. 'The problem is the press in England,' he said through Basher, the interpreter. 'They surely monitor every move made by Miriam Ali, risking further embarrassment to our government. To avoid this, I must insist that Miriam Ali leaves our country before her daughters.'

'What?' I protested immediately.

Ignoring my sudden outburst, the Governor continued. 'She must travel at least twenty-four hours in advance of her daughters.'

Basher translated and Colonel Al-Usifi looked directly at Jim, holding him responsible, somehow, for my reaction. Either that or he was bypassing me completely. In a fit of fury I began to holler and howl my protests. 'There is no way I'm going to agree to that load of bullshit! If you think, for one moment— '

Jim was up on his feet, at first talking over my objections, then shouting as I became more verbally aggressive.

'. . . marriages are illegal and you have to let my girls go now or else.'

236

I turned my aggression on Jim, who had grabbed my arm, squeezing my elbow. 'Take your paws off me. How dare you! What is this, conspiracy?'

Jim excused us from the Governor's office for a few moments. Impatiently the Colonel waved his hand, dismissing us.

In a small room adjacent to the main office Jim tried to take command of the situation. He spoke firmly. 'You can't keep arguing about the legality of these marriages, Miriam. It's like bashing your head against a wall, especially when both girls are saying what they have been told to say to keep the kiddies.'

'But it's all bullshit. "Saying what they have been told to say." Will you listen to yourself? Bloody hypocrisy! Told to say! Huh!'

Zana came into the office, leaving Nadia sipping fresh lime with Colonel Abdul Walli in the hallway. 'Mommy, calm down. You don't understand the Yemeni ways.'

'Who the hell does? Can't you see what they're doing? Bunch of slime-bags.'

Zana raised her voice then. 'We are nearly free. That's what they're doing. It'll be all right to travel separately.'

She was right. I had to concede. Jim had obviously found an ally in Zana.

However, I had to have the last say. 'I'm not having those two in my home. Never. I hate them.'

We returned to the Governor's office, where I sulked for the remainder of the meeting – all of ten minutes.

Jim took us for a tour of Taiz, taking us high up the Mogillia mountain for a panoramic view of the city. I largely ignored the conversation when it turned to the possible geographical location of Mokbana. I tutted at

Zana as she tried to lure me to join in. I was still in a serious sulk.

They were right. While we were here we should do this the Yemeni way. Mostly, that was playing our cards close to our chests and anything else by ear. To me, it was hardly a game to be played. The word 'compromise' stuck in my craw. I had to be grateful for whatever chance we had, no matter how slim it was. I found that difficult when so much heartache had been inflicted on my family. I had been in a state of panic at the thought of being arrested for espionage, knowing that these men would grab at any chance to side-step the main issue. My girls were still a long way from their freedom, but this was a chance, after all. So far the only chance.

A few weeks later I rang Jim.

'Bad news, Miriam. I think the boys will be turned down for their passports. Abdullah overstayed a six-month visa for medical treatment by three months, narrowly avoiding deportation in 1983, and Mohammed has lied about funds. The FCO have not taken too kindly to that. I have managed to get your visa extended, but only by one month, not two. The Foreign Office have said that if the marriages are illegal then these boys will not be eligible for visas anyway. They are holding an investigation. Can you come to Sanaa? I have your funds for you. At least that's some good news. And you will need your passport for the visa extension, too.'

What a blow. Straight in the kidneys. I suppose that now there was no chance that these men would be allowed into England. That thought had appeal, but at what cost?

We arranged that I would travel down next morning and Jim would meet me at Sanaa Airport. Initially we all wanted to go, just to relieve the monotony, so I decided that we should all fly down together.

Back at the flat Zana had reservations. 'They will never let us out of Taiz. I thought you'd have begun to understand these people by now. I'm not going. It's a waste of time.'

She was spot-on. When Nadia, Haney, Tina and I got to the airport all the walls were splattered with pictures of my girls as if they were criminals. The airport officials spotted us and all sorts of commotion began. We told them we were going to Sanaa, to our Embassy; we didn't have any intention of leaving Yemen. They shouted at us. We tried to drown out their objections with our own protests until, because their guns were bigger than our mouths, stronger than our 'rights', we were forced to turn back.

Zana had made food for us. It was ready as we walked in the door. She didn't say 'I told you so!' but her look said that and more.

I had to get to a phone and contact Jim. Zana insisted we ate. After our meal, which would have been enjoyable if we had not all been in such a dark mood, we walked to the nearby dug-out shop to use the phone.

A man stood just inside the door of the shop, his nose buried in a Saudi magazine. Nadia asked in Arabic whether we could use the phone. He looked up at us. His face turned white with amazement, his eyes boggling. Zana, Nadia and I all looked at each other, wondering which of us had three heads.

'What you looking at?' Zana snapped in Arabic.

Slowly, the man turned the magazine around. Spread right across the centre pages were photographs of Zana, Nadia, Muthana and myself.

Jim already knew what had happened, because of a call

he'd had from the Foreign Ministry in Sanaa. 'They are accusing me of trying to smuggle you and the girls out of the country. They have been going berserk at me for over half an hour and are now trying to report me to London,' he complained.

Chapter Thirty-Six

There was a knock at the door. A young man stood there, attractive-looking. He was dark, his eyes were a startling green instead of the usual brown or hazel. He had a nice warm smile. Casually dressed in beige trousers and a white shirt, he chatted to Zana. He reminded me of someone. She hugged him, much to my astonishment, and invited him inside. A local friend, perhaps? But Zana didn't hug friends like that. Then who?

The young man looked nervous despite his smile. I knew I was right in thinking that I had somehow seen him before. Grinning, Zana dragged him towards me. 'Say hello, Mom.' She urged the young man closer, then impatiently tried to pull me up from my seat on the cushion. 'Don't you recognise your own son?' she laughed.

Slowly I stood up, afraid to believe what my ears were hearing, my heart pounding loud and clear, thumping out a jungle rhythm. 'What . . .?'

'Mom,' Zana couldn't stand the suspense, 'this is Ahmed. You know, your son!'

'Ahmed?' I whispered. 'Is it really you?'

He couldn't understand me. After all, it was twenty-three years since he'd been taken away.

I opened my arms and he took a few steps towards me, shy or embarrassed, or both. 'God, son. You have grown!' I laughed as I embraced him tightly, tears streaming down my face.

He held me just as tightly, pushing me away to look at me, then hugging me fiercely again. He lifted me up, swinging me around the room. Zana and Nadia were laughing at us and crying at the same time; Ahmed and I laughed and cried even louder.

What an occasion! Having three of my lost children in the same room after so long.

Through Zana and Nadia, Ahmed and I tried to catch up on all that we had been deprived of for all those years. Of course, it was impossible. Ahmed told me how his grandfather, Muthana's dad, had been so annoyed with Muthana for not sending money to Ahmed and Laila, not even writing, that he had avenged himself by placing Ahmed in the Army for life when he was fourteen years old. Ahmed had had absolutely no say in the matter. In fact, his grandfather was so angry that when Zana and Ahmed had gone, unannounced, to visit him recently, to introduce him to his granddaughter, he had gone into an instant rage at the sight of a familiar figure approaching. Assuming it was his son, Muthana, he had come out of the house wielding a huge stick to beat his son to a pulp. Once his visitors had been identified he calmed down a little. He told Zana and Ahmed how much he hated his own son. Already all the land and property that Muthana would have inherited had been sold off or given to other relatives. Anything which had any connection whatsoever to Muthana had been disposed of. Including Ahmed, who was given to the Army for life, and Laila, who had been given to her cousin in marriage at the age of fourteen.

Zana had not seen Laila. She was no longer in the Marais village. She had been moved after her husband had been killed in a gunfight between northerners and southerners; married off, within months of widowhood, to another cousin who took her further south.

I told Ahmed that I would do whatever I could to help him, despite knowing that in this strange country I had very few options. But try I would.

Ahmed was on leave and had been to visit Muthana's cousin, Hagira, and her family in Taiz. He suggested we have a get-together. I didn't think much of that idea – meeting Muthana's relatives didn't exactly appeal to me – but before I knew it, Zana had agreed.

We all went with Ahmed to a shop in Taiz. I waited, pensively, amid an assortment of materials. A woman bounced in. Bright, beautiful and the exact opposite of what I had expected. She was dressed in a colourful array of exotic fabrics. Hagira embraced me, and a huge bundle of intricately tied materials wobbled on her head. I had never seen anyone like her before. I was awestruck.

Hagira, though born in Yemen, was Kenyan. Her mode of dress, her accent, her mannerisms, were typical of someone who had lived most of her life in Kenya. She was now in her mid-fifties and her own family were in their teens and early twenties. She missed Kenya as much as I missed England.

We were all soon chatting as if we had known each other for years. As we sipped fragrant cinnamon tea and nibbled sweetmeats, Hagira laughed heartily. I had confessed my previous reservations about meeting anyone from Muthana's family. Then, reflectively, her face darkened. She knew all about Muthana and what he had done to his family, and she was ashamed. She told me that he had left

243

Yemen all those years ago having stolen his mother's gold to enable him to get away from an arranged marriage. The last time she had seen him was in 1956.

Mysteriously, a couple of days later Ahmed was arrested and chucked in prison. He was called into the Governor's office, accused of plotting to kidnap Zana and Nadia and immediately placed under arrest. We didn't know where the order came from. No one would admit to it. We confronted Abdul Walli. After a hell of a lot of shouting, especially from Zana, we managed to get Ahmed freed.

Ahmed later told me that he had had a telephone call from a strange man in England. At first he was flummoxed as to who it could be. The person had launched into an immediate attack, ranting and raving on the phone, without bothering to mention his name. He had cursed continually, saying that Ahmed should hit his mother with a big stick, he should hate her. Then he said that the girls must not be allowed to leave Yemen. That was an order.

It was only then that Ahmed realised that this strange, demented caller was his own father, Muthana. But instead of recruiting Ahmed to his side, his call had had the opposite effect. This was why Ahmed had sought me out a few weeks before. Had Muthana not made this call, we would, perhaps, not have been reunited.

We spent most of our afternoons in Abdul Walli's house. One day we were in his lounge when the phone rang. Abdul Walli had just gone into the yard, so after a few rings, Nadia picked up the extension to answer the call. At that very same instant, Abdul Walli must have nipped back into his office and answered the phone there. Nadia heard the caller announce his name. She motioned us to

244

keep very quiet, mouthing that it was Gowad phoning from Birmingham. She listened to the conversation between the two men.

Gowad was shouting down the line that he absolutely forbade Nadia and the children to leave Yemen. He said he had written to his son, Mohammed, and talked to him on the phone; he had talked to Muthana and the Governor of Taiz, the Ministry of Foreign affairs and all important people.

As soon as we got back to our apartment, we searched Mohammed's pockets. We found three letters. The girls recognised Mohammed's handwriting in one. They read it to me. 'Don't under any circumstances allow them to leave with or without the children. We all forbid it. It would be *aib* [shameful] if they went to England with Miriam Ali and it goes to court.'

The second letter was in a different hand. It was from some of the villagers in Muthana's native Marais. Muthana had apparently instructed these people what to write to the Governor. Translated, it read: 'The mother is going to Yemen to run away with the girls with the help of the British Embassy. We have heard of this thing happening before with other girls. The father said his girls must stop in Yemen in the villages with their husbands. They cannot go back to England. The mother is trying to get the girls out without the father's permission. We wish for you to stop any movements from the British Embassy to get them out under any sky. They are Yemenis, left from England and were married with their permission the proper way. God's way. Thank you for your help.'

It was dated 15 January 1988 and signed by three people from Marais.

The third letter was a tatty piece of paper bearing a thick bold script. Nadia recognised it as a voodoo curse and threw it away. The other two letters joined my growing collection of evidence.

Chapter Thirty-Seven

As Jim had feared, the FCO turned down the boys' renewed appeal for visas. Colonel Al-Usifi was livid at the decision and announced that, notwithstanding, the girls could leave without the consent of the husbands. But the children were a different matter.

It was a terrible blow to us. Both of my daughters thought long and hard about the situation. The room gradually grew darker and darker as we sat and talked, yet we didn't bother to light the kerosene lamp. The evening shadows reached into the room and caressed us, comforting us in a blanket of darkness, hiding our anguish and tears from each other and the world. Honest truth filled this room, and we all needed the security of the shadows to hide in.

Abdullah had, under protest, consented to a quick divorce but he wanted Zana's son as his ransom. Mohammed insisted on a full Islamic *nakhar* (divorce) for the dissolving of a marriage that didn't exist. He, too, demanded that the children be his compensation.

Damn the British government! Why could they not agree to a visa for these stupid men? Why, after all these years of saying, 'The girls are Yemeni, married to Yemeni men,' did they now decide that the marriages were not legal? If they had done this in 1980, Zana and Nadia would not be facing this soul-wrenching decision. If the government had not neglected their duty to protect my girls, as they had honoured the hostages in Lebanon, my girls would not have borne children to their captors. If the government had not insisted that I kept quiet, kept the media out of this 'family matter', the pressures of publicity would have forced the captors' hands to relinquish their grip.

Now, in the darkness of this dingy room with the cold concrete floor, we talked and talked. Emotions were running high. I could do nothing to help. It was a decision. Zana and Nadia had to make alone.

'You have no idea what it's like. We've been prisoners all this time, and now we are free. I was happy just to get out of Hokail, into a real town, with real people. I can't go back there. Now you're here, I just want to come home.' Zana thought for a while, her eyes shut tight. 'When I do this and think, I can see Birmingham.'

Her smile faded. 'I have to leave Marcus. Thank God he is male, he will be all right. But I can't leave Nadia, Mom. She needs me. Gowad and Mohammed are putting so much pressure on her that she will crack up for sure. I promised that I would never leave her. I will die if she is alone with all this to face 'cos I don't think she can fight it for long!' Zana sniffed back her tears.

Nadia reached out and took her sister's hand. 'I said that I could leave my children, but as the time comes nearer, I don't think I can, Mom. Tina's still on my breast. I want to come home so much. I don't know what to do. After all this time of suffering in Yemen, in the village, I've got the chance to go home. I've got the chance to be me again, to

248

be free and with my family, but when I think of my babies, Mom . . . God, why? It hurts so much!'

'Can you live with Mohammed, Nadia? And know that Gowad has left you with his children, too?' Zana asked her.

'I hate Mohammed, and he knows it. This makes me prepared to leave my children, but when I think of my own experience in the village, being a slave for eight years and knowing that Mohammed won't or can't look after the children, I have a pain in my heart. Another woman can give food, like I have to do with Gowad's other children, but no other woman can love or care. I know this myself. Each day I'm with my children I feel like I'm betraying them. When Tina takes her milk from my breast I think of her being taken from me, and I know my heart's going to break. I just want the nightmare to be over with. I just want to go home, but Gowad keeps telling Mohammed that in no circumstances am I allowed to go home. He's *not* to let me go. He's even spoken to me on the phone, telling me, begging me not to go home. He said that Dad had been in touch and they know they'll be in a lot of trouble if we go home. And they said they'd do everything they could to stop it, stop us going!'

I was being torn apart, in my heart and my mind. 'That's why I think one of you should come, if both of you can't. We've got to show the world what these men have done to you both. Maybe we can get the other one out when the story breaks. It's the governments and the Shamiri men. The average Yemeni on the street has only pity for you and shame for what these men have done. They have to live with the shame, too, especially those in England, and they don't like it one little bit! I want both of you home. It's hard for me to think that one may stay behind for the children, though I understand that. I've been fighting for you, my children, all these years and now you want to do the same for yours. You *need* to do the same. I can't challenge that. However, I don't want you to have to face the same pressures I have faced for so long. It's hard and its taken its toll. I feel a great need to protect you, even now, just like you want to protect your own children.'

I clenched my fists again, drawing blood. Oh God, please don't do this to me, to my kids!

There was a long silence, an eternity, before Zana spoke. 'I've made a difficult decision to leave Marcus. I feel numb, sick! We're being tortured. Only we in this room can understand what it feels like. Others can only imagine what it's like. I don't think that I'm going to feel free after my divorce. I'll wait for Nadia. I could never leave her here alone, and they know that.'

'I'll wait too, then, and we'll all leave together,' I decided.

But this was not to be. The Yemeni government declined to renew my visa after I submitted my second application. I was told that they were deliberately not renewing it because they insisted that I leave before the girls. They didn't want the press angle to be our reunion in the Yemen and subsequent departure. I knew that Muthana, Gowad and Abdul Khada would be doing everything possible to stop the girls from leaving, with or without the children.

So we had to change our plans yet again. Now that my visa had been denied I would have to go back anyway. It was perhaps better in the long run. I could fight harder from England, with the press as my weapon, and right as my shield, plus something up my sleeve as insurance.

I knew that the girls wouldn't be permitted to leave Yemen with their children. If they both stayed then nothing would have changed, nothing would have been gained. They would have to decide for themselves. I had reached an impasse. I could do no more than wait for their decision. It was the most difficult decision in the world for a mother to make. Would they both stay, or would one come home? If so, which one? Which one would sacrifice her offspring for the overall benefit of them all? Their decisions went one way, then another.

They both became extremely irritable and emotional as the time for my departure drew nearer, knowing that the penalties of such a sacrifice could easily outweigh the reason for making them. I felt their pain and anguish, but I could do nothing.

Zana became increasingly frustrated and moody. She would be sullen, thinking about her dilemma. She was inclined to leave Yemen. It was hard to leave Marcus, I knew that, but she would also be leaving her weaker sibling to suffer alone in this part of the world while we fought on another. She tried her best to convince Nadia to leave instead, saying that she would care for her children until it was her time for her to go home too, and that she would bring all of the children out together.

Nadia held back. She had, she said, twice as many children as Zana and also Gowad's other children to consider, too. Her supporters in the village numbered more than Zana's. She would draw comfort from her kids and would be OK in Taiz until such time as her freedom came.

Before I left Yemen it was decided that Zana would come home. I knew that this decision would continue to rock back and forth for quite some time yet. It was only natural that the girls would be oscillating between their limited alternatives. I felt as if we were alone at the end of the world. And I had never been so frightened in all my life.

On 28 February Zana answered a knock at the door. Two men demanded to see me. As I sat with Nadia and the children, one of the men rushed into the room and immediately started to shout in Arabic. All the children started to cry. The man, in his forties and dressed in a long white *dishdash*, tried to shout over the screaming kids. His accomplice, a young guard in full combat-style uniform, fingered his rifle eagerly.

'Miriam Ali, I tell you visa to Yemen is finished. You break law now.' His English was poor.

'No, it hasn't. It still has four days yet.' He gave me the willies, yet I dare not let him see my concern.

'You in trouble big now,' he sneered menacingly.

His colleague petted his rifle.

'I said, it hasn't run out yet,' I repeated in slow, deliberate English.

'Give me bassabort. I want see!' he commanded.

I got my passport from my case and handed it over. He snatched it from my hands and fingered through it.

'Why you here?' he demanded, having found nothing to confirm his claim. He was angry now.

'Never mind why I am here. Why are you here? Who has sent you? Who has told you to speak to me?' I wondered about Abdul Walli.

'I no speak this. *Ma laish* [no why – never mind.' His limited abilities in English deteriorated even further.

'OK. Give me back my passport. Come on. Hand it over!'

He sniffed his refusal, acting like a child.

'I said give me it!' I snatched it from his hands. Slowly he backed away from me, but I closed in on him. 'I have four days left and you know it. Don't bother me again because I'm not leaving until my time is up. Now get out of this house! And take your little friend with you. Go on, shoo, shoo!'

He fled from the house, muttering like an old woman.

The very next day we discovered that the people in the tiny shop at the end of the dirt road approaching the house were spying on us. We had caught them reporting our every move to Abdul Walli. We had gone to his house to make a few complimentary calls when the phone rang. Abdul Walli was in the yard, his cheeks bulging with *qat*. Zana answered it.

A familiar voice gabbled in Arabic: 'They have gone out. Both girls, all the children and the mother.'

'Do you know where?' Zana asked in Arabic.

'No, but the taxi will be back to the shop soon and we will find out from the driver.'

'OK. I will tell my husband that you will call again soon.'

After fifteen minutes, the phone rang again. She picked it up first ring, hoping Abdul Walli hadn't heard it.

'The driver left them at your house, but did not see them go inside. Perhaps they have escaped.'

'No, I don't think so. I know they are here, with me. I am Zana!'

The phone clicked dead.

Zana grinned, but she was angry – as were we all. It was time to go.

The girls and their children came to the airport in Taiz to see me off. Abdul Walli drove us to the airport, and made himself scarce while we said our goodbyes yet again.

I wished with all my heart that I could just take the girls and the children on that plane with me; that we could shake the sands of the desert from our feet, for all time. We were all crying, making no effort to hide our tears. Nadia was shaking from head to toe, as if with ague. Was it a premonition?

'Not to worry, it's nearly over now,' I tried to reassure her, but I couldn't draw comfort myself from these platitudes.

Thankfully the plane arrived after just ten short minutes. I took a window seat to cry alone, unseen by my fellow passengers, until I could gain a little control.

My final visit to Jim had been just a formality so that he could reassure me of his intentions to keep things moving. On arriving I'd waited in the Embassy lounge to see Jim. I casually picked up an old copy of the *Economist*, dated September 1986. Lo and behold, there was a report on the Yemen. I read it eagerly.

It is a small country situated in the thinly populated Arabian peninsula, yet it is densely populated, 76 per square mile if not more, and the population is 9,274,173 according to the February 1986 census. The migrant workers total 1,168,000.00+. The earnings they send home are an extraordinary 30 times as much as the country's merchandise exports and account for 73% of its foreign exchange earnings.

I noted that some of the people who had been employed to carry out the survey had gone missing, too.

It was curious that my theory about brides for British passports seemed to be becoming more plausible than ever before, although it would never suffice as any form of excuse for the perpetrators of this pernicious crime.

I tore out the page, stuffing it in my bag along with my other little treasures.

Chapter Thirty-Eight

The most beautiful sight. England's pleasant pastures of browns and greens lay below, partially covered with an eiderdown of white hoarfrost.

I was so pleased to be home. As the plane made its final descent, I thought of my girls making this same journey in the very near future.

It's strange how deafening silence can be. And uncomfortable. By the following Tuesday, with still no news of travel for my daughters, I was frantic. The promise of their freedom twenty-four hours after my own departure now seemed to have been merely a ploy to get me out of the way. I had damning thoughts about all those people who had told me not to worry, that this would never happen. I rang Jim at the Embassy in Sanaa.

'The girls have said that they don't want to come home now. It was just the villages, apparently,' he said drily.

'Ah, the scruffy bit of paper proclaiming their acceptance of the marriages. Of course!' I surmised.

'Quite. Well, the only other news is that Abdullah is in jail. He was arrested for making off with Zana's gold. That could be interesting. Abdul Walli has been to see him in jail a few times. Something is brewing. Miriam, you are not to worry.'

Not to worry?

In a gush of excitement, he said that it would soon be time for me to put all this behind me and start afresh. I was not so sure of that. I was thinking that heads should roll. It was just a few weeks before that a gun had been pointed at my chest and I was to get out because my visa had expired; meanwhile, from England, Gowad was controlling the strings of the British Embassy in Sanaa. They asked him time and time again for his naturalisation details for Mohammed's passport application. Gowad told them to go to hell. The cheeky sod even had the audacity to apply for another little creep of a son, Shiab, to come into Britain by forging his son's date of birth. Now, all of a sudden, would all this come to an abrupt end? No questions asked? No fingers pointed in accusation? No slapped hands?

The phone never stopped ringing. Tom Quirke rang, the BBC and ITN, a German magazine offering £50,000 to speak to me, countless journalists. It drove me crazy keeping quiet. Personally, I felt that I needed media support, but James Halley said that I would have to keep quiet until after the release of the girls so as not to agitate the governments in question.

Agitate? In extreme frustration, I paced round and round the house, trying to block out the sound of the phone's insistent ringing. Pessimism had set in. I couldn't shake it off. It told me all was to no avail. Everything, everywhere, was illegal: the marriages, the ages. The purchase price of the girls was considered to be 'bargain of the week', although I expect their buyers regretted it now, and would have paid more for brides who were less 'politically embarrassing' than Zana and Nadia.

Muriel Wellington had been looking after Mo all the time I stayed in Yemen, as well as keeping a close eye on Ashia and Tina. Muriel's daughter, Lynnie, was Zana's best friend. In the previous eight years Muriel and Lynnie had been a close and sympathetic source of support. They knew we had been promised that Zana and Nadia would be home within days of my departure from Yemen in March 1988. I became frantic with worry as time crept on. Weeks passed. I drew comfort from their company and support. All the time we were bombarding the various official bodies with letters and telephone calls. Mr Cantwell of the Geneva charity kept up his constant diplomatic pressure throughout, especially now that we had a little hope.

Then, in the second week, I had a letter from David Cotton of the Home Office informing me that Zana had made contact with James Halley. He said she sounded relaxed and had informed James that she was now divorced. It was estimated that she would be free to leave Yemen around 6 June. She also told James that, as she understood the matter, Nadia would have her husband's permission to travel to the UK some time after Ramadan. David Cotton trusted that I would find this reassuring.

Why, oh why could they not understand? Imagine a man raping your daughter; blackmailing her with her own children to keep quiet. Think of his hands touching her intimately. These same hands beating her. Now do something about it! Do something about it in a country like Yemen. I enlisted all the help I could get, although it seemed pointless.

258

Chapter Thirty-Nine

On 19 April 1988 I had a call.

Jim, ringing from Sanaa, told me that he had been contacted by Basher, the Colonel's interpreter, from the Ministry of Foreign Affairs. 'Zana Muhsen is free to travel. We have her divorce papers here. She can leave whenever she wants. Give her passport to the Ministry and it will be stamped with her exit visa.'

I was elated.

I have never prayed so hard in my life. It bordered close to willing Zana onto a plane and out of there. She was just leaving Yemen, at almost that very minute. I was eternally grateful. I thanked God and cried aloud in my joy, but deep down in my heart, the rent widened. What about Nadia?

I listened in silence as Jim told me how he had been at the airport seeing off an official visitor when he saw Zana and Abdul Walli arrive in his jeep, closely followed by a group of about fifteen armed guards. Jim had slipped behind a column for concealment to observe her departure. She appeared downcast, her head hung low, her eyes red and swollen. Papers had been thrust at her to sign. For the most part she had been left alone, staring impassively at the ground. He could see that she was shaking.

As she was going through the departure gates she had been stopped. One of the guards had bawled at her in Arabic and his colleagues-in-arms had had to smooth over the ensuing argument. Finally she had disappeared behind the doors, apparently to the departure gate. Jim had waited until the flight had taken off to make certain that she hadn't been held back for some reason. Satisfied that she was on the plane, he dashed home to ring me.

I rang Muriel Wellington and talked to her about bringing Zana to her house.

In a state of euphoria, I met Zana at Gatwick Airport. It was, of course, an emotional reunion. Zana was ecstatic to be home at last. But the circles around her eyes were dark and etched deep, her body constantly shook and her fingertips bled where she had ripped off her nails with her teeth. Anyone could see that this was the most difficult time of her life. Her emotions were ripped to pieces.

We were reunited in the company of Eileen MacDonald and photographer Ben Gibson from the *Observer*. During the previous year, they had both made a trip to Yemen and had interviewed Zana and Nadia at first hand in the Mokbana region. In December 1986 they had a major scoop for their paper. The interest generated by their article had been a major contributory factor in the newly found determination of the two governments to intervene in what was strictly a 'family problem'. With Eileen's assistance and support over the previous year, I had made great progress in my struggle to liberate my girls.

After an anxious rest period at an hotel, we prepared for the car journey to Birmingham. Zana looked more like her old self in her trousers and blouse, although she would never be the same old Zana ever again, nor would she remove her scarf and mac. She bubbled with excitement as we approached Birmingham, fidgeting in her seat. The closer we got to home, the more she shuffled around. Her breath was clouding the car window as she strained to see everything she had left behind all that time ago. The closer we got, the more Zana recognised and the more excited she became.

We detoured into the city. Birmingham was changing a lot. New offices and centres were popping up all over the place, making the city a main attraction for an assortment of venues and enterprise schemes. Yet, unlike London, it had maintained its population and people-orientated policies. Zana spied the Rotunda building and sniffed back the tears.

'Do you remember it all?' I asked.

Her face was a picture of pure joy. She could hardly speak. 'Oh yes! Where are we going now?'

'Muriel Wellington's house.'

'Lynnie's?' Zana clapped her hands together, smiling from ear to ear, then became engrossed while she watched the kids in the street. She grinned.

'What are you thinking, Zane?'

'I can't wait to see the family.'

We made our way to the A34, the Stratford road, and drove into Sparkbrook. Within minutes, we were parked outside Muriel's house. The front door flew open. Out rushed Ashia, Tina, Mo, and Muriel's three daughters, Gaynor, another Tina, and of course, Lynnie, Zana's best friend, and Muriel herself. Charging down the path they hurled themselves in greeting on Zana, hugging her and crying. I had never seen so much collective emotion.

Zana was a little reserved with one of the girls until she realised it was her own sister Tina, whom she hadn't recognised at all. She had grown so much. She gave Tina two hugs as compensation.

We tried to get through the front door, a very large bundle of intermingled bodies, no one willing to relinquish their contact with Zana, and she equally unwilling to let go. Somehow, we managed it and piled into the lounge.

Zana looked at each of her family and friends and sighed. Ashia was still crying with the joy of seeing her sister again. Suddenly, in all this gaiety, this celebration of liberty, the mood took a sombre turn, when someone asked after Nadia.

I felt a weight pressing down on me. Nadia should have been here for this. Of course we were all pleased, more than pleased, that Zana was home but Nadia was in more danger now than ever before. I knew it and so did Zana. She was confused. Lynnie tried to cheer her up, then finally took her upstairs to chat out of earshot of Eileen and out of Ben's camera range.

The rest of the family understood very well how Zana felt. An outsider would never have understood. We understood Zana, she was family. Her friends understood her, they had been close since childhood. It was Nadia and Marcus. We hadn't expected her to be any other way for we all felt the same.

We stayed with Muriel for a week before going back home to King's Heath. Zana explored the house from top to bottom and really tried to settle. She hardly ever smiled and I could hear her crying all through the night. If I made any approach to comfort her she would feign sleep and refuse to acknowledge that she had been crying at all. She had changed so much. Her fortitude was amazing, but underneath it all she was heartbroken, for Nadia and Marcus. Zana could not let go of Nadia, or of her feeling that this homecoming should have been for the two of them to enjoy and cherish together. No one ever said it would be easy, nor did we expect it to be so. Zana would have loved to have introduced Marcus to the family as Ashia had done with Laina, her daughter. Now all Zana could do was wonder if she had done the right thing, although she had had no real choice. Could anyone understand how she felt? She had left behind her beloved sister in a country run by a government which had no respect, no mercy and certainly no morals. She understood how weak her sister would become as she continued to be pressurised by these selfish, immoral people. And there was poor little Marcus. What had he ever done to deserve this? He had lost his mother. His world was so very small, all centred on Zana. Now he had been taken from her, classed by his own grandfather as nothing more than a 'trophy', a 'souvenir' of illicit deals struck by godless men for selfish reasons.

Zana hardly left the house. As I had expected, a few reporters called, but when I explained that Zana was still a little shaky they always showed every respect for her privacy, understanding her quest for readjustment.

Tom Quirke came round and met Zana for the first time. He took us to his office at the *Birmingham Post*, to phone Nadia and Mohammed at Abdul Walli's house in Taiz. We were told, time and time again, that it was just a matter of time before Nadia would follow Zana, along with Mohammed and the kids. Earlier in

April Gowad had telephoned and Mohammed had agreed to go to Sanaa for a visa. He had made this promise in the presence of a judge and Colonel Al-Usifi and, furthermore, he had promised that if his own visa was not granted he would give Nadia permission to travel alone after Ramadan, which we were now in. May.

We both knew that Gowad was being pressurised by the media but he held fast, refusing to succum. It was because of this that Zana decided to go and visit her father.

I must admit that I was more than a little shocked when she appeared one morning dressed as a Yemeni and told me that she was going to visit her father that morning. She knew how I felt about it – it was written all over my face – but I understood that it was for Nadia. Muthana had always said that if he believed that his girls were unhappy, he would demand their immediate return from Yemen. Now was the time to challenge his view.

Muthana cried in shame before Zana and promised that he would demand Nadia's release. He said he had been to see Gowad, who had assured him that all would be well. But nothing ever came of it, despite Muthana's promises and Gowad's reassurances. Zana soon realised that what I had told her about her father was not my prejudice and she would have nothing more to do with him.

My world darkened again as the summer brought the sunshine. Nadia had suddenly been moved back to the villages, and Colonel Abdul Walli had been hounded out of Yemen. All those empty promises. My poor Nadia. We were back to square one.

I took this very badly, but no more so than Zana. She started a job in a factory and worked herself into the ground, coming home night after night to cry herself to sleep. We had an awful time with our own communications. I understood what she was going through – it had been the same for me. I, too, had lost my own children to a village in the mountains of Mokbana. I, too, loved Nadia and worried for her. Zana's worry was paralleled by my own. Her guilt, or rather anguish, was the same.

She seemed to have come back to England as a fifteen-year-old girl, mentally. She had taken up where she left off, seeing the same old friends, going to the same old haunts. She started to see her old childhood sweetheart again. It was as if the terror of the eight years in Yemen were being pushed from her mind by willpower. Yet when she looked at her hands, the disfigured fingertips and scars from grinding corn and cooking chapattis, a darkness would creep over her face. Of course, she never forgot Nadia and Marcus. But she would try to convince herself it was all a bad dream and, finding this a futile exercise, her true memories would flood in to terrorise her and plague her with nightmares and flashbacks.

Watching her in this pitifully awful state left me feeling enervated, withered. Zana's decline, Nadia's incapacitation and my own devastation. Hors de combat. We didn't stand a cat in hell's chance like this.

Zana refused to see a trauma therapist, choosing instead to vent her frustrations on me. I sat alone night after night on my sofa, wondering where all those promises had gone. How it had gone from certainty to contingency, then to all chances seemingly eradicated?

Late in February, 1988, Dr Alaryani, Foreign Minister, had called in to see the British Ambassador, Mark Marshall, in Sanaa. His country was 'fed up to the backteeth of the situation' and the matter had been passed to him to clear up as quickly as possible. Zana's husband, Abdullah, who was in prison, was to be brought to Sanaa and forced to sign either a permission slip to allow Zana to travel alone – or divorce papers with no court case. (This applies only if the divorce is contested, when a *nakhar* is necessary. Otherwise a simple 'I divorce thee, I divorce thee, I divorce thee' stated before witnesses by either partner is all it takes to dissolve a marriage.) If Nadia's husband was eligible for a passport, the Yemen Government was going to make sure he used it. If he was forced back from Britain on arrival Mohammed, too, would be forced to divorce Nadia. Jim Halley said this intervention from high-calibre officials was 'way out of proportion to the case'. But he too was convinced that both girls would be home – and free – soon.

Where had all those people gone? Dr Alaryani, Colonel Al-Usifi, Colonel Abdul Walli? I was so close then. What was happening now? Was I really supposed to let this all go by the by as they had done? Is that what they hoped for? Expected?

I was too shell-shocked to react, as was Zana. God alone knew how Nadia felt.

Ahmed had arrived in England. We were all surprised to see him, but delighted, obviously. At least Abdul Walli had managed to secure Ahmed's release from the Army before he left Yemen to crawl under a stone somewhere. Ahmed had been given his passport while Zana and Nadia were in Sanaa, but had refused to leave his sisters behind and come home straight away. He had stayed behind for Nadia but she had been moved somewhere else within weeks of Zana's departure and the government had refused to allow Ahmed to see her, going to the extreme lengths of threatening further imprisonment if he dared to defy their orders to look for her. Without Abdul Walli to 'protect' him he had no choice but to obey.

Now he was home at last and was warmly greeted by his siblings. He managed to settle to a new and completely different way of life in a very short time.

One day he came to visit and voiced his deep concern for Laila. She was extremely ill and needed to come to England quickly for treatment. I did all I could to arrange a passport for her and she arrived soon afterwards.

Laila cried as we embraced for the first time since she was a small child, not letting go for quite a while. She had her four small children with her and Zana helped them out of the minibus we had hired to fetch the family and ushered us into the house out of the cold. We fed Laila's kids and put them to bed. They could hardly keep their eyes open they were so tired.

Laila and I sat and stared at each other, the conversation difficult because of the language barrier. She was the image of Nadia – so much so that my first thought was that someone had smuggled Nadia out by pretending that she was Laila. Laila was pale and ill. It was easy to see that she had not come a moment too soon.

They were with us for over a month before she decided that she would like to stay in England to be with the family from which she had been separated for all this time.

So for the most part things were great. I had regained

three of my long-lost children: Laila, Ahmed and Zana. I was three-quarters of the way there. All I had to do now was wait for the imminent return of Nadia – which, of course, was another matter.

Chapter Forty

Since that first day back in Birmingham at Muriel's house Zana had been depressed. She felt that she could trust no one: that if anyone offered help he or she obviously had an ulterior motive. The shameful part of this was that, so far, she had rarely been proved wrong.

I had been talking to her about life without her and Nadia. She told me then that she felt as if Nadia and the children, and her own son, were slipping further and further out of reach.

Both Zana and I went into awful fits of depression which we were desperate to shake off – it was imperative that we resumed our fight if all was not to be lost.

Zana was told by a travelling Arab that he had heard that Nadia had given birth to another baby. Did this mean that Nadia had gone back to the village to endure another painful birth after she had been told by the doctor in Taiz that she shouldn't have any more children? Neither of us felt any joy about the birth especially when we received confirmation of the new addition to our family from the Foreign Office.

I was so worried about Nadia. Time was passing, and time was of the essence. My concern increased daily. We had to find another way. I reminded Zana, unnecessarily, how essential it was to get Nadia out. Zana whipped back at me that it was more than just Nadia. She missed Marcus too.

I was silent. This made me aware of something that I was in danger of overlooking, namely the great sacrifice made by Zana. She was suffering so very much. She became snappy and anxious whenever I attempted to broach the subject.

By August we had had enough of waiting. We sought legal advice. We were advised to go to the police to make a complaint about Muthana and Gowad and Abdul Khada.

The charges which emerged were serious: kidnap and forcing to co-habit were the two at the top of the list. Muthana and Gowad were taken in for questioning and later charged. Now we had something else to concern ourselves with – a major court case.

There were delays with Muthana's Legal Aid application and Gowad, being his ever-deceitful self, claimed that he could speak no English! The process was held up a little while the police found an interpreter who could speak to Gowad and translate the charges. Finally the wheels of the law were set in motion for them to appear in court but the Legal Aid problems and difficulties of representation made the whole process lengthy and extremely slow-moving.

After the first magistrates' hearing in Birmingham the case was referred to the Crown Court. It was now in the hands of the Director of Public Prosecutions in London, Mr Allan Green. After six months of 'due consideration', he turned down the case on the grounds of insufficient evidence. I was horrified; more so on being told that there was no chance of appeal. Was there anything left to hope for? If so, what? When?

After Zana's return I had thought it would be only a matter of a few weeks, a couple of months at the most, before Nadia would be home. I'd tried to be patient, as nearly everyone I spoke to urged me to be, but where was this patience getting Nadia? She was still having babies by her captor.

Muthana's words, impressed indelibly on my brain, rang loud and clear in my ears. 'I kept you pregnant to hold you down!' I knew, I *knew*, that now this was what was happening to Nadia, too.

Chapter Forty-One

In a desperate bid to cheer Zana up, I arranged for a night out with some of my family (well, most of them, in fact). They were eager to see Zana again and she had no qualms about going out with her family.

We met Henry, Derek, David, Rhonda and Ann at my brother Billy's house. Then we converged on the local pub where we let our hair down. Zana got a little tipsy and had a great time. We all did our best to cheer her up, keep her going, and although it seemed to work at the time it didn't last long. She smiled and fooled around for a while but, all too soon, she slipped back into her depression. We had a marvellous time with my brothers though, and took lots of photographs. It isn't easy to be miserable in the company of my brothers, anyway, no matter what ails you. Trouble is, there is always a time to go home.

Zana and I had been to visit Ann Sufi. She had found out through a friend that stories referring to Zana and Nadia were circulating in the Arab press again.

'You should write a book to put the matter straight, Miriam!' Ann suggested.

'Why me? Zana should write a book, not me. At least she can tell the world how much she suffered out there!'

'I can't write a book,' said Zana. 'I just want to forget the past and get on with my life. Why should I write a book?'

'Nadia and Marcus, for a start,' I reminded her.

'What have I got to write about? Every day was the same!'

'Oh no, Zana, it wasn't. It wasn't the same. You should talk about what happened to you out there, get it out of your system.'

Nothing more was said about it. It was better for Zana to decide for herself, in her own good time. Over the next couple of weeks she would shut herself away in her room and attempt to write. It was proving very difficult for her. She would just start crying and throw the paper across the room. She managed to write a few pages but the trauma was so intense that she would collapse in tears and be depressed for hours.

The next time I saw Ann she mentioned that a colleague at work knew a writer whom she thought could help Zana. His name was Andrew Crofts, a successful ghost-writer. A meeting was arranged and Zana told him her story. He decided it would be better for her to get away from her surroundings and tell her the whole thing on tape, right from scratch.

Zana thought about it for a while. 'What do you think, Mom?'

'It's been nearly two years since you came home, Zana. Your sister could benefit from this because, despite the court case and everyone's assurances and promises, nothing seems to have helped so far. I'd hate to think it'll be another year before we get her home. It's a chance you can't afford to miss, and Nadia can't wait much longer.'

Zana needed no further prompting. She contacted Andrew Crofts. 'OK. When do we start?'

He said he would make some arrangements and be in touch soon.

Andrew and Zana went to an hotel and, over a period of time, made a series of ten tapes covering her life and experiences in the Yemen. It drained Zana emotionally, but she kept at it, breaking down occasionally, then recovering and continuing. It was one of the hardest things she had ever had to do, second only to leaving Nadia and Marcus. It was possibly a way of solving that, too; of keeping the story in the public eye.

The book was published in 1991 and received limited response because publicity was banned due to the pending court case, which we had managed to resume despite the former DPP's findings. By this time, Allan Green had been cautioned in one of the sleaziest parts of London against kerb crawling for prostitutes.

We gave the book no further thought until it fell into the hands of Editions Fixot, the renowned French publishing company. They had read the book, realised the interest there would be in France, with its large Muslim population, and decided to publish it there. They invited Zana to appear on television in France. *Sacrée Soirée*, hosted by Jean-Pierre Faucault, was one of the most popular programmes on the French station TF1, and went out live at prime time.

Initially, Zana was far too shy and withdrawn to accept the invitation but after gentle coaxing she accepted. After asking preliminary questions about her experiences in Yemen and a little about her book, Jean-Pierre asked Zana for her trust as he introduced another guest.

Abdul Amir Chawki, the press attaché for the Yemeni

Embassy in Paris, had contacted the presenters of *Sacrée Soirée* when he heard of Zana's forthcoming appearance. He insisted that he be allowed to participate.

Chawki took a seat next to Zana. She squirmed away from him, recoiling into the furthest corner of the sofa, her body rigid, her face angry. From my seat in the audience, a row behind Zana, I could feel the tension. I glared at Chawki, forming an instant dislike for him. He represented Muthana, Gowad, Abdul Khada and the Yemeni government on the programme.

'Mr Chawki Abdul Amir, can you answer this: is it possible for Zana's son, her sister and the children to come back to Britain? What is your position and your country's position?'

'It is a terrible and dramatic situation and I sympathise with Zana. It is a drama and it is her father's fault. A lot of time was wasted when they were hidden in that village in Yemen.'

'What can you do to help Zana and her sister as you find the situation unacceptable?'

'I am very upset by this story. I am a human being. My department and Yemen have done a lot to resolve things.'

Zana couldn't contain herself. 'They should have worked on this twelve years ago! They knew, very well, what was wrong.'

'The government learned about it when it all came out. We tried to resolve the problem and immediately we put Zana and her sister under protection, to take them away from family pressure.' Chawki rested his arm along the back of the sofa, behind Zana. She squirmed further away.

Jean-Pierre looked concerned for Zana. 'Can Zana go back to Yemen freely and see her sister?'

'Zana was free from day one as she is a British citizen. Her mother went to Yemen twice to see the child and Zana could have gone there, too.'

'If tomorrow, or the day after tomorrow, or even on Friday, I went with Zana, and obviously *Sacrée Soirée*, to Yemen, do you guarantee that we will be able to meet her sister and the children, so that, humanely speaking, all is resolved quicker?'

'Officially speaking, on our side, there is no problem.'

Jean-Pierre turned his attention to the camera. 'Nadia is in Yemen and she has not spoken to her sister for four years.'

Zana's eyes widened. 'Four years ago, she told me to get her out of there as soon as possible!' Tears started to fall down her cheeks. Tears of anger, with Chawki and his nonsense. Jean-Pierre capped that poignant moment by revealing that he had managed to link up with Yemen on the telephone.

'In Taiz, Nadia is waiting on the telephone to speak with you, Zana. Say hello to your sister . . .'

The whole audience was hushed. The sound system filled with static. It was near impossible to hear what Nadia was saying over the crackling and hissing of the amplified line.

Tears trickled down Zana's cheeks. 'Hello, Nadia. Hello? We can't hear you.' It was no use. It was too difficult to pick out anything Nadia said.

Jean-Pierre announced a short break during which Zana could speak to Nadia from the offices. I went with her. Music filled the air as we left the stage of the live programme to take the call, local musicians singing their hearts out to a swinging rhythm.

Zana was still in tears so I took the receiver from

Jean-Pierre. Nadia sounded as Brummie as ever. I fought hard to hold back my tears, a losing battle. I held the phone out for Zana to speak to her sister. I heard a few pleasantries then, 'What?' Her face was deathly pale. 'You've what?'

I tried to take the phone away from her. She slapped me away angrily and gabbled furiously in a mixture of English and Arabic.

A floor manager popped his head round the door to call us back to the stage. Zana slammed the phone down.

'What's happened, Zane?' I whispered.

'She's had another kid. They are back in the bloody village.'

We were interrupted by the floor manager shepherding us back into the studio. I tried hard to stem my flow of tears. My poor Nadia now had four children, this last one coming quickly after the third. I was still reeling from the news as Jean-Pierre greeted us effusively. Our entrance must have been good emotive television. The whole show had gathered on to the centre stage, including Chawki and all the musicians. Jean-Pierre asked Zana about the phone call. She swallowed hard and took a deep breath.

'Nadia is back in the village. She has been there since just after I left Yemen. She has had another baby now.'

'And Marcus, what about him?'

'He was taken from her just after I left Yemen. She hasn't seen him since. He is gone!' Her voice rose. 'He's disappeared!' She gritted her teeth.

'What will you do now? Will you give up?'

'No. Never! I'm never going to give up. I want Nadia to come to England with the children and prove that she is free. If she wants to go back afterwards, that's up to her, because she is free. Until that happens, she isn't free. How

277

can she be free? I'm not giving up. I'm more determined than ever now. I'll never give up until she comes home. Until she is free.'

'Thank you, Zana. We wish you all the success in the world with your book and hope that Nadia will be free soon.'

The monitors round the studio were filled with a close-up of Zana's tearful face. Jean-Pierre focused his attention on the other guests as the final piece of music played and the credits rolled. The audience clapped in time with the music.

I was distraught. I couldn't take any more. Poor Nadia. Poor Zana. Sobbing inconsolably, I put my head in my hands. Zana pulled my hands away. 'Don't let them see you cry, Mom. Don't let them see you cry!' I realised I was on camera. She was as solid as a rock despite the hurt she had inside.

I glared across at this person, Chawki, my most penetrative basilisk glare, mustered to turn him to stone on the spot. He made the mistake of smirking at me. I took off. Before anyone could move, I had him. By the scruff of his neck. 'You bastard. You lying Arab bastard!' I screeched.

My other hand was round his throat. I tightened my grip. His eyes bulged. The audience, still in their seats, applauded loudly.

'I won't have your lot destroying my children any further. I'll have your job for this. Do you understand? You're next!'

I remember thinking that I would prefer not to have to wait that long for justice. I could kill him right now, without the slightest compunction. Bernard Fixot, Zana's French publisher, was the first to react. He pulled me away, urging calm in his limited English. 'Come, Miriam. We leave now.'

I was still shaking with rage as we left. Chawki, also shaking, was ushered offstage by another route, embarrassed as the audience heckled and booed him.

When Zana reappeared to 'claim' me, the audience clapped and cheered, shouting 'Nadia libre, Nadia libre' – free Nadia – drawing instant public support and sympathy.

Chapter Forty-Two

Following the programme, the TF1 studio and Bernard's publishing company were flooded with telephone calls and letters, all sympathising and all supportive. Petitions were being drawn up and letters had begun to flood the Yemeni Embassy, addressed to Chawki.

Such was the public outrage that Zana was once again invited to appear on *Sacrée Soirée*, within weeks of the first programme. Bernard and Jean-Pierre had decided to put Chawki on the spot. We had a brief meeting, the outcome of which was that they asked Zana whether she felt she could return to the land that had almost destroyed her.

During the second programme Chawki, once again joining Zana onstage, made various sweeping statements. He said that Zana was completely free to visit Yemen if she were so inclined and there was no earthly reason why she shouldn't meet Marcus and Nadia. After all, they were family. Now Jean-Pierre was calling his bluff. He smiled, turned to Zana and asked. 'Zana, do you accept to come with us, to Yemen? Tomorrow? To sort things out?'

Zana's eyes flickered towards me in the audience. I held my breath. 'Yes. I accept.'

He turned to Chawki. 'If you were in Zana's position,

would you have done everything to get this story out in the open, in front of the whole world?'

Chawki nearly croaked. He coughed, fidgeting like crazy in his seat, adjusting his suddenly too-tight tie. He chose not to reply directly. 'Your dad's problem is dramatic. The Yemeni government took away his passport from him.'

The audience hissed.

'It's not true! My dad had a British passport.'

'He still had a Yemeni passport!' Chawki sulked.

Jean-Pierre shook his head. 'If we don't have enough publicity to this story, the problem will never be resolved. Zana, the author of *Vendues*, ['Sold'], will go to Yemen with *Sacrée Soirée*.'

We were to be flown out in a private jet on Sunday 11 February 1992. My passport had expired in the previous couple of days. The invitation to appear on French TV had caused such a rush that I hadn't realised how close to expiry it was when we left Birmingham. I had all the hassle of getting a new one but our Embassy in Paris were most helpful.

Then there was the problem of the Yemeni visas. These had to be obtained from – yes, you guessed it, from Chawki.

Obviously there had been some sort of behind-the-scenes smoothing over, or maybe he'd had his knuckles rapped over his antagonistic attitude, which had reflected on Yemen itself. There was no problem with the visas.

Chawki promised Bernard that the visit would include Zana seeing Marcus, her missing son. Furthermore, there would be no government interference; Zana and I would be given time with Marcus and Nadia and her children at a private venue chosen by Chawki, away from the public, the media, the government. This all reiterated what had been said on TV, broadcast to the French nation, so he wasn't going to renege on that, was he?

In return for their concessions the Yemeni government extracted the assurance that we would not try to snatch Nadia and the children. Chawki said that if Nadia and Mohammed wanted to leave Yemen, they could do so freely with the children, but if Mohammed objected, Nadia would have to leave alone. There was to be no media coverage with the exception of that of *Sacrée Soirée*, which would consist of a sound man, a cameraman and one technician, Jean-Pierre and Bernard Fixot. In addition, Bernard would have to take Chawki along to Yemen to oversee the visit.

All agreed.

The flight was quick. I was busy taking in the comforts of this plush jet, Bernard had gone to the cockpit to talk to the pilot. He had an avid interest in planes and jets and was taking full advantage of the situation. Zana watched the monitors recording our progress. The nearer we came to our destination the more edgy she became. We all knew that she was uncomfortable going back to a land of misery and cruelty, as she saw it. Jean-Pierre asked her if she was OK, his concern apparent.

'I'm all right. I'm telling you, though, I know these bastards. It won't go as planned. You can't plan anything with these people. They'll have the place crawling with government officials and the army or police too. It'd be too much to expect them to bring all the children. They probably think that if Nadia and all the kids come, she'd say she wanted to come back with us. That would scare them. I know! You watch. I'm not wrong. You watch and see!'

She dragged furiously on her cigarette and stared through the window. She hardly spoke again for the rest of the trip.

In no time at all we began our descent into Sanaa Airport. We would be flying on to Taiz, but international regulations required that we land first at Sanaa. With a gentle bump we touched down on the tarmac. Zana shuddered. There was no going back now.

Bernard and the pilot went to see the airport police and officials to register our arrival. Another group of officials came to attend to us and we were ushered to a room to wait until all the formalities were completed and the paperwork had been done.

Zana gnawed at her nails constantly, viciously, her eyes darting around the room suspiciously surveying the corners and dark areas. She shook visibly. The enormity of what we expected of her began to sink in.

After a couple of hours we were back on the plane, heading for Taiz. It was a very short flight, making a mockery of the six-hour car trip. If Zana had been nervous in Sanaa, it was nothing in comparison to her state as we approached Taiz.

We disembarked from the jet and were enveloped in the cool dusk. Zana looked around. She hung her head in an attempt to regain control of her emotions, her tears silent, the memories flooding back in an unwelcome assault on her mind. She took a deep breath. Bernard touched her shoulder reassuringly then escorted her to meet the inevitable officials congregated on the tarmac.

We were not tourists this time. Here we were, British trouble – as they saw us – accompanied by French media. The red carpet was almost out. Funny how people the world over react to the presence of TV, isn't it?

We were taken to a waiting Land Rover. The men piled in the bags and equipment, over-burdening the luggage area of the huge vehicle. We were to be taken to the Sheraton Hotel, where we would await the new day and the promised visit of Nadia, all four of her children, and Marcus.

Neither Zana nor I slept much that night. We sat smoking and drinking gallons of tea long after the others had retired for the night. She repeated her fears that the visit would not go as assured. I felt such compassion for her then, but I, too, worried that we'd had to go to these lengths to see our family. Zana's fears triggered all my suspicions that the whole story had not been told. It was much more than sisterly love that drove her to this. All through the night and into the early hours of morning, we worried in silence, lost in our own thoughts, gripped by our own fears, willing time away, until once again we were in the Land Rover.

We were taken a short distance to a small garden where we were told to wait. On a patio were three seats and a small table, surrounded on three sides by a high, whitewashed wall. Zana and I stood talking quietly as the three-man *Sacrée Soirée* team arranged the camera and lighting equipment. We heard what seemed to be a convoy arriving.

Curious and not a little perturbed, we craned our necks to see why there should be so many vehicles. A huge Land Rover had parked next to ours. Behind that were five other cars. Men piled out like ants from a nest. I could see Chawki among them. Three video cameras were in evidence. Armed guards wandered about, trying to pretend that their presence was purely coincidental. We knew we had made a big mistake. Our exchanged glances confirmed that we both realised we had played right into their hands.

Originally, and in good faith, Bernard and Jean-Pierre had arranged a reunion for our family. The camera crew was included to protect us as much as anything else. In order to gain the confidence of the Yemeni people, Bernard's wife, Valerie-Anne, had offered herself as surety that no snatch would take place if they would just leave us alone to see Nadia, which at the same time protected us should anything go wrong. Her value was great, not merely because she was Bernard's wife, but also as the daughter of the former President of France, Valerie Giscard-d'Estaing, a very influential politician worthy of great respect.

All those agreements and promises made by Chawki on prime-time television, witnessed by thousands of people all over France, suddenly seemed to be crumbling before we had even seen Nadia. Bernard and Jean-Pierre were totally confused. They didn't know whether to start a protest or start the camera rolling.

A figure came slowly into view, completely clad in black, save for a small slit around the eyes. Zana and I clutched at each other, huddling together as it came closer. A man carrying a child appeared, following her.

'Marcus?' Zana whispered, holding on tighter to my arm.

I couldn't tell whether Zana thought that the child was her son, or whether she instinctively knew he would not be there, and was calling his name in desperation.

The man was Mohammed, we could see that now, so the figure in black must surely be Nadia.

Together, Zana and I stepped towards her. Nadia held her hands in a palms-up expression of questioning.

'What's gooin' on?'

Her Brummie accent boomed across the patio. Zana and I were a little stunned. We so much wanted to rush at her, hug her, kiss her, but . . .

'What do you mean?' I gasped.

'What's all this? Why are all these lot here?'

'It's not us, Nadia. It's them. They promised that we'd be able to visit you, all the children and Marcus. Where are all the kids?'

Nadia's eyes glistened as she flashed a look behind her to Mohammed. The officials, including Chawki, had gathered at the gate, blocking what they thought to be an escape route.

'They're all at school!' Nadia lowered her head and stared at the ground.

Zana had walked across to Mohammed and greeted him, meeting Nadia's fourth child for the first time. The atmosphere was electric as the tension built and Nadia fretted.

At last we were able to talk together. Mohammed stayed close all the time, listening to Zana talking to Nadia in Arabic, which she did in an effort to involve him, bring him round.

I thought it might be a good idea, and joined in. Through Zana, I actually told Mohammed that I accepted him as my son-in-law. And if this was so, he should respect me as his mother-in-law. I swallowed a build-up of bile, cringing as I offered peace. He remained, as always, implacable, the differences irreconcilable.

Deeply engrossed in strained conversation, we suddenly noticed that even more people had joined the officials. Now there were about thirty Yemenis. Nadia was becoming more agitated and nervous.

Bernard and Jean-Pierre approached and asked Nadia for an interview. To our utter astonishment, she readily agreed, without looking for approval from Mohammed and Chawki or any other interfering busybody. Of course, we were pleased.

But it was too easy. She was far too willing to comply, but in the strangest manner. She had been primed, robotically, ready to speak. She even took a deep breath, composing herself for her prearranged speech. But Nadia was totally thrown by Jean-Pierre's interview technique. Unprepared.

Zana and I were flummoxed. We talked all through the interview, whispering our opinions of this obvious set-up, and missed everything she said.

We were asked to go inside a nearby building, part public café and part government conference rooms. In a medium-sized room were four chairs, placed in a line for us. We sat, as requested, and were shocked to see four Yemeni women, dressed in the same depersonalising garb as Nadia, taking four more seats directly opposite us, no more than five feet away. These women, obviously linguists, leaned forward if we spoke in hushed tones, and sat back if we spoke in normal pitch. I was absolutely furious.

The privacy we had been assured of was a non-starter. This was a public building, no privacy was possible. But, of course, they didn't intend it. They even had a little insurance for themselves in the form of at least thirty of their own intimidating squad. They had known from the outset that if Nadia said she wanted to come home with us she would have to be granted her freedom. I told Nadia that there was a jet waiting to take her home, if that was her wish. They'd known that was a possibility and were

287

using every trick in the book to prevent her from saying anything that she had not been preprogrammed to say, First by making her leave all her children behind, then by using armed guards as an implicit threat.

I wouldn't have been at all surprised if they had warned her that they would open fire if she said the wrong thing. In her frame of mind she would have believed anything they wanted her to.

Nadia was so upset. Petrified. The whole meeting had an underlying plan, to put added pressure on Nadia. 'The kids are at school,' she'd been ordered to say. Schooling in Yemen begins when children are seven years of age. That could account, perhaps, for Haney and Marcus, but the other children were five and under. School wasn't as important as seeing their grandmother or aunt, was it? For only one day?

Throughout the two-hour visit Zana and I were never permitted to talk to Nadia alone, nor could we even go to the toilet without the four black-clad women as escorts. Nadia fretted about the children the whole time and constantly looked at Mohammed as if for confirmation that she hadn't stepped out of line.

'*Haya Bina!*' We go! Mohammed simply stood up and started to walk away. Nadia jumped to her feet and began to follow him, about ten paces behind. Mohammed had decided that the meeting was over and Nadia would be returned to the village, *now*! He spoke to her in Arabic, perhaps forgetting that Zana was able to understand him, perhaps in blatant disregard.

'Nadia!' I called after her. 'Please, Nadia!'

'I have to go now, Mom.' She looked at me, her veil wet with tears.

'Nadia, you don't have to go now, you can stay. Come

288

and have dinner with us at the hotel first. Please!' I implored.

'I can't!' she almost shrieked as she hurried after Mohammed.

We managed to catch up with her. Zana put her hand on her arm. She stopped. 'Nadia, don't go. We can speak to Chawki. He will order Mohammed to let you stay with us,' she offered.

'Oh, no. No, no!' Nadia panicked at the very thought, her eyes darting around to look for anyone listening to this conversation.

Seeing her like a trapped rabbit in a snare made my blood boil. 'You will see, Nadia. Gowad will pay for this. I'll kill him, the bastard!' I growled, more than spoke.

'I don't give a fuck about Gowad!' Nadia spat his name out, venomously.

I stood back, shocked. The mere mention of his name had provoked that spontaneous reaction of white-hot malice. 'We love you, Nadia. Please tell him to let you come home.'

'I know Mom, I love yous, too. I'll come home, soon.' She quickly composed herself again.

'Soon? When?'

'Soon. I'll come home soon!'

'You've said that before. You always say soon,' Zana cried.

'I will come home, but not yet. It's not me, it's him.' She pointed to Mohammed. 'He's scared of all the press.'

'So he should be!' Zana snapped.

'You shouldn't have brought all these people.' Nadia was scared.

'Look, Nadia. The last time I was here you said you wanted to come home. You asked me to do all I could

289

to get you home soon. I've done that. I didn't bring all these people. It's them. The Yemeni government!'

'Them?' Nadia asked with definite astonishment.

'Yes, of course! Do they look English to you? Do they look French?'

Mohammed had been listening to all this, trying to follow what was going on. He realised his male authority was in question as Nadia stood talking to us. With a glare he focused on her and with a simple jerk of his head, ordered her to hurry up. Like a dog to heel, Nadia scurried off, closing the gap between them, and out of the building.

Chawki appeared and stood with his arms folded, his weight resting on one leg, the other slightly bent at the knee. He smirked. If there is one thing I cannot tolerate, it's a smirking Arab. I rushed up to him.

'You bastard!' I screamed. 'You said I could see my grandchildren whom I have never seen! Where are they? You said we would have privacy! Where is it? You said we would be allowed time together – alone – and it's all bollocks. We have flown thousands of miles because of you! Now, what have you got to say for yourself?'

He raised his eyebrows. 'Why not go to the village?'

Zana froze on the spot. 'No! Never!'

'But you can, you and your mother. You have a problem with this, Zana?' Chawki chortled to himself.

From the depths of her soul, Zana summoned every Arabic profanity that she knew and threw them all into Chawki's face in a cobra strike of damnation.

His mouth dropped open. Memories of Paris must have flooded back. He fled to safety behind the armed guards. He said not a single word.

Nadia was out of my sight and we had achieved nothing.

Zana ran to catch up with her. By now she had climbed into a jeep, supposedly leaving for the village.

'I love you, Nadia!' Zana cried.

Nadia leaned forward to kiss her sister. 'I love yous all!'

Then, as they embraced, she whispered in Zana's ear. 'Zana, did you forget me? Please, Zana, don't forget me. You promised you would never forget me. Don't leave me here! Not too long. Please!' She gripped Zana's arms with astonishing strength, as if to add emphasis to her plea, and breathed deeply to control her tears, compose herself.

'I'll never forget you, Nadia. I made a promise. I know what's happening. You will come home soon,' Zana smiled. She stood back and waved to her sister as the jeep started its return journey to hell.

Bernard and Jean-Pierre were flabbergasted. They stood motionless on the gravel path as they witnessed the whole episode.

Zana ran back then, her face streaming with tears. 'See, I told you what would happen! I told you they'd lie and do everything they could to make sure it all went wrong. And I told you that in France!'

'Yes, you did,' Jean-Pierre said reflectively.

Chawki sauntered over, grinning. He announced that dinner was ready in the great banqueting hall.

'Choke on it, you bastard. Do something right in your life!'

'Miriam,' Jean-Pierre coaxed, 'perhaps it would be a chance . . .'

'No way! There is no way I'm going to sit there and eat with these Arab bastards. I didn't come all this way for food! I came to see my daughter and my grandchildren.

I'm going to the hotel. You stay if you think some good will come of it.'

'No good will come of it, Jean-Pierre,' said Zana flatly. 'I'm going back with Mom.'

We went to the hotel. We clung to each other and wept. We realised now that this trip had put Nadia in danger. The Yemenis had told her that we had planned this whole thing. They told her what she was to say during the visit. Her children had been held to ransom to ensure that she obeyed.

To me, her apparent obsequiousness provided more evidence of her total fear. This was going to cause her many problems now. Mohammed and the Yemeni government would make her pay dearly for something which was of their own doing. This was what they must have had in mind all the time. It was all so blatantly obvious now, but it was much too late to do anything about it. Desperately, we drew strength from her words to Zana.

Early the next day, we were airbound for Paris. We all had a thousand and one thoughts racing through our minds. Most of all, we had an overwhelming sense of disbelief. Had it really happened? Jean-Pierre had taken it badly. He told us that he wanted Zana to appear once again on his show when he ran the film of the trip. She agreed.

292

Chapter Forty-Three

On 12 April Zana reappeared on *Sacrée Soirée* before a supportive audience. Jean-Pierre introduced a videotape of the visit to Yemen in February. The film began with our departure from Le Bourget Airport in Paris on an overcast Sunday morning, picking up the arrival at Taiz on the Monday at midday and the meeting with Nadia.

The French audience sat awestruck throughout.

As the film finished, Jean-Pierre introduced Chawki, inviting him onstage. The people hissed and shouted abuse, some gesturing with their fingers. As Chawki took a seat next to Zana, Jean-Pierre began.

'Zana? What did you wonder?'

'When she approached me, she was looking around and was surprised to see the cameras that she had not seen for twelve years, and she must have been wondering what was going on. I told her that that was the way they had planned it. Obviously, it was hard for Nadia to understand. She was not allowed to be unveiled. We sat down and talked and told her that she could go freely, with us, and the children, but she only had one with her. The rest of the children were not there. The excuse was that the children were at school. The promise was broken by the government. In Yemen, children go to school at the age of seven, and the eldest is eight. Nadia has a daughter who is six, a three-year-old son and a fifteen-month-old son. I was shocked at the lies and manipulation, which I expected anyway.'

'Mr Chawki. I showed you how the trip went. It was agreed that the children would be there. Now, based on Zana's strong accusations, what do you have to say tonight?'

'When I decided to come to your programme it was not for a duel. All I wanted was to help Zana, and I still do. I understand the pain she is going through, and you were with us, Monsieur Jean-Pierre Faucault. You saw it. You showed a film which will show things very clearly. Nadia is Yemenite and it's her choice. Zana is British, and it's her choice. I respect both of them.'

'Why were the children not there?'

'Because, Monsieur Faucault, our idea was to go to the village, to their home. Zana refused to go to the village. She didn't want to bother to travel for two hours.'

Jean-Pierre stiffened visibly. 'I agree. Zana did not want to go to the village, but can you understand why? She had suffered for so long. It is human and normal not to want to go there. Why didn't we see the whole of the family together?'

'As far as I know, that was not the issue. The issue was the meeting between Zana and Nadia and they came with the youngest son in the father's arms. It is not Nadia's children's problem. The most important thing was the meeting between Zana and Nadia. And in any case, communication is difficult between Zana and Taiz by telephone. It was a communication problem, but the meeting between sisters was the most important thing.'

294

'Don't you think that if all the family were there, Zana and her mum would not have been suspicious?'

'I don't think so because the children issue is secondary. They were at school.'

'But do they go to school at the age of seven in Yemen?'

'Oh yes, of course!'

Jean-Pierre glared at him. 'The children were *not* seven!'

Chawki shifted uncomfortably in his seat. 'The eldest was seven.'

'And what about the others?' Jean-Pierre snapped.

'Er . . . em . . . the others? But why drag them with us?' Chawki offered, flippantly.

Jean-Pierre became angry 'Don't you think that they would have wanted to see their grandmother and aunt? Surely it's more important than missing one day at school!'

'When they met, you saw it yourself, Monsieur Faucault. Did you feel that Nadia wanted to throw herself in her mother's or her sister's arms?' Chawki patronised while he had the opportunity.

'I do not judge!'

'You do not need to judge, it's observation.'

'Indeed, I expected them to kiss!' He turned to Zana. 'You did not kiss. There was no physical contact. What prevented it? What happened?'

Zana, cool and composed, explained. 'Because I'm so strong. I had told Mr Fixot beforehand what would happen and it turned out the same way as I told him. When I reached Nadia I saw the shock on her face. All the officials were around. There was me, Mom, her and the others. It was the shock. We were told we would be alone. It was not the case. Anyhow, you do not need to touch someone to show emotion. My sister told me what she wanted when we were on our own. It made me stronger. I understand what she told me and I *know* what she wants. Nothing can change that for me.'

'Well, in spite of all this, on the plane on the way back I felt you were different from what you were on the way to Yemen. I felt you were better. Is this first step, that we started eight days ago, as important for you?'

'I did feel better. I saw her alive and now I know what she wants and until she comes out of that country – and the Yemeni government needs to tell me that she is free to leave Yemen, then she will be able to leave the country, and I will be able to thank the Yemeni government—'

Chawki jumped in. 'Zana must understand that her sister is a big girl. She is free to express herself, free to choose.' He sat there, waving his hand back and forth, chauvinistically dismissing Zana's opinion.

The audience jumped as Jean-Pierre shouted at Chawki. 'OK, she told *me* that she would like to come to England, with her husband and children, for a few days. When she decides, let us know, as we are the ones who started these meetings and we would like to see that she *can* leave the country! Don't you think that for children it is important to see their grandmother and aunt, four years later?'

Chawki turned up his nose. 'They have to *ask* to see them! Nadia was virtually shouting at her mother, telling her that she was the cause of it all. It's a family that has changed a lot over the years. You have to take into account the change. You cannot force the situation!'

'Don't you think that, as a father, it would have been easier for the whole family to have been together?'

'Yes, But it is an internal problem.'

Jean-Pierre turned to Zana. 'You stayed together for a

hour and a half. We did not hear what you said, then your sister allowed me to interview her, let's listen to what she answered.'

A film began showing Jean-Pierre talking to Nadia. 'How did your meeting go with your mum and your sister?'

'I feel happy, very well. She's my mother, she's my sister!'

'Are you happy to live in the Yemen with your husband and children?'

'Very happy with my husband and my children. I have a big house. I have food. Nothing is missing. I'm OK.'

'Have you finished with your life in Birmingham, in England?'

'When I was in Birmingham . . .?'

This was the point where Nadia's preprogrammed speech was to begin, and now she is suddenly thrown off track. A voice asked Nadia if she remembers Birmingham, if she has forgotten Birmingham?

'I do remember some things. But not a lot. I was only small, young . . .'

'Do you have any regrets about life when you were younger?'

'No, no. No regrets. I was only young. I used to go to school. I was only eleven, twelve. I was playing. I was only young.'

'Would you like to spend a few days with your mum, sister and children in England?'

'It's impossible!'

'Why?'

'Because it's not possible for now. I wouldn't like to, because it's too much. Too many people. Too many worries and because I'm a Muslim now, and I have learned Islamic law. I don't like all this. Too many people!'

'Are you happy, Nadia?'

'Very happy. Very happy with my children. They are the *only* things in my life!'

Nadia stared into the camera, then looked away. Such an emotive look in her eyes. Anguish, desperation; deep, deep sadness, fear. This look said a thousand things that words could never manage.

'When you met your sister Zana, an hour ago, why didn't you kiss her?'

'It was the shock.'

The film finished. Jean-Pierre turned to Zana. 'What do you have to say about the interview I did with Nadia?'

'They left her children because they knew it was a threat. They did it to me when I was in the Yemen and I refused to live with my mother because I wanted to go back to my boy. I know how fond Nadia is of her children and that's all she is living for. As for Mr Chawki saying that she is a big girl; nothing has changed for Nadia, she is still the fourteen-year-old girl who left, because her life has not changed. She has not had the chance to grow up. She doesn't know what growing up means.'

Jean-Pierre tilted his head, quizzically. 'Did she feel obliged to say what she said, or is it because she felt she could not say it? Don't you think that there is a glimmer of hope that she might come to see you in England with her husband and children, and she might make a decision then, without feeling suspicious?

'Mr Chawki, she can come to England, can't she? The salary is not in the way, and I asked her husband, who told me that he could not come because he would lose his job. Would you, as an authority, facilitate their coming to England?'

'Of course! I would not have gone to the Yemen with you if I didn't have in mind that possibility. But before we finish, I would like to say that everyone has heard Nadia. She is an adult. She is now a mother. She is twenty-four and she got to the Yemen only young. Under obligation, it is true. And then she got used to life there and enjoyed it. She loves her children. Zana talks about her sister, just as if it were her mother, or grandmother. Nadia is over eighteen and deserves respect, that is the difference.'

'We hope that you can see your sister, your son and her children soon,' Jean-Pierre smiled at Zana.

'I would like to thank you and your team for making it possible to see my sister. I have a lot of hope and until she comes out, nobody can tell me that she is free. It's in her eyes. There is too much anguish. I *know* she wants to come home and she will one day.'

The show finished. As I rejoined Zana from my seat in the audience people became very aggressive towards Chawki. He rushed away towards the stairs leading to the exit.

Chapter Forty-Four

As I sat in my lounge I reflected, as usual, on past events. The facts never changed, of course, but I continually searched for a hidden solution, something I might have missed, perhaps. The court case was going well. Muthana had been making rash statements to the press and getting himself deeper and deeper into the mire. Gowad and Abdul Khada had also been served with papers. Properties were seized and accounts frozen. It wasn't enough. I wanted something more. I spent most of my time now sitting here, going over all the information I had accumulated. I had done a little research, too.

I discovered that I wasn't the only one to have suffered at the hands of a Shamiri. I now knew of at least five other mothers who had had their children taken to Yemen. This had accounted for at least ten other children, the majority female. I knew that there were many more like them.

Zana had met so many girls taken from the Midlands by force who were now in Yemen. One was a petite blonde from Derby. She was nine years old when she was taken and had already had three miscarriages when she became pregnant a fourth time. This time the child had been stillborn. The death of this little baby had taken the child-mother's sanity. She was twelve years old. Another, also twelve years old, often chatted to Zana, telling her that she could still count to ten in English. She told Zana how desperate she was to go home to England. As they talked together, she suckled a child of her own at her breast.

I was beginning to meet many women who had been left to patch together the tattered remains of their lives, their children gone, desperately clinging on to hope and sanity. I began to get letters every day from women all over the world in the same position as myself. I wrote back to them all, trying to give support and encouragement.

Zana's book was remarkably successful now, and on an international scale at that. The people of France, God bless them all, began writing to Zana and offering prayers and support. These correspondents were everything from eight to eighty years old. Some would send pages and pages of signatures supporting Nadia, others would send sweets for Marcus. The story was spreading across the world. Zana and I had appeared on several television programmes and were constantly in the national papers.

I was also a grandmother several times over. Zana had had a child, a son named Liam; Tina had two boys and had settled down to a life that suited her perfectly; Ashia was waiting to give birth to her second child; Laila had four children. Ahmed was now married and Mo was going steady too. If only I had Nadia at home to see her nephews and nieces. If only her children could play with their cousins. Throughout all this none of us ever forgot Nadia. Nothing would ever be the same again and nothing would be right until we had her home to complete the family.

In April 1992, Ann Sufi, her daughter Yasmin and some

friends, Chris and Jana, and myself met at Yasmin's house. We had all decided that something would just have to be done about all these abductions. Together, we formed a non-registered charity called Lost Children International, designed to reunite children with their parents in their homeland. We set out our tasks and objectives in a professional manner. Very soon, we had a chairman, Peter, and several members. We appeared on local TV and radio and gained instant support from local businesses, who donated equipment, time, money and stationery.

We all converged on Yasmin's house for meetings. We managed to raise funds and began to counsel other parents who had suffered abduction, kidnap or separation from their children. It was not long before we had active interest from overseas.

Jana introduced us to her friend Nancy, from New York, who had come to visit her in England. We all took an instant shine to Nancy and she became an honorary overseas member of the charity, meeting some of the estranged parents, helping with fund-raising and generally getting stuck in. She represented our cause in the States.

My life became radically different. No longer did I just stay in the house, brooding. Jana was full of ideas and would insist on testing the field herself, as long as I went with her. We went out regularly for the charity, spreading the word and getting other people involved. My family could not believe that I was actually going out again; what was more, I was hardly ever in the house. Jana called it 'networking'.

In June, Ashia had an encounter with her father while she was mooching round the market. He told her that Nadia was pregnant again and happy. The Yemeni government had paid her £10,000 and had given her gifts.

When Bernard Fixot rang us at home we told him of this turn of events. A meeting was arranged and Zana once again appeared on *Sacrée Soirée*, this time with Ashia.

Chawki was invited to participate but after the last débâcle he had arranged, he declined in the strongest possible terms. I don't think he expected the announcement by Ashia that money was again changing hands. He rang the studio in the middle of the transmission and blew his top, demanding to be allowed to join the programme.

To Zana's utter disgust, Chawki stomped on to the set and plonked himself down next to Ashia. Both girls turned sideways, so that Chawki could only see their backs. Jean-Pierre Faucault tried to hush the hissing audience then turned his attention to Chawki.

'You have come, as you said when you phoned us earlier on in this show, because Ashia said that the government had given Nadia one hundred thousand francs, which represents thirty years' work for the average Yemeni. You grabbed the phone and we heard that you were not happy. Now, is Nadia going to be able to go and spend a week with her family? Yes or no? You are going to think that I am not minding my own business, but I heard promises, including from you! Where do we stand?'

Chawki could hardly contain himself. 'Of course she can, if she wants to. As a free individual. But allow me to answer you generally! Tonight, I am indignant and rightly so. Because it is thanks to us that Zana was able to see her sister. It is thanks to the government that Zana is free, because when the government knew about her story, it is them who freed her. The Yemeni government has other things to do, other tasks, other problems. Now, if Zana enjoys turning on the waterworks on stage to resolve her problems, that's just great. But it's not right!'

Jean-Pierre persisted in trying to get his answer. 'When will Nadia be able to spend a week in England? I am under the impression that we have just been going round and round, for months and months!'

Zana came in then, addressing Chawki. 'If it were not for Jean-Pierre, the French people and the media, I would not have been able to go to Yemen, and I thank them very much for that. I thank you and your government for letting me see my sister. But excuse me – you had a document promising me that I would see my sister and all her children, and my son Marcus. I didn't see them. You made promises also, but you lied to me.'

As she confronted Chawki, I really thought she was going to clobber him with her microphone.

'Allow me to say something to that! I have the letter, which you can read out to the public, Mr Faucault. I would like to remind the viewers that we left Paris to go to the village. I made arrangements to get to the village. We did not get there, because Zana did not want to see her son in the village!'

'No! No, it was not. I was told it was too dangerous for me to go to the village.'

'You were not in any danger,' Chawki growled.

Ashia squirmed to the back of the sofa as Chawki and Zana sparred.

'Do you really think that I could face that nightmare again?'

'But listen, you were with us! With Jean-Pierre Faucault! You were with everybody. There was no danger, absolutely no danger!'

'Mr Chawki,' Jean-Pierre interjected, 'we have not been able to go the village.'

'But it's *her* fault! I must be firm,' the press attaché sulked.

'On this point, yes! I did want to go to the village, but it is true that people and the authorities said to us that they could *not* assure our safety. Yes, Mr Chawki, you agree with me? You agree with me?'

Chawki could not challenge Jean-Pierre on this point. He was cornered by the presenter and he knew it. He sank into his seat, blushing.

Jean-Pierre continued: 'Mr Chawki, since you are saying that this is a minor problem in your country, you don't want to spoil the image of your country, and rightly so, for a family problem, *let them out!*'

'Of course! The answer is in the letter!' Chawki insisted.

The presenter read: ' "Following the confusion and the strange mixture that Zana Muhsen's family brought to our attention, the Yemeni Embassy in Paris certifies the following: one, Miss Zana Muhsen, can go and see her son and sister and may write to them. Two, Miss Zana Muhsen may appeal against the judgement of the custody of the child given to the father, and may compile a file that may be submitted to the Yemeni court." '

Annoyed, Jean-Pierre waved the letter about. 'We knew that!' He shook his head. ' "Three, Mrs Nadia Muhsen[sic], her children and her husband are Yemeni citizens and as such have always had the freedom to leave the Yemen, for any country of their choice which welcomes them. The appropriate Yemeni authorities will be pleased to help Miss Zana Muhsen and her family to obtain a happy conclusion to their problem." '

Jean-Pierre then read out the accompanying letter. '"The Embassy of the Republic of Yemen sends you its best compliments and in the event of the programme representing the problems of Miss Zana Muhsen Wednesday fifth of February is honoured to inform you of the following.

' "As soon as the Yemeni government heard of the problem arising from the forced weddings of Zana and Nadia Muhsen, both minors and of British nationality, they were told to leave their villages of Hokail and Ashube to come to Taiz. A flat was made available to them and their problem legally undertaken as they were put under the protection of the governor away from their family and their husbands. The court of Taiz decided by a court order that the marriages were illegal and consequently Zana and Nadia are considered by the Yemeni law to be British citizens. They had the choice to stay in Yemen or to leave on their own, leaving the custody of their children to the fathers. Zana left the country leaving her son. The Yemeni government, aware of the importance of the family gathering, and in order to solve the problem arising in the separation of parents offered the possibility to the Yemenite fathers and to the children to go to Great Britain or any other country of their choice with Zana and Nadia. All agreed and an application for visa was issued to the British Consulate in Sanaa, which unfortunately refused even with the agreement of their ex-wives.

' "The Yemeni government confirms today its agreement for the departure of Nadia, her husband, her children and the son of Zana to a country of their choice, in this case Great Britain, especially as Nadia's father-in-law has also obtained British citizenship. Despite the fact of the departure of Zana and the refusal of the British government to grant visas to the Yemeni fathers, the government helped Nadia's husband to find a job with a reasonable salary in order to maintain a big family as well as the son of Zana,

306

being in their custody. A flat was provided in Taiz with a telephone in order to facilitate the contact with their family in Great Britain. The mother of Zana and Nadia since the departure of the former managed to visit her daughter twice with the help and the co-operation of the Yemeni government and the British Consulate." '

Chawki raged on. 'It's a problem of freedom! We must not forget to say that the husband is free to leave if the British government gives him a visa. Until now, it has been refused.'

'I have a letter from my solicitor saying that the Minister for Foreign Affairs has a visa ready for him,' Zana challenged Chawki.

In a fit of pique he exclaimed: 'Zana is a victim!'

'Many of us are still suffering in the Yemen,' she reminded him.

'I would say to those who are selling their books, they have sold enough! One hundred thousand copies is very good. They have poisoned enough people and enough is enough. Now we need to live in peace!' Chawki's leg twitched in a spasm.

'I am *not* going to stop until she is free! The picture on the front of this book does not show freedom!'

'If your sister is angry, it is because you do all the publicity. That is why she is angry!'

'It's not! It's because she is unhappy!'

Jean-Pierre concluded the argument. 'May your sister and her family spend their holiday in Birmingham.'

Although, during the transmission of *Sacrée Soirée*, Chawki had promised a safe passage to Yemen for myself and one other, he had no compunction in forgetting that when out of the range of the camera. Obtaining yet another visa was awkward, but by no means as difficult as deciding who should or could come with me into that hellhole.

It would have to be a man. A solicitor, maybe, or a professional who could witness the charade that I was convinced would be awaiting my arrival in Yemen. To this end I spoke to my solicitor, who was looking into the possibility of sending a lawyer or representative from an international organisation such as Amnesty.

Feelers were put out; all I had to do was wait. I hate waiting. It is something that I always have to do, but I never accept it lightly, always reflecting on the time that has been consumed already. I was very busy, arranging my schedule.

I asked Jana to inform the FCO of my impending visit and to get the facsimile number of the British Embassy in Sanaa. The conversation between Jana and a senior Foreign Office person, Michael Pauley, revealed that the opinion of the FCO was that Nadia should be left in peace. As far as Pauley was concerned, it was unfair to disturb her and her children just to appease her mother. 'This is a matter between husband and wife,' he stated, adding: 'We have always made our view clear, that this is a family matter. Tell Miss Ali ring Heather Taggart on Monday.'

Jana rang me immediately, hopping mad, and relayed the conversation. As I listened to her condemnation of his attitude, it was like putting the clock back yet again.

'Now you know the sort of people I have been fighting for the last twelve years. I wonder I haven't pulled all my hair out over the years!' Oh, it bothered me. It bothered me a lot. But this conversation revealed something more worrying than an apathetic minister.

She came out with it. 'Mim. I hate to be the one to tell you . . . Nadia is pregnant again.'

I can't remember concluding that conversation with Jana. I couldn't fight the nausea that overcame me. I didn't make it even halfway to the kitchen before it overwhelmed me. I fell to my knees and was violently sick. Tears of illness mixed with tears of pain and sadness. I continued to retch long after there was nothing left to expel. I cried hysterically, shouting aloud for mercy for Nadia and for her fifth child until eventually a burning anger evaporated my tears. I was lost then, as a deep, black depression took over.

Against my better judgement I had to ring Heather Taggart, to find out how they had come by this information. At first she refused to acknowledge that a Consulate official had gone into the Mokbana region and paid Nadia a visit. Then it came out that he *had* seen Nadia and noted that she was pregnant. Noted? How observant. She was eight months pregnant! She had apparently told this official that she was happy and also said that if Mohammed was allowed to come to England too, then she would come.

I wanted to finish this conversation quickly. Things were urgent now. I told Heather of my intended visit to Yemen and asked her for Consulate assistance. She said she would arrange an hotel and asked when I intended to leave.

My reply was the only one possible in the circumstances. 'As soon as possible!'

This left me in a quandary. First, there was the question of my companion for the trip. Now that I knew Nadia was pregnant and near her time of confinement I would have to leave very soon. I felt that I would have to do whatever I could to get her into Taiz for the delivery of the baby. She'd had such an awful time with Tina. I recalled the doctor's warning that she shouldn't any more children. Now she was about to have number five.

I rang Jana. 'Jana, Nadia is in trouble. Oh, yes she is pregnant again. But eight months! I have to go *now* to Yemen.' It was all I could manage before the tears started again.

Jana tried to talk me into a calmer state. She suggested a colleague who might be able to go with me. I rang him. He said he would be only too pleased to come, but that he could only do so with enough notice to apply for vacation leave. I couldn't wait. Nadia couldn't wait.

I rang Jana again. 'I'm going! He can't come with me so I'm going on the next available flight.'

'Mim, you can't go alone!'

'I have to go now, and I can't find anyone to come. I can't ask just anyone.'

'At least ring around first. Give it a try! If all else fails, I'll come.'

'You can't come, Jana. You have enough to worry about.'

'You would do it for me, you said so before. I know you would.'

'I can't ask you. It should be a man, anyway.'

'Well, try for a man, then, but the offer is there. OK?'

'OK. Thanks, Jana. I've got to keep trying. I'll get back to you.'

'Ring around first,' she had said. Who? Yellow Pages? What do you say to people? Oh, are you doing anything special tomorrow? Can you come to Yemen? Hmmm?

I rang as many people as I could think of. It was the time factor that caused the problem. All the people I asked for help were willing but had to give notice for work. I tried all day. Mo offered to go, but I said no. I sat in my lounge

310

and thought. As the time ticked past, I knew it could be only one person.

I dialled the number slowly, giving myself additional seconds to rethink. To no avail. The phone rang.

'Hello. It's me.'

'Oh, hello. Any luck?'

'Get your passport ready, Jana. You're coming to Yemen. We go to London tomorrow for visas.'

'OK, Mim. What time do you want to leave?'

'Early. I'll meet you at the front of New Street Station at half-seven. You'll need your passport and two photos.'

'OK. See you there.'

'Jana?'

'Mmmm?'

'Thanks!'

Chapter Forty-Five

We arrived in Sanaa on Friday 31 July 1992.

After the usual customs procedures we were soon in a taxi en route for the Al Hamd Hotel, which had been booked by the Foreign Office via the Consulate in Sanaa.

While we were taking tea in the lounge, this character calling himself Jimmy MacGregor, who was really an Arab called Abdul Hamid Salam, introduced himself as a taxi driver who knew Sanaa like no other and said that, if we required a taxi at any time, we should call on his services. He could be contacted at any time via the hotel staff.

He started to make conversation about working for the British in Aden, which was how he got his name. He would do anything for the British, his favourite kind of people. He smiled, every single tooth in his mouth covered in gold.

After a great deal of insistence, he managed to convince us that we needed a tour of Sanaa, especially the older part, which, according to Jimmy, was splendid for tourists. Especially British tourists. Most of the money donated for the restoration and upkeep of these grand old buildings came from British coffers. Because of this claim, we allowed ourselves to be persuaded and spent an horrendous hour and a half in the local marketplace, or *souk*, as it is called locally.

We went back to the hotel and retired to our room to sleep the day off.

We woke at eight. Jana was covered in bites from over-zealous insects. We washed and went down for early tea, intending to visit the Embassy.

Jimmy was waiting to pounce as soon as he heard that we had ordered a taxi. We went to the Embassy. It was open, but no staff were available to see us. Disappointed, we returned to the car. Back at the hotel we tried to contact Paris. The lines were down.

That evening, Jimmy took us for a drive to an old Chinese graveyard. It sounded an awful place to visit but in fact it afforded a magnificent view of all Sanaa. It was curious that on the horizon we could see two satellite dishes of huge proportions. We wondered why Yemen would have such communications equipment when their economy could not afford either to run or maintain any system that would warrant dishes of this size.

On our way back, we decided to go to a restaurant for dinner, not feeling able to face the offerings at Al Hamd. Jimmy said that musical entertainment was planned for the evening at the Ramada, where I had stayed in 1986.

On Sunday, we arose early, had tea and checked out of the hotel so that we could make our way to Taiz after visiting the Embassy. We had planned to take a bus to Taiz, but there was Jimmy popping up again, insisting that he take us. I asked him about the cost and he said that we could talk of that later. I didn't like the sound of that at all. However, we accepted his offer to take us to the Embassy.

313

It was open, so I asked to see the Ambassador. I was seen, in fact, by Phil Whitmore, a consular aide, who said he would try to assist but could not afford me any protection at this time. But now that he was aware of my presence, he would welcome contact and help me if at all possible.

We left the Embassy and endured the six-hour drive to Taiz. Jimmy drove us there, despite my objections. It was the Arabic way to persist, and I really was not in the mood to haggle too much. We stopped several times for Jimmy to show us a sheer cliff face or buy *qat* for himself. We drove until around three o'clock, when we stopped for lunch and to answer to the call of nature.

Children ran to the car as we pulled over, and stopped dead in their tracks when they saw Jana. They had never seen anyone like her before: a white woman, auburn hair uncovered and not wearing purdah. I was less strange: coming from a mixed family I have darker skin tones and black hair. I suppose I blended in to a certain extent, although I was not covered up either. Jana stuck out like a sore thumb. The kids were very curious about her.

The worst part was using the toilet. It was dark, smelly and the door had no lock. It was one of those squatting toilets, which had Jana in fits of laughter as she tried to balance and aim in the right direction, never having used one of this type before.

It was time to go. One last bid by the kids lost Jana her pens. Jimmy now contentedly chewed *qat* as he drove us over the mountains and close to the sheer drop.

'This is it, Jana! Taiz!'

We gazed out at the surrounding rubble that remained since my previous visit.

I told Jimmy to take us to the Al Gnad Hotel.

'Closed!' He shrugged his shoulders. 'I take you good hotel!'

'Not the Mareb!' I insisted. 'It's too expensive.'

'No, but near this.' Jimmy dismissed any further conversation and concentrated on avoiding the locals, who were on the road trying to avoid the camels, who were on the path trying to avoid the rubble.

Huge craters still made the road near impossible to negotiate and Jimmy swerved in and out regardless of the oncoming traffic, pedestrians and animals, his old tank of a Mercedes growling in objection to the hard punishment it was taking. On several occasions he had to brake hard to avoid a child or a car and at one point an Army jeep, all the time swearing at his adversaries, green slime escaping from his *qat*-filled cheeks and dribbling down his chin. We finally began an ascent up a huge hill and suddenly turned left into what looked like a disused building site.

'This Al Funduq Al Ikhwa. Hotel Al Ikhwa! Good. No?'

In disbelief, Jana stared out of the Mercedes window at the ugly concrete lump. Too fatigued to argue, we disembarked and made our way to the entrance. Goats roamed free, munching on discarded predigested *qat*.

Jana dodged the animals who had taken a fancy to her clothing. Dogs barked, assorted mongrels, skinny and scurvy-ridden, running wild. We hurried on ahead as Jimmy collected our three bags from the Merc, which was steaming from the strain of the drive. This was where I had met Colonel Abdul Walli all those years ago, and still nothing had changed, either with the hotel or the staff as far as I could tell. Inside the hotel was dark and dismal. No decoration had taken place since my last visit here in 1988.

We started to settle down. There was a knock at the door and Jimmy stood there. He had come to inform us of the café-cum-restaurant downstairs. He handed over our bags and quickly disappeared. After the long drive, we decided to have a good, hot, long shower and of course tea. Tomorrow we would travel on to Mokbana and Nadia.

We made our way down to the restaurant. The room overlooked the natural basin where Taiz city had been built, surrounded by high inhabited mountains. The view was quite breathtaking. We became so engrossed that we didn't notice how time flew or what was going on around us. We had ordered food over an hour ago, but the waiter preferred to serve everyone else first.

Jimmy came into the café and pointed out a group of young men who were watching us very closely. We were far more intrigued by why he was still around. He took a seat at our table and explained that his family had problems with a dispute over land ownership. A feud had erupted and Jimmy had come here to see the local sheik, who could sort it out. He pointed to the biggest of the surrounding mountains and said that the sheik lived at the very top. He had booked into this hotel and had arranged to see him tomorrow.

I told Jimmy that I wanted to hire a jeep for a hard drive to the Ashube mountains. Jimmy looked around suspiciously and leaned forward. 'You are her? The one with two daughter in village Shamiri?'

My suspicions were immediately aroused. He was making the connection far too quickly. 'So I have relatives in the village. What of it?'

He slumped back in his chair and sucked air through his golden teeth. 'You want to go in? Tomorrow?' He raised a white eyebrow, 'Maybe you take them out?'

He had made the connection easily, but didn't seem to acknowledge that Zana was free and in England.

'Just get the taxi for us, Jimmy,' I said flatly.

'I take you to jeep station. You want anything else?'

'Only to change sterling for ryals.'

'OK. When you want go?'

'After tea. We order food, but no come!' I started to sound like him now. It seemed usual to speak in pidgin English, a habit formed whether you intended to or not.

'Forget food. I take you good restaurant. No good here!'

'Fine. Let's go.'

The three of us walked to the car. We had to wait while a jeep made a very tight three-point turn on the rough forecourt of the hotel. It backed up a side road and flashed its lights for Jimmy to take his chance to drive off first.

It was a close squeeze. Jana looked out of the window and watched the car creep past the jeep with only an inch to spare from the jeep's front bumper, holding her breath as Jimmy calculated the gap between the jeep and the wall. A flash of light caught her attention. She thought Jimmy had hit the jeep, but the men in the jeep laughed and waved. Ignoring them, she faced the front. 'Did you see that flash of light?' she asked me.

'No. What flash of light?'

'It's just . . . Oh, never mind.' Jana dismissed the light and concentrated on the road, more so than Jimmy. Being a driver herself, she said it was out of habit. That was true. I don't drive, but on the way across the mountains, I had seen Jana pump imaginary brakes many times.

'There it is again!' She suddenly turned around in her seat and looked behind us.

'There's what again?' I asked, puzzled.

'That flash of light. I saw it in the rear-view mirror!'

We both looked out of the back window of the car and, sure enough, a series of flashes came from the car behind us. It was the jeep from the hotel. Suddenly the driver switched his headlights on to full beam. Jimmy winced as the car was flooded with light. In fear, he put his foot down hard on the accelerator and we sped into the cover of the mainstream traffic at the end of the road. We monitored the jeep as it weaved in and out of the traffic trying to catch up with us, then suddenly they gave in and turned in a wide arc in the middle of the road, heading off into the traffic going in the opposite direction, regardless of right of way, fear or caution.

Jimmy swore and cursed in Arabic. He put it down to 'bloody kids'.

That little episode over, we slowed down and cruised along the street called Jamal, turning off near the end. The roads were even worse here – it was stretching the imagination to call them roads, really. After a short time, Jimmy pulled over and stopped the engine. 'Wait here, I will see if this is good.' He slammed the door behind him.

We were in a dark alley. We sat trying to blend into the shadows inside the car. Dogs scavenged along this small turn-off and kids chased them, trying to rip off their legs if they were quick enough to catch them. We sat and watched in horror as the children played this game time and time again, the dogs yelping in terror and pain and, on occasion, snapping at the bare legs of the kids. This prompted the children to collect large sticks to beat the offending animals.

'This not good!' Jimmy announced suddenly, making

both Jana and I jump out of our skins. We had been so hypnotised by the kids and the dogs that we didn't see him approach the car. Thankfully, his return meant we didn't have to witness the punishment inflicted on the dogs, or the danger that the kids were putting themselves in.

'So, now what do we do, Jimmy? I have to go to Ashube!' I demanded.

'No problem. Okey-dokey! There is one more in *souk*. We go there now!' He started the car and negotiated the potholed ground. We drove for about ten minutes before he parked the car outside a brightly lit jeweller's shop in the middle of the *souk*. He told us to stay where we were. We had no intention of moving anyway.

Jana and I peered out at the shop. It was so strange to see it open the way it was. We stared in, admiring the solid gold belts, bracelets and rings while we waited. Jimmy returned with a small man in tow. He opened the door of the car and looked in.

'What is this village, Miriam? They don't know it!'

'Jimmy, I told you. It's Ashube.'

Jimmy turned and muttered the name to the small man. He shook his head. He and Jimmy disappeared. Again Jimmy returned with this small man. 'Where is village? He no can find this. Come see map!' Jimmy thrust a map into my hands.

'I can't even see this. Why don't you know where it is?'

'Yemen is very big,' Jimmy defended himself.

'Some tour guide you are, Jimmy!'

'I can with Sanaa and Taiz and most places, but nobody ever sees villages. Come outside. Look with this.'

I got out, then turned. 'Come with me. You know I need glasses. Come on, Jana!'

She slid out of the car and followed me into the bright light of the gold shop. Jimmy unfolded the map and placed it on the counter. 'Now, what is village?'

'*Ashube!*'

Jimmy, the small man and the jeweller shook their heads as they scanned the map. 'No. I no can see. What is near, do you know?' Jimmy grinned, his teeth glinting full beam in the bright lights.

Jana tugged on my sleeve and whispered in my ear. 'Mim!' I looked up to see a crowd of about thirty men which had gathered around us. They were all wearing *jambias*, very long curved swords worn around their waists, supposedly for decoration, but functional in every sense.

'I can't tell you where it is. I don't read maps!' I snapped. I felt a great sense of foreboding.

'But you have been before. You can remember what is close?'

'Er, yes! It's off the German road,' I remembered, irritably, as Jimmy traced a trail on the map with his gnarled finger.

'Campais – Mocha – Hokha – Mokbana!' he read aloud.

'Yes, that's it. It's near Mokbana!' I was ashamed that I had not recalled the name of that dreaded village.

The small man shouted his obvious astonishment. 'You want go to Mokbana?'

'Yes.' My tone of voice urged him to back off.

A voice in the crowd shouted. 'It's her! It's mother of Mokbana sisters!'

By now the gathering had swollen to about fifty and still more were joining the throng. Arabic voices, curious, angry, filled the air as the men closed in on us. Jimmy called my name, which only added to the problem, as now he had confirmed to this growing crowd that I was *the* Miriam Ali.

The noise grew. I clasped my hands to my ears, trying to drown out the sound of the ever-increasing crowd.

'Oh, shit! Mim, move, come on!' Jana shouted at me. She pulled me close, practically carrying me through the crowd, making use of the path that Jimmy had created. In a joint effort we pushed irate Arabs away from us as they grabbed at our limbs, clothes and hair. Holding each other close, we barged right through the middle of the mob, having no alternative route. Jimmy made for the car and opened the rear door. Jana pushed me inside, following closely herself. She reached over me and slammed the lock on the door and did the same to her side of the car while Jimmy ran to the driver's side and hurled himself into the seat, slamming the door behind him.

Suddenly, the mob succumbed to mass hysteria. Moving as one, they began to rock the car from side to side, screaming abuse and threats and opinions. Jana and I were thrown around in the car as Jimmy desperately tried to start the engine. Faces pressed against the windows all round the car, only to be pushed away by the return rocking motion. *Jambias* were produced, some of the men making slicing motions at their throats, some thrusting the swords into the air in a stabbing gesture. The engine of the Mercedes coughed and spluttered, but wouldn't start.

I started to pray. Jana shouted at Jimmy to get the car started and get the hell out of here.

The passenger door was ripped open and an Arab wielding his *jambia* clambered into the car. Jana and I sat

321

shocked rigid in our seats. He held the sword at Jimmy's throat and spoke rapidly in Arabic. At that moment the car burst into life. Jimmy tried to force a way through the crowd. Men were on the roof, bonnet and boot of the car. As we started to move they began to jump on the soft metal of the Mercedes.

'Move it, Jimmy!' Jana hissed.

He hesitated and then suddenly the car leaped forwards, throwing the pirate Arabs into the crowd and on to the ground. Another Arab managed to open the front passenger door. Jimmy kept his foot down regardless. We rushed forward. The crowd scattered in all directions to avoid the moving car as it gained speed, converging again as a solid mass as they chased after us, determined in their pursuit.

The Arab in the front seat next to Jimmy was still with us. He turned to us, speaking in broken English. 'Why you here! Who speak you can come? You come with me to see Police Colonel and you ask him if you can come here. You speak why you in Yemen. You— '

We lurched forward. Jimmy had suddenly slammed on the brakes. We watched, amazed, as he pushed the intruder out of the open door of the car. As we shot off again Jana and I spun round in our seats to watch our unwelcome visitor bouncing along the street.

After putting a good few miles between us and the mob, Jimmy pulled over and collapsed across the wheel of the car. He breathed deeply and finally turned to face Jana and me. It took him several moments to gather his wits. 'My God, Miriam. I hope Allah looks after you. This very bad. Yes, very bad. You are OK?'

I nodded.

'You, Jana. You are all right?'

'Yeah. I'm OK. What did he say to you?' Jana gestured behind her.

'Oh, er, he want take you to sheik. Speak why you in Yemen, what you want here!' Jimmy lit a cigarette. He sat smoking quietly until he had finished it. Only then did he feel calm enough to take us to another part of Taiz to exchange money.

Again he left us in the car, but this time he parked on the main road before disappearing into the crowd. I chose to let him exchange the money on our behalf, first to protect us from further exposure, and secondly to get a decent rate of exchange.

'Do you suppose Jimmy had tipped them off, Jana?'

'Can't say I'm at all sure he didn't, Mim. But then it could initially have been that they were curious. Maybe that's why they all collected around us, that plus us being out of purdah, Western women.' Jana lit a cigarette.

'So why did they mob us only when they heard the name of the village and my name? It was Jimmy who shouted out my name. He didn't need to do that. Even a fool would realise what it would do! So either he is a fool . . . or he isn't!'

I took Jana's lighter and lit my own cigarette. 'And if he isn't a fool, then what is he?'

'You can't trust anyone, Mim. Now they will all know that you're here. Your element of surprise has gone.'

'Oh, Jana. You think that the Ministry hasn't told them I'm on my way into the village?'

'I'm sure everybody knows all about it, but many of these people wouldn't know what you look like. But with me around, you will easily be spotted no matter where we go.' Jana blew a cloud of smoke out of the window into the face of a staring Arab.

'Are you saying that you want to go home, Jana?' I sank into the seat dreading the answer.

'Nope! I'm saying that perhaps we should invest in a couple of those Jasper Conran exclusive purdah ballgowns!' She turned and grinned at me.

'You would wear one of those?'

'So would you, if the need arose, and I think it just did. At least we will melt into the crowd.'

I could see the sense of it.

As soon as Jimmy returned with the ryals Jana and I slipped into a shop and chose two purdah outfits. I watched, totally amazed, as Jana started to transform herself into a Yemeni. She still stood out as she is a lot taller than the average woman in Yemen but, other than that, it looked rather convincing.

I nodded my approval and agreed that it was a pretty good idea. Jana peeled off the purdah coat, with the help of the assistant. He grabbed at her breast, a perk which he obviously thought went with the job. She hissed at him menacingly, swearing at him in proficient Arabic. Wide-eyed, he backed off, shocked and a little intimidated by her imposing size and stance. I thought she was going to clobber him one for the insult. She later admitted that she would have, had it not been for the fear of starting another incident.

Then it was my turn. The male assistant was very careful not to touch any part of my body, darting apprehensive glances at Jana, who glared at him no matter what he did. He seemed grateful when he had bagged our new threads and we had paid up and left.

We returned to the hotel, taking the purdah coats and veils straight to our room. We would have worn them immediately but they were badly creased after being in their packaging bags, so we just hung them up and left them to air for a while.

It was only then that we realised that we still had not eaten. We headed for the restaurant.

Chapter Forty-Six

Jana and I made our way to the hotel restaurant. To do this, we had to go through the foyer, out across the forecourt and take a giant step off a dead-end path, a drop of some two and a half feet. From there, we followed a small gravel path for a couple of yards into the open space of a concrete garden. The restaurant was an annexe at the end of this garden, a cantilever construction – propped, just in case – built on top of a sheer cliff face.

We walked in. The restaurant immediately hushed into an uncomfortable conspiratorial silence as all eyes looked our way. We held our heads high as we walked to the table by the huge window that afforded the view we found so enchanting. We sat down and waited to be served. We had not eaten all day and our poor stomachs churned noisily. We stared out of the window. The dark outside was alive with thousands of tiny lights. The constant bibbing of car horns had abated a little. We didn't speak much. We were both wrapped in our own thoughts.

'Hello, Miriam and Jana! How is the life?' It was Jimmy.

'Devoid of food – except, of course, if you happen to be a mosquito!' Jana slapped a gorging mozzie off her arm.

'You have good blood! Don't worry, they take only a little.' Jimmy flashed his golden gnashers.

'I fully intend to keep as much of my blood as I can.' Jana applied Savlon to her new wound.

'What are you doing now, Jimmy?' I asked, not really interested.

'I have business to do, Miriam. I will maybe see you later when I have news of your jeep.' Jimmy casually saluted and bid us farewell.

'Thank God! I though he wanted to join us,' I confessed to Jana.

'Maybe not him, but I think these over here have their own ideas.' She gestured with her head in such a discreet manner that at first I couldn't see what she meant. Then I saw them, a group of perhaps six young men winking and blowing kisses in her direction. Ignoring them, we chatted for a while. A waiter had actually taken our order and eventually returned with some stale bread, rancid cheese and fruit, which was all he had left. We accepted the food out of desperation and tucked into the fruit but were unable to break the bread with our teeth. All the while, the group of men in the corner of the restaurant tried to attract Jana's attention. Absolutely fed up with the situation, she suggested we leave.

We walked quickly into the dark night, back through the garden and hauled ourselves up to the path and on to the forecourt. The day had been a hell of a strain. I didn't know what we were going to run into next as I took the stairs in the foyer two at a time to escape from the dogs foraging on the forecourt. Jana was close behind me. As we rounded the corner to the second flight of stairs she muttered just loud enough for me to hear that we were being followed by the men from the restaurant. In haste we scurried down the dark hallway to our room. I fumbled with the key to open the door, cursing the hotel for being so dimly lit. The door sprung open and I more or less fell into the room. Jana was just entering behind me when a hand clutched at her shoulder. She spun around to face a young Arab man.

'Excuse me. This for you.' He handed her something small and square, turned and went into the room next to ours. Jana closed the door behind her absentmindedly as she peered to see what it was. Walking into the light, she shook her head and handed it to me.

'What the hell is this?' I asked.

It was a photograph of Jana looking out of the back window of Jimmy's car.

I gave it back to Jana. She didn't give it a second look as she threw it contemptuously on to the coffee table. She flopped down on an overstuffed chair and sighed. As we settled down for the night, we talked about the mobbing incident. It had bothered me a lot, and I could tell that she was uneasy about it too. We decided to ring the Embassy first thing in the morning, report the incident and seek their advice before venturing into the nether regions of Mokbana.

I wouldn't risk Jana's life in this, no matter how important it was for me to see Nadia, nor would I expect her to put herself in jeopardy. Jana knew how important all this was for me. She understood exactly how I felt. Of that I had no doubt. I was glad of her company and her support. Her instincts were as keen as mine. I knew that if we went into the village without taking every possible precaution we would be in danger. My own survival instincts prevailed. I wanted to see Nadia; that meant I had to be alive to do so and

alive I was going to stay. Was this why Phil Whitmore
had mentioned protection?

At half-past ten a knock came at the door.

'Who is it?' Jana called.

'Jimmy!'

Jana groaned inwardly as she got up to open the door.

Jimmy took it upon himself to sit down. 'Miriam,
Miriam, Miriam!' he dramatised. 'Why you go to Mokbana?
Many people want to know why this! All say now,
"Jimmy, why this woman want to go for trouble in
Shamiri village?"'

'I am going to see my daughter. She is to have a baby
soon, and I want to be with her.'

I asked myself why I was explaining things to Jimmy, of
all people. However, it seemed a little late for that now.

'This Nadia, yes?' Jimmy raised his eyebrow.

'Yes, Nadia. Why?'

'Nadia happy here. All Yemen know this. She speak for
television to say she has good life, good husband and good
children.'

I couldn't believe that Jimmy actually expected me to
justify my visit to Yemen, or that he should be privy to
information about my family.

'Don't even bother me with that, Jimmy. You think that
I don't know my own daughter? You think that Shamiri
knows best for my daughter?' I snapped. 'If Nadia really
is happy, then there is no problem for her husband to come
to England and have a holiday with Nadia and the children
in my home, is there? Gowad, father of Mohammed, is
living in England, near to my own home, and has been
for many years. He has been to Yemen maybe two times
in twelve years! His wife is with him in England and they
have a child born there. Gowad left two children behind

329

many years ago and Nadia is looking after them, as well as four children of her own. Gowad is wrong, he is *haram*, he is the one who will not allow Nadia or Mohammed to leave Yemen, because he is scared for what will happen to him.'

I turned away from Jimmy, angry at his curiosity and even angrier at his expectations and meddling. He soon realised that I was going to add nothing further to this, and, indeed, had nothing more to say about anything. Not quite knowing what to say now to justify his presence in our room, he lowered his head and glared at the coffee table.

'What this?' he suddenly shouted.

Jana and I looked at Jimmy in surprise. He was holding the photograph these men had taken of Jana.

'It's a photograph, Jimmy. Taken by those young men next door. They gave it to me when we returned from the restaurant,' Jana explained.

At that moment another knock came at the door. Jana glanced at her watch. 'It's quarter to eleven. What the hell is this?'

Jimmy took the initiative and opened the door. From where I was sitting I could see a young man, camera aimed, ready to surprise the person answering the door. I don't know who was more surprised, Jimmy, the young man or Jana and me. Jimmy immediately launched into a verbal attack on him in his own tongue. He tried to shout Jimmy down. Finally, with a tremendous slam of the door, Jimmy turned to face us. 'He want picture of you. He see many tourists and want to collect you.'

'Tell him to go to hell! By the looks of him, he was going to take a photo, no matter whether we agreed or not. He was aiming the camera as you opened the door!' I shouted, feeling that enough was enough for one day.

Jimmy said that he had told this man to go down to Reception and fill in a form asking for our permission, stating his name and other details, which Jimmy claimed was his way of obtaining proof for a complaint of harassment. He then telephoned down to Reception and demanded that the manager of the hotel meet him in the foyer.

'Jimmy, leave it will you? This is getting out of hand!' Jana snapped.

'You no understand Yemen. You must have permission for everything,' he growled. 'One of these men followed me before to my room, to ask which room you were staying in.'

'Is that why they are now next door to us, Jimmy? How much did they pay for that?' Jana was getting angrier. Jimmy looked directly at me, saying nothing, and left the room, slamming the door behind him.

We hoped we'd seen the last of Jimmy for the night but twenty minutes later he returned. He sat down and helped himself to Jana's cigarettes as he told us his tale. We sat in silence as he reeled off an incredible story of identity parades, Kalashnikovs, heated arguments and apologies.

The budding photographers were soldiers, staying at the hotel with their Colonel. Jimmy recounted his victory over the Colonel following his complaint as our emissary.

The Colonel had castigated his men in front of Jimmy. 'Men, you are wrong, they are right. What you have done is *haram*!' Then turning to Jimmy, he had added: 'Do what you want with this gun. If you want to shoot their heads off, so be it! If not, an apology. I will have two cows slaughtered in the morning to feed all the people in the hotel.'

Jimmy declined both of these options on our behalf

and settled for telling them all off. 'Just because they are Western does not mean that you can do as you will with them!'

He returned the gun to the Colonel who, out of a newly formed deep respect, made the offending soldiers kiss Jimmy's head and apologise for their insult.

Jimmy had said: 'It's to them [Jana and me] that you should be sorry!' and marched out of the room to meet the manager in the hallway. He had heard everything whereas Jana and I, despite being only in the next room, hadn't even heard voices raised.

Jimmy wiped his brow. He was sweating with excitement.

Having had more than enough for one day, our first in Taiz, Jana and I made our excuses and got Jimmy out of the room.

The biggest poser was why Jimmy would go to all this trouble anyway, elaboration or not.

Chapter Forty-Seven

We rose at eight. We were going into Mokbana but we decided to ring the British Embassy first, to alert them to yesterday's bizarre events and inform them that we were off to see Nadia and the children. We'd showered and packed our small suitcases while waiting for the Embassy to open for the day. The phone contact was really just to cover ourselves in case of further conflict. As added insurance we had to think of a way to get a message to Maddie, my solicitor in Birmingham.

Jimmy, our genie without a lamp, appeared to interpret our request to the manager for a call to England. We were informed that outgoing international calls were not possible from the hotel but they could accept incoming ones. Jimmy added that no hotel in Taiz had this facility, so he placed a request with our first hotel in Sanaa, the Al Hamd, and through them relayed a call to Jana's friend Dee in London to ring Jana in Yemen at the Al Ikhwa hotel as a matter of urgency.

Dee rang back within the hour. Jana briefly explained events, and the need for her to contact my solicitor as soon as the office opened at nine BST. Then Jana rang the Embassy in Sanaa and spoke to a Martin Cronin.

Once Martin had the facts, he promised to get back to us as soon as possible and asked us not to leave the hotel in any circumstances.

It was Gordon Kirby, the acting Ambassador, who called back. He gave me the number for the Governor of Taiz, Colonel Iryani, who had been appraised of the situation.

Kirby said: 'It is my opinion that you are in great danger if you go to the village. The villagers are very agitated. If Colonel Iryani is of the same opinion, then you *must* listen to him and take his advice. If he says you can go he will do everything in his power to protect you and at least find you an escort, although that may take some time. You have to assure him that you have come in peace and it would not be your obvious intention to take Nadia away.'

So we were to wait. The Embassy would do all they could to arrange a visit by Nadia to Taiz, which would be a lot safer. Just after one o'clock, Faisal Abdul Aziz, the private secretary to the Governor of Taiz, telephoned to say that he would arrange a visit from Nadia and all of her children. He hoped that the visit would take place later that day or the next.

There was something vaguely familiar about his name. Try as I might, I could not concentrate long enough to place where I had heard it before. I had other considerations to occupy my mind.

At a quarter to two Martin Cronin rang again. He confirmed to Jana that Nadia would be coming to visit us here. He also mentioned that Gerald Ryan, the head of the Consular Department in Sanaa, had seen Nadia recently at the request of the Foreign Office in London. Martin asked Jana to assure me that it was his intention to offer protection to us if we stayed here in Taiz. He asked to be kept informed of the outcome of the meeting with Nadia and the meeting with Faisal Abdul Aziz. He mentioned that Heather Taggart from the Foreign Office had contacted him after getting a call herself from Maddie, thanks to Dee in London. Martin said he would keep the relay going between me, Maddie and Heather and the relevant officials in his own department.

Jimmy came to the room, laden down with fresh fruit and tins of condensed milk. He mentioned that he had managed to dismiss the prebooked driver, who had been waiting downstairs in the foyer since nine o'clock, charging us 100 ryals for his trouble.

'You are talk of Taiz, Miriam,' he chuckled.

He proudly handed over a clapped-out cassette-player which he had managed to negotiate out of the hands of its evidently proud owner. Jana was pleased as punch. Seeing as we were more or less confined to quarters, albeit for our own protection, I was as pleased as she was that we could at least listen to some music of our own selection.

We waited and we waited.

It wasn't until six that evening that the telephone rang again. I grabbed at it, desperate for the announcement of Nadia's arrival. No chance. My heart sank as the manager announced that Mr Faisal Abdul Aziz was here.

He was with us moments later and introduced himself. He grinned like a Cheshire cat – and stank like a polecat.

Jana took an immediate dislike to him as he helped himself to fruit and walked around the room, prying. For over an hour this man slimed his way through a conversation that I took little part in. I didn't want to talk to the man, yet we had to do it for Nadia. His conversation was dull, and had very little to do with Nadia. He spoke

335

mostly of his career, a little of his family. He had served his country in Russia for many years and was completely sympathetic to that government's problems.

He had a daughter, Lillian, and several sons. His daughter had become sick and he had promptly sent her to Jordan for urgent medical attention. He droned on and on. At long last he announced that he had business with the manager of the hotel. As he rose to leave the room he dropped the news he had brought with him, that he had sent a friend to fetch Nadia and all the children from the village. He gave us his home telephone number. If we needed anything all we had to do was call.

Hunger demanded that we risk the restaurant again. Believe me, we had to be really starving before we could consider food in that place. We casually walked to the only nice place in the hotel and took our seats. True to form, the food was awful. We ordered tea and watched the lights twinkle for a while. An Arab casually walked over to our table and mentioned that he had seen us before, in Sanaa earlier that week. We didn't remember. He announced that he had taken the liberty of paying for our dinner, but noted that we had left most of it. He offered alternative food elsewhere as his guest. As politely as possible we declined. He took a seat anyway and talked about America, where he had attended military training a long time ago.

Jimmy came in. When he saw us he came over to our table, obviously uptight about something, then departed in an unusually unfriendly mood without a word. The man who had covered the cost of our uneaten meal informed us that he was the local sheik.

We asked him whether he knew our driver, Jimmy. He

said that he knew nothing of him and had never seen him before.

Jana and I spent the rest of the evening searching for listening devices, convinced that our room was tapped. We even dismantled the phone looking for bugs that could be hidden inside.

Chapter Forty-Eight

At half-past one the next day, Tuesday 4 August, Faisal called into the hotel again. Nadia was on her way with Mohammed and all four children, and should be here at any moment.

I was elated. I rushed around the tiny hotel room, gathering together all the gifts we'd brought with us for the children.

Sure enough, an hour later Nadia arrived with Haney and Tina, her two eldest children. Mohammed followed them in.

Suddenly the room was full of men. I recognised one as Shiab, his brother, but had no idea who the others were. I didn't care. Nadia flew into my arms and embraced me joyfully. I cried, she cried, Jana cried. Everybody else stared blankly at us.

Jana disappeared to collect herself and gather tissues. She returned just as Faisal Abdul Aziz barged into the room, without knocking, followed by armed men.

The men took it upon themselves to plough into the sweets I had put out for the children. Nadia became visibly petrified and confused as the men in the room shouted at her in Arabic, in between gobfuls of chocolate. She sat down with them and our reunion was reduced to me looking at her across the room. I sat down heavily. The atmosphere was electric.

Jana chipped at the invisible barriers Faisal had put up between us by introducing herself to Nadia. 'How are you, Nadia? I am Jana. I'm a friend of your mum and of your family.' She extended her hand to Nadia, who looked her up and down suspiciously, then returned the gesture and shook Jana's hand.

'I'm fine. I'm OK,' she answered, relaxing quite visibly. Then, in response to a shouted command from Faisal, she turned her back on Jana and entered into an Arabic conversation with the men.

Jana was undeterred. 'When is your baby due, Nadia?'

Nadia turned around again. 'Soon. In about a month.'

'What will you name the baby?'

'I don't know. It took a long time to name the children. Mohammed picks the names.'

'What are the names of your children who aren't here?'

Nadia looked Jana up and down again. 'Nasser and Uthman.'

'So this must be Haney and Tina, yes?'

'Er, well, Tina is Shadia now. It's – it's more Arabic.' Then she was back again in conversation with the men.

I managed to catch her eye. I indicated that I was going into the small bedroom annexe off of the main room. She followed me and we hugged again. As we spoke softly she removed her veils to reveal a haunted expression. She was pregnant and nearly at full term. Her fatigue and anxiety were clearly apparent on her face and she kept glancing at the main room. 'Who is that woman, Mom?'

'That's Jana, Nard. She is my friend.'

'Is she a reporter?'

'No, Nard. She's come with me because I could not travel alone. She's got her own family and she's my friend.'

Nadia relaxed at that and pulled herself on to the bed where we sat to enjoy photographs and conversation. We were alone for a full two minutes before Faisal Abdul Aziz marched in. He harangued Nadia in Arabic for a good five minutes, leaving only when Jana came in to say that tea had arrived and she wished to change her clothes, so he'd have to leave the room. As he was going she asked him who the men with the guns were.

'They are friends of Mohammed, from Mokbana. They heard news that he was in town so they popped in,' he smiled.

'Why are they disturbing a family reunion, without even having been invited into the room? Is this the way in Yemen, Faisal?' She shooed him out of the room and closed the door none too gently.

'She only did that to get him out,' I whispered to a startled Nadia.

Nadia grinned widely at Jana, in obvious approval.

'I wonder what he'll do for a face when Quasimodo wants his arsehole back?' Jana muttered.

Grinning, we went back to the photos of the family waiting for Nadia back in England. Nadia looked intently at her sisters and brothers, asking how they were and the names of the children in the photographs. Zana had written a message on the back of one or two, and Nadia read them over and over, crying and hugging them to her chest.

'Can I keep these, Mom?'

'Why don't you come home and visit them all? So many

340

people who love you are waiting for you to come home and see them. We won't forget you, Nadia. We all love you and want you to come home, even if it is only for a visit.'

I fought my tears as Nadia smiled warmly and touched my hand. 'I'll come home soon, Mom!'

'You always say that, Nard, and never do!'

'Oh, Mommy. Please. You don't understand. It's him. I can't come while he is afraid of the press. He won't let just me come.'

'Nard, they can't get away with this. You knew what would happen when you made that tape with Zana. What they did was wrong.'

'Forget that, Mom. It's all in the past. It should be buried. It doesn't matter any more.'

'Are you mad? Of course it matters. How else can I get you out?'

'Mom, it can't go on like this. Forget the press and I can come home soon.'

'They've been lying to you, Nadia. All the time, they've lied. All of them, including Mohammed and the Shamiri!'

'I have to respect some things, Mom, if I like it or not.'

'But Nadia, I'm your mother. Why can't you respect that? I won't be around forever. I would like to see you free in my lifetime. You've got family who love you and miss you. We want you to be happy, Nard. I want to see you in your own home, free and happy. You can come for a holiday and if then, you still want the Yemen, it will be over. Why don't you stay here for the night? You look so tired and pale. I'll pay for your room, there is no problem.'

'OK. I will ask Mohammed.'

Faisal Abdul Aziz reappeared at that moment, without knocking, and took command of the conversation, again in Arabic.

Nadia told him that she was tired and would like to stay overnight. His face visibly darkened and he called to Mohammed. Her 'husband' came through into the annexe. All trace of Nadia's new-found relaxation quickly disappeared. She looked at Mohammed with disdain and told him the same thing.

'*Lat, lat! Haya bina!*' No no, let's go! He turned and went back to his friends. Nadia lowered her head and heaved a sigh. 'Don't worry, Mom, I'll come again, probably next week.'

I had no option but to allow her to leave. I wouldn't make her life more difficult after what had happened when Fixot and Jean-Pierre had been with me. 'I'll wait until you do come, Nadia. I promise!'

We hugged again and she rejoined the men in the main room. They were still chomping on the sweets meant for the children. At least Haney and Tina had managed to have some.

Faisal Abdul Aziz turned to Jana. 'Miriam will be fine now that she's had her visit.' He added that he was now expecting Jana and myself to get the first plane back to England.

It was time to say reluctant goodbyes. I asked Nadia, again, if she would come to England for a holiday. She replied that she would like to and would ask Mohammed who, right on cue, came into the room to tell Nadia to hurry up.

Faisal asked him if he would be willing to bring Nadia again, with all of the children, for a visit next week.

'*Inshallah!*'

I wondered why Mohammed wasn't struck down by the very wrath of God there and then.

They took Nadia away. I watched her limp out of sight, her burden heavy and telling in her gait.

The room became still and quiet, the only evidence of the visit was the empty sweet-wrappers and the spilled tea.

I went through and sat on the bed, feeling the warmth that Nadia had left there. Each time I closed my eyes I could see her face, weatherbeaten, drawn and pockmarked; her haunting eyes, looking lost and bewildered, her teeth rotting in her mouth. Her frightened expression when Faisal came into the room, her suspicion of Jana, her contempt for Mohammed. And her very apparent distance from her children.

I shook my head, trying to picture Nadia as the happy woman looking at family photographs but, as hard as I tried, I couldn't shake off that first look.

Jana came to the room and put her arms around me. She said one word only. 'Bastards!' A huge lump formed in my throat and I fought a useless battle against my tears. Jana could do nothing. She sat by me as I began to cry, helplessly, her own tears streaking her face too.

The visit was duly reported to the British Embassy. They were flabbergasted. Negotiations for a more personal visit were launched immediately, a severe complaint about the conduct of Faisal was recorded and he visited us again to sort it all out.

Although I had been party to the whole farce I still couldn't believe what had happened. I had come from England to see my daughter and her children. She had travelled, in her last weeks of pregnancy, all the way from Ashube over very rough terrain. For what? An interview with Faisal Abdul Aziz, and a chummy reunion with the people of Mokbana in our apartment, lasting for just half an hour.

I was so angry. I wanted to say so much, but I was also numb. It struck me that the mountains of Ashube and Mokbana must be relatively empty these days, what with all the men either working in other countries, creaming off wealth to invest in *qat* plants in Yemen, visiting friends in Taiz or mobbing people.

Faisal had warned us, 'Don't go into the city. It's too dangerous for you!' Of course he was referring to the mobbing. The people who'd mobbed us were from Mokbana, he'd added. Previously he'd asked if we knew who the people were. Of course we replied that we had no idea, so how he found out we didn't know.

I asked him if Nadia could be delivered of her child in a Taiz hospital. He laughed. 'She'll be fine, Miriam. She will need no hospital, no doctor. She has the women of the village and a floor. It's not her first child. *Inshallah*, it's not the last!'

I wished that we could have had someone follow Nadia and her company as she left the hotel. I firmly believe that she stayed in the house of Nasser Saleh, the postal agent of Gowad who had stopped my mail getting through to Nadia and Zana all those years ago. Were we really supposed to think that they would have made Nadia endure a long and arduous journey into Taiz, then return after half an hour, only to face a long climb up a mountain? There is a limit to anyone's credulity.

Why wasn't she dirty? No dust from the road, no grime from the mountain. I had seen her on this mountain many times. The purdah coat would have become encrusted before she reached the bottom, her feet filthy. The journey

344

along the dusty track out of the mountains would clog her lungs with a fine dust. Nadia and the children were too clean to have made that journey and come straight to the hotel.

So when had they arrived? Yesterday, when Faisal said that they would be here at six o'clock? Was that why they didn't believe that Nadia was too tired to make the return journey? Why couldn't they let her stay with me? Did they really think that I would kidnap her? I suppose they must have done, hence the armed guard at the door of the hotel room. They had, of course, got their guarantee in the village. The other children. It was always the way.

Martin Cronin was the first to return our call. After all was explained he urged us not to go into the city. Why? Would we see Nadia?

Martin said that he would telephone the Governor as soon as he could. 'What shall I tell him it is that you want?' he asked.

'We want Nadia and *all* of her children to visit on Monday. With Mohammed, if needs must. We want a free visit with her for the whole day. We have come in peace and just want her to be happy and healthy. We would like to know that she will deliver this child safely. Once we are sure of this, we will leave Yemen.'

Martin agreed it was a reasonable request.

Wednesday. We waited for anticipated calls from Martin, Bernard Fixot, Faisal, whoever. We stayed in that room all day. Only in the evening did we venture out, to cross the road to the Mareb for a change of menu.

As we sat in the rooftop restaurant we saw Jimmy watching us intently from the forecourt of the Al Ikhwa.

By Friday, Jana was down with dysentery.

Chapter Forty-Nine

We were in constant contact with the Embassy. Gordon Kirby rang to say that it was 'up to the young lady', whether she would want to come out of the village or not. I told him that she did want to come, and that I had promised Nadia I would wait for her to do so.

'It would not be right for the Yemenis to see that you, Miriam, might abduct Nadia,' was his reply.

Insulted and frustrated, I reminded him of the legal position regarding the marriages. Both by our standards of law and the Yemeni standards the marriages had been deemed illegal long ago.

Later in the day Faisal Abdul Aziz rang to say that Nadia would be in Taiz to see us at noon the next day, 10 August. He invited us to go and chew *qat* with him and some of his friends. We could not think of anything that we would like less, so we declined. He said he might 'pop by' later anyway. That upset Jana for the rest of the day. It left me apprehensive, too.

She rang Gordon Kirby to inform him of the visit and asked his advice. Kirby said that he was pleased about the planned visit and he had already spoken to Faisal Abdul Aziz about it. He quoted Faisal as saying: 'Your

346

Eminence, this is Yemen. Here, what the husband wants, the husband gets!'

Kirby suggested that we approached Mohammed and said, beggingly, beseechingly, that we wished to talk to Nadia about women's problems and so get some time alone. We must try to remain calm and 'clear the field' for any future visits to Nadia in Yemen. Kirby said that he had spoken to Maddie, my lawyer, at great length and added: 'God forbid that you can't get that young lady out of here. Do what you think is right, despite the feelings and opinions of other people, but remember that what you do will reflect on whether or not you can see Nadia again.'

We woke up early and anxiously waited for any sign of Nadia, with or without Mohammed. By half-past two there was still no sign. I was so edgy by now that I asked Jana to contact the British Embassy. They said they would make inquiries and call back. They did. To tell us that Nadia would be here by nine tonight, according to Faisal Abdul Aziz. Kirby had spoken to Faisal, who said that he had sent the police to fetch them early that morning.

'I have also asked Faisal to allow Nadia to give birth there in Taiz, and he said he would see what he could do. Let me know how the meeting goes, OK?' Before he rang off, Kirby told us that he would be in the Embassy on Friday and Saturday, if we needed him.

At eight o'clock Jimmy knocked on our apartment door and told us that Faisal had just telephoned Reception to inquire whether Nadia and all her children had arrived. Jimmy had taken this call himself and told Faisal that there was no sign of them. Faisal rang ten minutes later and said that the person he had sent to the village had just informed him of his arrival there, in Ashube. Not to worry, they would be here in the morning for sure.

I asked him why he had sent anyone at all if direct contact was possible. Faisal completely evaded this question. 'Don't worry, they will be here for sure tomorrow. I will phone again!'

Jana got rid of Jimmy for me. She looked troubled. Neither of us could establish why Faisal would have talked to Jimmy about my business. Our anxiety and concern for Nadia kept us walking the floor until the small hours of the morning. Sleep became impossible. The clock dragged its arms around the face of the dial and the fear that Nadia would not come became a fact. She never did come.

It was half-past five on the afternoon of the following day before we were told that Nadia was not coming. 'Due to ill health', according to our inevitable source, Faisal Abdul Aziz. Now I panicked. Was Nadia seriously ill? I began to fret that something might go wrong with the birth, as it had when Tina had been born. I wanted Nadia moved to a good clinic in Taiz where she could have immediate treatment if the birth got difficult, where it was clean and relatively germ-free. If necessary I would pay all the expenses myself. I put this proposal to the British Embassy for them to negotiate on our behalf with the necessary people. Again the answer came back, 'Your Eminence, this is the Yemen, what the husband wants, the husband gets!' This, of course, came from Faisal Abdul Aziz, who also repeated: 'There is nothing wrong with the floor in Nadia's home. There are women who help all over the mountain, and Nadia has now much experience in giving birth.'

We waited in that damned hotel room for three days, never moving from the room, always being told that Nadia was on her way. We didn't even know for sure whether all our calls were being put through. Gordon Kirby had told us that he tried to contact us several times only to be told by the Reception staff that no English people were staying in the hotel. Finally, fed up, he told them: 'This is the acting Ambassador of the British Embassy in Sanaa. Get your finger out. Come on, put me through!' We managed to take out a lot of our aggression on the hotel staff, by chewing their ears off for incompetence. It passed a bit of time, anyway.

Faisal rang me shortly after a quarter to six. He claimed that Nadia was in labour. We begged him to get her to a hospital in Taiz.

'No, she has a clinic nearby,' he snapped.

'But it's no good there, Faisal, you know it!'

'It's same as Taiz.'

'No. Even Gordon Kirby said it was no good.'

'No matter, she has babies before.'

'Yeah, and she was cut from arsehole to breakfast time with a rusty razor, and badly infected. She was told by a doctor not to have any more!'

'Telephone your Consulate and inform them of this labour.'

'Will you contact Mokbana tomorrow and ask how Nadia is?'

'No! I'm too busy.'

'Then you ring the Consulate and tell them yourself how busy you are!'

However, we did ring Kirby. We told him of Faisal's news and attitude. Kirby said he would try to get the Governor to assist, but he might say no as he had given us a lot of Faisal's time already. 'We would rather Faisal helped Nadia than spent time with us chewing *qat*. Please get us the number for the Mokbana Police Station or the clinic, or both preferably. We will make our own inquiries.'

Susanna rang from Fixot. It seemed that the Yemeni authorities were worried that Jana and I would rush Nadia to abduct her. How the hell could we have done that? I suppose the best people to ask for advice on abduction would be them – Gowad, Muthana, and Abdul Khada. After all, they had the experience.

On the Thursday Jana and I went to see Colonel Iryani himself. He was welcoming and, to all intents and purposes, helpful. He offered to do everything that he could, adding that he would bring Mohammed into Taiz and get him a job and also persuade him to come to England with Nadia and all the children. Colonel Iryani liked Britain very much; he had served there as a diplomat and Ambassador for Yemen.

He listened to my account of the only visit I had had with Nadia. When I finished he called Faisal Abdul Aziz into his office and castigated him, in front of us, for the terrible behaviour he'd displayed during a delicate meeting between mother and child. The Governor impressed us further by ordering Faisal to make all the arrangements for a private meeting between me and Nadia, plus all the children. Pronto! I was delighted with this development, as was Jana, but for her, she told me later, it was the deep joy of seeing Faisal cringe with embarrassment at being reprimanded, right before our eyes.

All in all Nadia seemed to be nearer to gaining her freedom. This time our waiting was not so traumatic.

On Saturday evening, Faisal came from the shadows of the night and surprised us as we were on our way to the restaurant in the hotel grounds. He had been waiting in the darkness specifically for us to pass by. Why hadn't he come to the hotel room, or Reception?

'Good evening, Miriam. Good evening, Jana. How are you?'

'Waiting to see Nadia, or hear that she is well,' I replied.

'Well, now, I have news for you. Mohammed will be here, in the morning, to take you to Ashube in a jeep.'

I staggered, stunned. Jana grabbed my arm to support me.

'This is good, no?' Faisal kept checking to his left and to his right and he spoke so softly.

'It's too dangerous, Faisal. You said that yourself.'

'Don't worry about it. Be ready at six.' He grinned his Cheshire cat grin.

Jana jumped to alert then. 'Faisal, does the Governor know about this? Has he been told about this trip?'

'Of course!' Faisal's eyes darkened when he addressed Jana. He wrung his hands together, turned to me and spoke quickly. 'So, Miriam, you will be ready at six?'

'No! I'm not going into the village. Everybody keeps telling us how dangerous it is. That is enough to know. Tell Mohammed to not bother!' I turned to Jana, who was chewing her lip. 'Come on, Jana!' I sniffed aloud and we walked away from Faisal, leaving him to dissolve back into the darkness.

We sat in the balcony overlooking Taiz and ordered tea. 'Mim, you have just turned down a visit to Nadia. That is what you came for.'

'It's too dangerous, Jana, you know that. How many times have we been told this, by how many people?'

'Is it me, Mim? Are you trying to protect me? Am I making it too difficult? Maybe they think I'm a reporter, like Nadia did, and they are acting accordingly. Don't stay behind because of me, 'cos if you are, I can wait here for you. I *will* wait.' Jana touched my hand reassuringly.

'No, Jana. I know what you're saying. In a way, it's you who's protecting me. It would cause a lot of trouble if they harmed you. I think they know that, but I don't think they care. It's me they want. It won't be the first time they have tried to kill me, or at least threatened to. But accidents can happen, you know. I don't like the way Faisal just appeared out of the dark; I don't like the idea of us being collected so early, before the Embassy opens. I don't like the way so many people have warned us not to go into Ashube, and suddenly we are supposed to go there. I won't risk you, Jana. I don't know what is going on any more.'

'Mim, do you think that this is all Faisal's idea? Do we know for sure that the Embassy know about this trip into Ashube?'

Just to make sure, the British Embassy were duly telephoned. Gordon Kirby responded: 'Yes, there is an element of risk, but you are in constant contact with us and our phone calls are monitored. I doubt if they would dare harm you or get up to monkey business.'

'And if they did,' he added, 'there would be hell to pay!'

Jana pointed out, oozing sarcasm, that this would be too late. There would be no benefit to us from posthumous protests. And contact would not, could not, be as constant, from Ashube.

Monitored? Our calls were monitored? Why?

On Sunday Kirby rang us for an update on the news. We told him that we had decided to decline the offer of a visit to Ashube – it was far too dangerous, a feeling that seemed to be confirmed by the attitude of the British

Embassy. Kirby said: 'After further thought I could not imagine that an Arab would invite you to his home, escort you there, only to attack you.'

He was reminded of the fact that the relatives of these Shamiri Arabs had done something very like that to Nadia and Zana way back in 1980. How could he overlook that?

By noon on the same day, however, Kirby had a change of mind. 'Even if Mohammed promised, on his life, to protect you with his life, it does not mean that someone else will not take a shot at you. You are in danger. I think that you should phone the Governor and tell him that you fear for your life.'

This sudden change of attitude confirmed to me that Kirby must have found out what I had already suspected – this was to have been a one-way trip for Jana and myself. That now seemed certain. A cold shudder crept up the length of my spine.

About half an hour later Faisal rang to say that Mohammed was now at the office of Colonel Iryani. We should get there as soon as possible for an urgent meeting.

When we arrived, Colonel Iryani slapped his chest to emphasise his personal assurance. 'I am sure you will be safe in travelling to Ashube.'

Not to be outdone, I responded with a slap to my own chest and a confident 'I am not sure. Therefore the risk must not be taken.'

Surprised by my attitude, but apparently respecting it, he said that he would arrange for Nadia to be here in Taiz by tomorrow. I was deeply concerned for my daughter's condition and her health. After all, she had been in labour since 12 August, according to Faisal. I said it would be far too much trouble for Nadia to travel so we would wait until after the birth, since it was imminent.

With a look of incredulity, Colonel Iryani said it could be two weeks or even a month before I would see Nadia. I gave him every assurance that I would wait. Turning my attention to Mohammed, I asked through Iryani when he would visit England.

'Next year, *Inshallah*!' He grinned at Iryani, not daring, even now, in his obvious new-found confidence, to look me in the eye.

I protested that Mohammed had been saying that for at least five years and still he had not left Yemen. Iryani challenged Mohammed, who replied that he would go to England when the propaganda had died down.

This was getting us nowhere. I tried a different approach, telling them all that I wanted it to stop too, so that I could be free to live my life and have some peace, but that until Nadia proved to the Western world that she was free, there would be no peace for any of them or us. 'When you all come to England, it will stop,' I assured all the men in the room.

Mohammed smirked and would not commit himself any further, and Iryani appeared to have lost interest in the conversation.

Jana and I left, despondent and depressed, having achieved nothing at all in this urgent visit to the Governor of Taiz, apart from saving Nadia from an exhausting journey over rough terrain for five hours in the last month of pregnancy for what would, most likely, be a very brief encounter.

At half-past three Faisal rang. We had booked Nadia and her family into the same hotel as us and she was due to arrive *at any moment*! It was no trouble. 'Just a one-hour trip,' he said, as if I had never undertaken that same journey myself. He said that Mohammed had already left for the village to inform Nadia. That didn't make sense, either, as he had just said that she would be here 'at any moment'.

Playing along with him, I told him that, in that case, Nadia would have to stay in Taiz until after the birth. All this travelling was no good for her. In a fit of pique, Faisal expressed concern that this would be too expensive. I countered that by reminding him that I would cover the cost myself, with pleasure, both hotel and medical fees.

He was silent for several moments. Then, in his own gesture of oneupmanship, graciously informed me that the Governor had already given Mohammed money for the trip. And for the expenses. And had promised him a job in Taiz. And he was expecting a call from Mohammed in the morning to say that they were on their way. And he could not now stop the visit.

With the greatest of pleasure I told him, 'OK, then, I expect Nadia and her family to be my guests for the next month or so.'

A sepulchral silence followed until Faisal muttered that he would tell Mohammed to comply with my wishes.

Sure he would. And there was I, supposed to be believing his claim that they'd be here 'at any moment'.

Chapter Fifty

Monday morning, at nine sharp, I rang Martin Cronin for a full briefing on the situation. He gave us the phone numbers of new contacts to help us with the changing of ryals, as we had now really fallen out with Jimmy, who would not go away and leave us alone. They were Jed and Dave.

Dave was the sort of person who loved company, so that he could talk his head off. He jumped at the chance to meet us. 'Us Brits have to stick together, especially in a godforsaken hole like this.' We gratefully accepted.

During our only encounter Dave rushed around in shorts and flip-flops with a mobile phone attached to his ear. He was fifty-something, fairly short with grey hair and pale eyes. He lived in one of the good areas of Taiz, up the Mogillia mountain, directly opposite Abdul Walli's old house. It certainly brought back a few memories seeing that place again.

In retrospect, I suppose, to be fair to Dave, I should have explained who I was. But I didn't see the point. Having said that, it was a fair assumption that Martin wouldn't have given us his name as a contact if he'd thought there would be any problem. Anyway, we said nothing as we sat in Dave's lounge, drinking rotten beer and good gin. He just could not sit still or keep quiet, so there wouldn't have been much chance of telling him the purpose of our visit in any case. We were grateful for a change of scene, a familiar language and an informal chat about anything and everything.

Later in the evening, his friend came round. Fred was a lovable guy, funny and uncomplicated. Before we left Dave invited us to look around his factory one day next week, and stay on for dinner. We accepted his promise of 'bangers and mash', drooling at the thought of it already.

Fred took us back to the hotel. When he discovered it was the Al Ikhwa he asked why he had never seen us in the Mareb, the 'good' hotel opposite. He said that the café doubled as a pub. It had beer and spirits. Jana and I looked at each other and grinned. We knew where we were off to as soon as Fred dropped us off. We were drinking lager before he'd managed to turn his jeep round.

In the Mareb we discovered an international telephone line and a fax machine. Jimmy had got it wrong again, with the result that we had gone through the Al Hamd switchboard to make all those calls back home, which cost us a fortune.

Early the next day I rang Faisal to find out where Nadia was.

'Nadia had baby now,' he said. I could just feel him grinning, smirking.

'You know if this is a boy or girl?' I asked apprehensively. Please God, not a girl, I hoped with all my heart.

'This is a boy. You cannot see Nadia now. Maybe one week, maybe ten days, *Inshallah*, she can come to you.'

I had no objections. I would much rather Nadia recovered fully. Her health was a matter of great importance to me. No matter what the gender of the child, I was glad it was over for her. Yet I couldn't help but thank God that she had given birth to a boy. I worried about the labour and the actual birth, wishing that I could have been with her, to comfort her, help her. Really, it was all that I had asked for all along. Well, she would rest now, I hoped. Maybe this next time we would see the whole family together at last.

Fred rang a week later. If we were interested, he could take us to meet a married couple who lived across the mountains from us. It turned out to be a most illuminating visit.

Their names have been changed, out of respect for their safety. They will know who they are. Richard and Jenny are a pair of the nicest people you'd ever wish to meet. They welcomed us, complete strangers, into their home despite the fact that they knew who I was as soon as they saw my face. Once my identity had been confirmed, Fred said something very interesting. Dave, with whom we'd had drinks, had that morning been trying to warn all the expats in Taiz that they should not see us, speak to us or have anything whatsoever to do with us.

We asked why.

At the time Fred really didn't know. Dave had been very cryptic, unable to speak freely on the phone because of the monitor, but now that Jenny had identified me, Fred, of course, realised. He rang Dave there and then to find out what the score was. The message was relayed that we were being watched and followed by security police and had been since we had landed in Sanaa.

The original warning had come from a meeting in Sanaa. Dave had been on one of his lightning visits to catch a play in Europe – the day after we'd met him, in fact. On his return he'd met up with a group of expats. He would only give Fred their initials. P., M., P. and D. There was one other present; he would tell Fred who it was later, not on the phone.

Riddled with curiosity, we sat and talked.

Jenny knew that there was a book about my daughter's experiences in Mokbana, and had somehow got a copy from Britain and read it. It was currently being passed around the expat community. Fred was still in shock as he realised what the implications of talking to us could be. However, we had a nice time. Jenny invited us to go to the *souk* with her, to have a look around. We expressed our concern for her safety, after what Fred had relayed to us, but as her attitude was 'to hell with them', we accepted.

We went over to the Mareb that evening to have a few beers. The heat was intense. We were minding our own business when an expat came over and asked if we would join him for a beer or two.

Peter was OK. He had been in Taiz for so long that he had to fight constantly against the habit of dropping into pidgin English. Originally he didn't have a clue who I was, but, as we chatted, he began to scrutinise my face. It took only moments to click, without me ever mentioning Nadia or Zana. I hadn't even told him my name.

Once he had recognised me he became uncomfortable, moving away from the huge windows of the Mareb. 'For fear of being shot,' he explained.

'What on earth is wrong with you?' I asked irritably.

'I'm so sorry, ladies. I'm afraid I've made a terrible mistake. I can't remain here with you. You are trouble and the police are watching your every move. We have all been warned not to associate with you, for our own safety. My God, I should have known. There aren't that many people here who fit your description. You're being watched! Me too, right at this very moment, probably!' He was getting quite hysterical.

'We had no idea. If we had known we would have warned you off. If you've been told, why haven't we?' Jana had a point there.

He scanned the room with suspicion, his eyes narrow. He stood up to leave.

'I swear to God we didn't know until today!' I said honestly. 'Was it Dave in Mogillia who warned you?'

'Yeah, but he got good information in Sanaa.'

'Even Dave hasn't had the decency to tell us we're in danger. That leaves us a little vulnerable, don't you think Peter? Would you bear it on your conscience if we were harmed and you could have at least warned us,' Jana cornered him, 'even if Dave couldn't be bothered?'

He looked around cautiously. 'Do yourselves a favour, forget it! Forget it all. Shit, you don't know how lucky you are to be sitting there. Maybe your ignorance has saved your arses. Your cards were marked as soon as you got here in Yemen. You were supposed to be disposed of last week, and, I tell you frankly, here and now, I'm absolutely amazed to find you still in one piece.' Peter picked up his keys and files from the table. 'Stay that way, ladies. Go home!'

'I'm not leaving Nadia. They don't scare me!' I announced, more confidently than I felt.

'You should be scared, me old fruit. May God be with you, and protect you both! I wish you all the luck in the world. You are going to need every ounce of it.' Peter walked off, not looking back. He was too busy scanning the room to left and right, probably scared that the bogie man would leap out at him.

We faxed Fixot to alert them that it seemed to be open season on Jana and myself. Just in case . . .

Staying on at the Mareb, alone, we drank too much beer and ate nothing. We were in low spirits and getting very morbid. Why bother to shoot us? The stresses that they were creating would have me six feet under in no time!

We staggered back to the Al Ikhwa and commiserated with each other, sulking until dawn.

Our gloom hadn't lifted after a fitful sleep. Jana had been having bizarre dreams, and it was my turn for an attack of dysentery. And the water had been cut off, which didn't help at all.

We had been through quite a lot together by now, mostly defending ourselves against marauding males of amorous intent. We had made a few friends, too. I had become friendly with a Syrian called Abdul. We had met on a few occasions, either at the restaurant where he worked or at our favourite café, which was run by Syrians. It had taken considerable effort on Abdul's part to get me to notice him, but his efforts paid off in the end.

I had mentioned to him that I needed to get away for a while. Now that Nadia was in confinement it seemed to be a logical time. Abdul asked if he could escort us. He was different from any other man I had ever known, Arab or otherwise. I felt the first stirrings of love. I really felt that at last there was room in my life for love.

Of course it was up to Jana. She'd been such a brick, I really don't know what I'd have done without her. I braced myself and asked her whether Abdul could escort us to Aden. She laughed, saying that it was my choice. She would be fine staying in Taiz on her own. The implication that she did not not want to play gooseberry was plain, but

I managed to talk her into coming too. We both needed the break.

Aden wasn't really that far, geographically. It seemed to be worlds away when we were stuck in the intensified heat of a car, but it was, by all accounts, a vastly different and much more civilised place, in all senses of the word, where we would be able to relax and forget the traumas of Taiz.

Chapter Fifty-One

We stayed in Aden for four days, letting off steam. Jana spent most of her time alone after Abdul arrived apart from when we all went out to a cabaret, or to have a meal in a restaurant. She didn't mind; she had her nose in a good book, completed her puzzle book on the Gold Mohr beach, drank beer, relaxed and spent up to five hours at a time bobbing about in and out of the sea. She preferred her own company, which left Abdul and me alone to develop our relationship, which we did.

I was so scared of my feelings. I knew that I had fallen deeply in love with Abdul and was trying hard to camouflage my emotions as gratitude for his support. Ever since the first time I had spoken to him in the restaurant I blushed like a schoolgirl at his flirtations. Of course, I had convinced myself that it was just a game. When East meets West, there are always cautionary tales to be told. I should know. But Abdul was different from the start.

It was Jimmy's big mouth that had led to our first meeting. Finding the food in this restaurant the only edible stuff to be had in Taiz, Jana and I frequently ate there. Jimmy had told the manager of the restaurant all about me and my 'family problems' during one of our later visits; the manager, in turn, told everybody else.

Abdul had made a point of talking to me one day and had suggested a few people of influence to ask for assistance. Soon we were sitting together. It cost him his job. I felt awful. Undeterred we began to meet, as friends, in a local café. His attentions became more and more serious. I dismissed them as infatuation, or a game, perhaps.

One day, out of the blue, he told me that he loved me.

It was all so sudden, so unexpected. I didn't believe he was sincere. Then he kissed me. Ardently. In the middle of the café, to the astonishment of all the diners there.

I flushed from head to toe but not from embarrassment or fear – even though in Yemen it is the most serious offence to even touch in public. I was glowing with pleasure. I had never, ever, experienced such strong emotion before. I felt alive. I knew I was in love with him. I didn't know what to do about it though – I hadn't come here for this. I was angry with myself that I could feel pleasure in such awful circumstances. Abdul treated me with respect. He was so dependable and although he reminded me daily – hourly – of his love, he never forced the issue.

Now we were in Aden together. I was hopelessly in love and feeling totally guilty. Until I thought of Nadia. She had every right to feel the same way: to experience the deep and burning love of a man and her own pleasure in returning it. She had the right to choose her own man. She had the right to feel as I did, protected, loved, supported, respected, precious – not to be forced into a loveless, cruel dictatorship.

Now I had the fuel I needed to carry on. I had a wrong to right and Abdul had made it all so clear to me. And I loved him all the more for it.

The time came to return to Taiz, where there was unfinished business. The hotel staff were very surprised to see us back, so much so that they presented their bill immediately.

'Probably want their ryals before we get bumped off!' Jana laughed.

We moved to another hotel that same day.

I was spending a lot of my time with Abdul now. Jana held the fort, listening to music on the cassette-player I bought, staying in our room, ready to take any calls that came in.

I passed alternate days with her and Abdul. Time was running out. We had been here twenty-eight days. There wasn't much light relief about. We had very little time left on our original visas. A few days. We took our passports to Faisal for extension visas on his suggestion. He asked if we had enjoyed our stay in the hotel in Aden. Yes, they were following us all right.

On 29 August we went back to Faisal to pick up our passports with the renewed visas. He had not moved them from his drawer. We ran around like blue-arsed flies for three days, going back and forth to six different places chasing our extension visas, using the routine that Faisal said was obligatory. In the end we had to go back to him and ask why we were going round in circles to no avail. He grinned and looked at his watch with great exaggeration.

'You have to go to the Ministry and explain why you are in Yemen with no visa. Maybe you cannot leave now!' And he was so smug and proud of himself that he laughed himself stupid.

Fate took a hand. We were lucky, very lucky, to have a good taxi driver who knew where to go and what to do. The driver was supposed to take us back to Faisal after we'd had a letter from the Ministry, but instead he took us straight to the Passport Office. The formalities were minimal. We were given an extra two months and the most sincere wish from the charming clerk that we enjoy our extended holiday. We had been down to the very last day on our old visas. Faisal went crazy with frustration.

We had met a young Syrian couple, newlyweds Ali and Hallah, and saw them regularly in a small restaurant run by another Syrian. If we could not socialise with British people, then we had the Syrians. Ali tried to teach Jana Arabic. She had us all in fits of laughter at her attempts. This small café became a focal point in our daily routine.

We decided on Thursday to take a taxi down to the seaside resort of Hokha for the day, wondering if it was any closer than Aden, or any cooler. We were on the German Road, so named because it had been financed and built by Germans, heading out of Taiz. I recognised the side road as soon as I saw it.

'That's the way to Mokbana!' I called to Jana as we passed the turning which led in the direction of Nadia's village. I felt an overwhelming desire to tell the driver to turn and head towards the mountains. Common sense told me I couldn't. It didn't stop me wanting it so much. A huge lump formed in my throat as I thought of Nadia up that mountain.

'All this Mokbana,' the taxi driver informed us in shaky English.

The Mokbana mountain range is vast. It stretches from just outside Taiz to Hokha, and is just as wide. We drove for miles and the driver, parrot-fashion, repeated his phrase over and over.

After five hours' driving we pulled over into a small café for fresh lime juice. Our driver announced the place as Campais.

Campais. Where Abdul Khada had brought Zana to work in his 'café'. So this was it! She had contracted malaria here. I explained to Jana where we were, what it meant to me. Just imagine Zana in this dirty rotten dive of a town, serving food, slaving in this heat for Abdul Khada while she fought against malaria.

Looking around the area there was not much to see. The whole place was wide open, a single row of dwellings and shops. Old tyres and the foundations of never-to-be-finished buildings littered the side of the road. The café was a wreck. The roof slid off unaligned walls, which crumbled and rotted under the weight of the warped roof. Cars and lorries had been abandoned and their rusty carcasses were strewn about all over the place.

Jana took photos of everything. Of all the nothingness. It was a far cry from Birmingham. The whole country was dead, dry and dead. Would anyone in their right mind really want to choose this place in preference to any corner of England when he or she knew the difference? If she really had a choice?

Three days later I rang Faisal to ask where my daughter was. Faisal said he had sent an assistant out to the village. The man had taken the opportunity to visit his own family and was, in fact, still with them in a neighbouring village. Maybe he would know something on Friday or Saturday. 'I want to see Nadia, Faisal.' I was determined.

'But, Miriam, what is your hurry? You have a visa for

another two months. You will be here until October.' He shrieked with laughter. I slammed the phone down.

After I'd calmed down a little I rang Kirby. He said the Yemeni government was busy these days. It was probably because the Governor had the Korean Deputy Prime Minister and representatives of the Japanese Development Bank as his guests that Faisal had been left to his own devices. But he also conceded that this was no excuse.

That evening I went to the café with Abdul and Jana. We stayed until late in the evening talking with Ali and Hallah and swapping photographs. They were their usual pleasant selves. I usually found their company most relaxing because, surprisingly, they still had no idea who I was. To them Jana and I were simply tourists. But that night I couldn't relax. I was irritable and moody; I wanted to leave, to walk, alone, anywhere away from people. That upset Abdul. A lone female wandering around is definitely frowned upon in Yemen, of course. Wandering around is not permitted.

We returned to the hotel to find a fax from Fixot waiting in our pigeon-hole. Ahmed, the night shift manager, handed it to us, smiling knowingly to himself. We made our way to our room, asking him to send up coffee and tea.

Ten minutes later, Ahmed put the the tray on our table. He pointed his finger at me. 'I know who you are, Miriam.'

Oh, dear God. Not now, please.

'You are bad woman, to try to take Nadia!'

That was it. I exploded. All the pent-up aggression of the month was thrown in Ahmed's face in a volley of home truths.

He turned and left the room, crying, his head hung in misery.

'You see, Jana? You see what has happened? They force Nadia to say that she is happy for the benefit of these people, and they believe it. All those tapes that she was forced to make for Muthana are being played to these dumb people, to gain their support. They have even been playing Zana's first tape, to help their story along. God give me strength!'

I cried into the small hours until, exhausted, I fell asleep.

We were getting nowhere phoning the Governor's office. Trying to get hold of Faisal, through whom the calls were supposed to be routed, was impossible. Both at his office and his home the people who answered the phone were evasive; he had left his job, he had moved.

We took a taxi to Sanaa. First thing on the following Monday morning we went along to our Embassy and saw Kirby. We told him that Faisal had gone and God knew what was happening.

'Hang on. Let me get you some tea, then I'll ring the Governor.'

Surprise, surprise. Who should answer the phone but Faisal. The slimy, hypocritical scum-bag said: 'Oh, yes. Why of course, Your Eminence, Nadia is fit to travel. She will go to Taiz very soon. *Inshallah*.'

'Faisal should give us a full detailed plan of his proposed promised visit, including time of meeting, length of meeting, number of children. And assurance of no friends popping by and no armed guards.'

To encourage inspiration in his efforts to bring in Nadia we let it be known that Bernard Fixot and Jean-Pierre Faucault had arranged for a television broadcast to be scheduled at a moment's notice on *Sacrée Soirée* to expose the farce to which we had been subjected, should she not make it.

Jana rang Kirby at two o'clock the next afternoon in response to a message left at our hotel in Sanaa. Apparently Faisal had rung him at eight the previous evening. Nadia was still unfit to travel. Kirby told her it was a good idea to send in a doctor now, but only I should go with the doctor as Jana's presence would be seen as a provocation.

Chapter Fifty-Two

I had been expecting a telegram from Zana regarding a money transfer. It still hadn't arrived by 12 September, and we were concerned because nearly all our money had gone. We rang Kirby and asked if he had heard anything. He was curt and firmly unapproachable to Jana.

'I have heard that Zana is angry with the Yemeni government, the British government and this Embassy, and she has said that she will go on French TV and expose us all. I have not read the full report to you, to save Miriam's feelings, but if you go on French TV, I will be obliged to account in full that Nadia is a Yemeni citizen, loves her husband and wanted her privacy respected. I know where I stand. And I have my job to do. Now that the position has been made clear, and I have had my orders, I can have nothing more to do with the matter. Gerald Ryan is now back at work and he will deal with you in future. Hold on. I will try to transfer you.'

We were passed over to the consul Gerald Ryan without further ado. Kirby was 'washing his hands of the whole thing completely'. An appointment was scheduled for the next day at noon, at the Embassy.

Gerald seemed entirely different. His approach to the

subject was much more sympathetic and very diplomatic. He advanced us 2,000 ryals and talked about Nadia. It had been Gerald whom the Foreign Office had sent to see Nadia back in June. I'd told Heather Taggart not to send anyone. He had gone into Taiz, not Ashube, to see her. Mohammed had been with her but none of the children. Most of the talking had been done by a British woman, married to a local Yemeni, who could speak Arabic and was described by Gerald as 'nice'. During the meeting, both Nadia and Mohammed had appeared to be scared by the horde of Yemeni officials who were 'organising' and 'supervising'. The meeting had lasted a couple of hours, with no firm developments, although a statement had been taken from Nadia, who 'wanted her privacy respected'. Those were not words that my daughter would normally use but they were taken as gospel by our people.

Gerald promised assistance. Suddenly things seemed promising again and my spirits were high. Gerald said he'd try to negotiate for us and we had every faith in him. We arranged to meet again, a little later when I could repay the funds that Gerald had advanced.

It was around this time that we were given a document. Translated it read: 'This is to inform Zana Muhsen that she has been returned to her husband's custody'.

Dated 21 April 1988 and witnessed, it stated that her divorce from Abdullah had been cancelled. He was her owner again. So, to this day, according to the Yemenis, she is still married to Abdullah, and has been since her very narrow escape from Yemen on 22 April 1988. We were also given information about the French-assisted trip in February 1992. It really was just as well that Zana refused to go back to the village because, it now seemed, it would have been a one-way trip for her. I now understood a little more about how lucky she had been to get out. And why Nadia hadn't.

I married Abdul that evening in an Islamic ceremony attended by Jana, a taxi driver and an acquaintance of Abdul's.

It had been said by Faisal that Nadia was having the traditional forty-day rest after the birth of her son. This talk of a 'traditional' lying-in was totally preposterous, a fable, utter rubbish. There was corn to grind, water to carry, shit to shovel. I had asked Zana. In all those years she had been in Yemen no one had ever enjoyed this so-called 'traditional' rest. It was impossible, completely impractical. It would have been a luxury for a woman to have even a couple of days without fetching water up the mountain. Alas, this was something we could do nothing about. They said Nadia was enjoying the 'lying-in' and we had to accept it.

I was still concerned for Nadia's health. I counted the days. On 26 September 1992, the forty days elapsed. Would they now think of something else to keep me away from Nadia? I was sure that they would apply every effort to do so.

I was right. Day after day we waited. September melted into October. In desperation, we went to see Gerald on the 14th, telling him that we were leaving Yemen on the 22nd and would be flying straight to Paris, to *Sacrée Soirée*.

'In that case, I am going to tell the Ministry that I will be taking a back seat from now on. I have done everything I could to get this meeting to take place. I don't intend to end up with egg on my face. If it is a case of laying blame, I can be confident that our Embassy has done all in its power. I wish I knew where things were being held up.'

In unrehearsed unison, Jana and I said, '*Faisal!*'

I spoke to Martin Cronin on the Monday. Faisal had told him that a driver had been sent to Ashube to collect Nadia. Perhaps she would come straight away; perhaps she would come tomorrow. He said he was going to contact Faisal again that evening between five and seven and then he'd ring us. We hoped that the knowledge that Jana had booked a ticket to England via Paris would galvanise them into action.

At a quarter to eight we couldn't bear the strain of waiting any longer. I rang Martin. No news. Fifteen minutes later he rang back. The driver Faisal had sent this morning was lost! Faisal Abdul Aziz had sent in another driver. Martin would ring us again in an hour.

It seemed that suddenly people were going into Mokbana left, right and centre to see Nadia. We were getting calls from all the usual sources saying they had sent someone in, but they never appeared to come back out.

At 8.20 Gerald Ryan rang. He was told of the latest events and he cursed like crazy. He would make a few inquiries and get back to us.

I was in tears by now. I couldn't stand this torment. Why were they doing this? It was torture. Jana tried to console me. She rang Martin's number. The phone rang and rang before she gave up. I was frantic. I sat, rocking myself back and forth, cradling my stomach. I wanted to rip my hair out and hurt myself. The pain inside my tortured soul was unbearable. I wanted relief from the pressure. It was too heavy. Dear God, help me. It bubbled inside my head relentlessly.

Jana sat up with me doing her utmost to prevent me doing any physical damage to myself. It was after midnight when the phone rang. She took the call – I was in too much distress. I watched her face, trying to anticipate the news, feeling the vibrations for mercy. It didn't look hopeful.

Martin Cronin was apologetic. 'Hello, Jana. I'm sorry to ring you so late. I thought you would prefer to know that since talking to Faisal earlier today, I haven't managed to locate him and, despite leaving many messages all over the place for him, he has failed to reply. I will go to the Ministry first thing tomorrow, and in future I will bypass Taiz and go via the Ministry directly. I will put in a complaint about Faisal and all the staff at Taiz. Faisal told me that a relative of Mohammed who has a shop in Taiz had gone into the village to deliver a message and had not turned up. Another version was that a goverment car had gone in and yet another version was a taxi!'

Jana replaced the receiver. 'Please try to hold on, Miriam. You have to. For Nadia. I know it's hard, but just a little longer!'

I didn't know if that were possible. My reserves were so very low.

Martin rang the next day after noon. No news. He said that not only had Faisal made no attempt to ring him, he had ignored all of the messages left for him. 'I think it is unlikely that Faisal sent a car at all,' he said. 'Apparently, Faisal said he "sort of" sent a car. I doubt if a meeting will take place at all.' Martin would try again the following day.

Gerald rang. He was deeply concerned about my state of mind and furious about recent events. He was 'leaning on' the Ministry of Foreign Affairs to investigate what was going on and who was involved in this fiasco. I drew little comfort from this. It seemed that there was nothing at all to be done.

We thought and thought and thought. Jana anticipated

375

that if we both left for England, Faisal would say that he had finally got Nadia into Taiz and she had nothing to do but watch our plane take off. Who would know if that were true or not, apart from Nadia, Faisal and us? I could imagine Faisal saying just that. We decided we would let everyone think that we were both leaving, but in fact only Jana would do so.

She left for Sanaa the next morning to arrange for her exit visa. Abdul tried to fill her supportive role.

It was a long day and a very quiet night. I couldn't go out of the door, and there were no calls from anyone. I felt so very alone. I missed Jana and her support, kind as Abdul was. And I needed to know what was going on.

Early the next morning I decided that I too should go to Sanaa, and push with all my might for this meeting with my daughter. I already knew it would only be a meeting, nothing more. Certainly not a reunion.

Abdul and I arrived at the British Embassy in Sanaa a little after one o'clock. Complete chaos reigned when they saw me. Gerald explained. 'It's Faisal. He rang this morning and said that Nadia was in Taiz, waiting to see you. Now, Miriam, please do not give this any credence. I made previous arrangements with Faisal that he would give me thirty-six hours' notice if Nadia and her children should come out of the village. He never did. Unfortunately, I was not here when Faisal rang Sameera, my secretary. She rang Jana, whom she knew to be at the hotel. Jana came here straight away to see me but I was tied up with something else. I had spoken to Faisal earlier in the morning and he told me that he was going to send a car in. He'd spoken to Martin and said he had already sent a car in, and he'd spoken to Sameera, telling her that Nadia was already here. Three people, three different stories. Jana is very upset. She actually spoke to Faisal herself, from our Reception.'

My mind was in a whirl. 'So what are you saying, Gerald? Is Nadia in Taiz or isn't she?'

Gerald shook his head. 'No. She is still in Ashube.'

'What's going on, then? Why did Faisal tell Sameera and Jana that she was in Taiz when she isn't?'

Gerald and Martin were baffled. I left immediately for the hotel to find Jana. When I arrived, I found Jana in a fury. She paced the room in agitation. She knew that I had spoken to Gerald, but I didn't know the full turn of events as Jana did.

'What happened?' I asked, helping myself to the tea on the table.

Irritably, she explained how Sameera had called her at half-ten and said that Nadia was on her way to Taiz to meet me at Colonel Iryani's office. Jana had left for the Embassy.

Martin, Phil and Sameera were frantic because I was not with her. Phil arranged for her to phone Faisal. Faisal told her that Nadia and Mohammed were with him in his office, waiting to see me as he had promised would happen. However, there were no children with them, and Faisal flatly refused Jana's repeated request to speak to Nadia.

According to Faisal, for Nadia to speak to Jana was *aib* (shame), and the children's attendance was 'too much trouble'. 'Too much trouble' – a phrase Nadia had used in the French TV interview. The word 'brainwashed' sprung to mind. He concluded the conversation with Jana – by confirming our earlier suspicions.

'Miriam must come soon. Nadia has to return for her children. Now Miriam cannot say that we did not bring

Nadia to see her. After three months, Miriam does not accept a meeting?'

'She isn't there, Jana. Faisal rang Gerald while I was there and said that Nadia was with him, but he wouldn't let anybody speak to her. It's a lie. We know it; Gerald does too. Faisal has blatantly lied to all of us.'

I'd had enough. The time had come to force the issue.

Two days later Jana left for England. We gave everybody the impression that she was heading straight to France for a rendezvous with Zana.

Chapter Fifty-Three

Saturday 7 November 1992. Three months and three days after my six-minute meeting with Nadia. We were to meet again, at long last.

Under the impression that Jana and Zana were due to appear on French TV, the Ministry of Foreign Affairs had sent two jeeps into Mokbana to collect Nadia and the children. Since 2 November the Ministry had ceased using Faisal as their intermediary and now, five days later, Nadia was on her way to Taiz.

Gerald took Abdul and me down to Taiz in his jeep at six in the morning. On the way Abdul and I talked about what he should say to Mohammed, if the opportunity arose, to get the prat to come to Birmingham.

We arrived at the offices of Colonel Iryani. I felt the strong stirrings of pure fear as I followed Gerald up the stairs to the Governor's conference room. The room was dismal, badly decorated and full of chairs lined up against the walls. It contained nothing of interest – apart from the chairs it was completely bare, hot, stuffy and uncomfortable. I was very ill at ease in this room, sure that an invasion force of creepy-crawlies was about to storm it. And so it happened. Faisal Abdul Aziz walked in.

We were taken to his private office. My gut feeling was that he would try to make us all meet here, in his office, under his salamander glare. I had to invest 100 per cent effort into not saying anything to him. My God, I really wanted to have a go at Faisal. Since we'd started our organisation, Lost Children International, we had found out a lot about little British kids in Yemen. I wished I could confront Faisal, tell him what I knew. But for the sake of so many children I could say nothing. I had to console myself with the inner knowledge that his time would come. I kept my thoughts to myself, saying over and over to myself what I wanted to say aloud. It had to suffice. The effort of my silence drew blood from my hands as I dug my nails in hard. I didn't hear Faisal ask me who Abdul was, why he was with us in the room.

Gerald sensed my mental agitation. He told Faisal that Abdul was my husband. Faisal practically stopped breathing and tried, with all his might, to keep his bulging eyeballs in his ugly face.

Gerald asked where Nadia was. Faisal didn't answer. He picked up the phone and made a call, speaking conspiratorially in Arabic. I assumed it was to Nasser Saleh, feeling very strongly that there was no other logical assumption.

Fifteen minutes later he rang again. Speaking in more casual tones, he gave the impression that he didn't have a worry in the world. I wished someone would shove a rocket up his backside. Inwardly I volunteered for the job. Any time!

Faisal arranged for fresh lime to be served and we sipped out of impatience rather than genuine thirst, watching the inevitable armed guards. One stood by Faisal constantly, another casually strolled in and out, inspecting impassively. Faisal's equally odious assistant stared at me. He was a horrid little man. His face was like a death mask drained of blood and he hardly ever let it show a flicker of emotion, except through the variable twitching of his moustache.

Suddenly Nadia and Mohammed appeared. Nadia, carrying her baby, quickly kissed me through her veil and slumped into a chair, breathless and struggling hard to get new air into her lungs. No one attempted to assist her. Instead, the eyes of my enemies turned her way and their look was of sheer contempt and hatred. Faisal tried to thicken the already oppressive atmosphere by introducing Nadia to her mother's husband.

Nadia smiled. I suppose she took it really well. She knew of my feelings on marriage. I had never married her father, thank God, and now both her parents were married, but to other people.

Muthana had made himself a nice little number back in 1991. He married Halima Manaser Hussein in Birmingham on 18 April. Muthana had claimed that he was paid handsomely for his 'hand', when the price probably reflected his damaged one. He didn't even have to pay for the wedding.

Money was his way of explaining it to his kids. His wife had been born in 1961, the year before his own first child. Young and fresh and fertile. We all pondered at the time on whether she, too, would get to know Muthana's darker side. It looked that way, because she quickly became pregnant and had given him a son. The difference here was that she was born in Yafai, Yemen. Perhaps it would be acceptable to her if this child were to go missing because of Muthana's material concerns.

But would I really wish that my worst enemy? Faisal's image flooded into my head at that instant, and I turned to look at him, wondering what he would do in my situation. He had been denied his attempt at alienating mother and daughter. He glared on.

Gerald audibly swallowed and cleared his throat. 'Is there a room where Miriam and Nadia can have a private chat?'

Faisal's nostrils flared, his face demoniacal. Gerald held his glare. The Arab remained silent, apart from general sounds of strain as he fought a battle with his invidious inner self. He was bound to honour the essence of the visit. With a sinister expression, he spat out that there was 'one' room. He spoke to the assistant with the hairy face, whose droopy moustache twitched in sheer pleasure as he received his order and tried to keep a straight face. The assistant rose and bade Nadia and I to follow him. He barged into the conference room and gestured us inside. He didn't move. He stood there, watching.

'*Barrah!*' Out! I emphasised it with a contemptuously dismissive wave of my hand.

He sucked air through his teeth as he went out. I slammed the door shut after him.

'Where is that woman, Mom? The one who came with you?'

'That woman is my friend, Nadia. That's Jana. We work together. She's had to go back to England. She's been here three months and she's got her own family to care for. Where are the kids?'

'In the village.' Her lips quivered. She looked away.

'Nadia, please come home! Can't you see what they are doing?' I launched immediately into my plea, not sure that the two-hour schedule for the visit would be honoured.

Nadia hugged her baby tightly to her breast.

'Just come home for a holiday with Mohammed and the children. Ask him! Ask Mohammed to come!'

'*No!*' Agitated, she cut off my pleading. Looking around, she went on, 'If I ask him, Mom, he'll go barmy. He said he'll throw me out and keep my kids, if I ever ask again.' She was terrified. In a single, swift swipe she removed her veil for the first time since her arrival. I gasped. She looked so ill. My nails dug into my hands.

'Do you *want* to come home, Nadia?' My heart beat began to pound in my chest.

'Yes, Mom. I want to come, but he won't. He won't!' She hung her head.

I closed my eyes, full of unwelcome tears. The rancid, acid taste of blood filled my mouth. 'What *is* his problem, Nadia?'

'It's because of the press, Mom.'

'The press? Nadia, I have not spoken to the press for three years. There will be no press, no television, no nothing. Just come home for a week to show everyone that you are free.'

'I am free, Mom,' she said, listlessly. She wouldn't look at me as she said it. Then she brightened a little. 'I can come if he comes with me!'

It was as if she was willing me to convince Mohammed, not leaving her to try the impossible. I knew what she wanted, it was so plainly obvious. Why God, was she under so much pressure? 'OK, Nard. If I get Abdul to speak to Mohammed in this room with us, is that OK?'

'Is that your husband, Mom?'

I nodded and smiled. I think I blushed a little, too.

'Can he speak Arab?'

'Yes. He's Syrian.' She smiled and nodded her consent.

I went back to Faisal's office and with a motion of my hand I called to him and Mohammed. The assistant rose to join them.

'No, not you!' I snapped.

We went back to Nadia. I braced myself for round two. 'Speak to him, Abdul. You know what to say.'

Abdul nodded. He squeezed my hand gently and followed Mohammed across the room, opposite Nadia. I sat next to her.

Abdul and Mohammed began the negotiations.

Nadia asked me questions about the family, which I only half answered as I shared my attention between her and the two men. Their voices were now rising.

'What are they saying, Nard?'

'Mohammed said no, he won't come to England.'

'But why? What's the problem? I've told you about the press.'

The men realised that we had stopped talking and were listening to them, with Nadia interpreting. Abdul told me that Mohammed said that he had been told that if he ever came to England, he would be arrested and put in prison. He also said, rather in contradiction, that he would consider a holiday, because he was free, but that Nadia would *never*, never go to England.

'Do you want money? A house?' I offered, through Abdul.

'He says, no, he has money, a house and a father in England, and Yemeni people here.'

God, I wanted to shake the life from the gutless little bastard's body. My heart was racing now at a frightening pace.

Abdul was losing all trace of patience. 'If you don't come to England with Nadia and the children after this meeting,

Bernard will speak to Ali Abdullah Saleh, the President of Yemen.'

'*Doss* Ali Abdullah! *Doss* Miriam!' (Doss is a contemptuous remark bordering on the 'fuck you' variety.) Then he spat. '*Laish Miriam hinna fe Nadia?*' Why does Miriam come here for Nadia?

'Oh, forgive me, I'm only her mother.' My words dripped with sarcasm. 'We are not all like your mother, leaving you alone to care for your brother and sister, after lying that she would only be away for a little while, and saying that you will be in trouble if you go to England.' I tried to calm him and instil some faith into the stupid little man.

Mohammed walked out in extreme agitation. He turned at the door and leered at Nadia, his stance menacing. He shouted at her in Arabic before he slammed out of the door.

Nadia sat, shellshocked, as she interpreted what Mohammed had just said. 'You tell Gerald, you *don't* want to go to England!'

The pulse in my temple was pounding at a phenomenal rate, my heart was crashing in my chest. I was dizzy. My mouth was dry, my blood draining.

'No, Nardie, please. Oh, please don't do this to me. Don't do this to your family. You can't. Please. Do you want me to die? Don't you love me, your family?' I teetered at the edge of my old friend, the black tunnel. My head swam, bile rose in my throat.

Nadia looked at me through dead eyes. 'I love you, Mom, and my family.'

The door opened and in barged Faisal, closely followed by Gerald. The room was silent. I held my breath. My world was crashing in on me. There was no air. I struggled

385

against the tears. I could not, would not, let them see me cry. I was dying . . . my God, please . . . help me . . .

'Stop it!' I screamed silently to myself.

Still the room was devoid of any sound. Nadia, her eyes downcast, stubbornly refused to speak.

Faisal cracked the silence wide open, his voice excited and shrill but his English perfect as he caught the scent of victory.

'Well? Go on, Nadia! Say what you have to say to Gerald!'

Silence.

I was very aware of the shameless sinister snicker in Faisal's voice as he repeated the order. 'Well, go on. Tell him!'

A small frail whisper. 'I don't want to come here any more.'

My head filled with a vortex of rushing blood cells. Bile burned my throat and my stomach churned violently.

'Pardon, Nadia. What did you say?' Gerald strained his head in her direction.

'I don't want to come *here* any more!' She spoke louder, emphasising one cryptic word.

My world stood still. She hadn't said what both Faisal and Mohammed had commanded. I looked at Faisal, fearing that he might order her to correct her statement. His face was frozen in a stare. I couldn't fathom his expression. Did he understand? Nadia's emphasis had suspended my feelings. I didn't feel any better than I had after Mohammed left the room, but I didn't feel any worse.

With a smile of triumph Faisal looked deep into my eyes. He savoured the moment, willing it to last. Mohammed shouted roughly at Nadia to leave. He ordered her out of the room as one would a dog. She slowly rose to her feet, her body shaking, perspiration beading her brow. Two steps behind her master, she left the room.

The meeting was over, the two promised hours curtailed to thirty harrowing minutes, but I didn't argue as Faisal ushered us all out.

We were outside the building. A jeep waited for Nadia to enter its hot interior. Faisal, jubilant, whispered something to Mohammed. Mohammed spoke in harsh tones to Nadia. She closed her eyes and sighed deeply. 'If you speak on French TV, Mom, I have to phone them and tell them I don't want to go home.' She looked me straight in the eyes. 'It's not me, Mom!'

I blinked at her as she voiced Faisal's order, which Mohammed had just endorsed. 'Who is it, Nadia?' I asked quietly. I desperately wanted her to speak their names.

Nadia wouldn't meet my eyes. I looked over her shoulder. Faisal, his assistant and an armed guard were waiting with the driver and Mohammed by the jeep. They all stared indifferently. 'I'm not leaving you here, Nard!' I said it loud enough for Faisal and his cronies to hear.

'It's the Islam, Mom. I am a Muslim. I can't come home with you. He said he will bring me, but it's not up to me if – if I can come home or not. It's up to him. I want to come home, but . . .' Nadia turned away from me.

'I love you, Nard!' I said.

Suddenly she turned back and reached out to me. I held her close, showering her with kisses. She held on tight and I could feel her body shaking with silent sobs.

Without speaking, she turned and slowly made her way to the waiting jeep, each step laborious and difficult as she limped towards the open door.

I watched Mohammed and Faisal take their seats,

387

one each side of Nadia. The armed guard got in the front.

Faisal turned to me. One smirk. I vaguely remember asking myself why. The driver put the jeep in gear. Why all of this? Where were they going with Nadia? They were moving. I was beyond all reasoning. I was promising my daughter that I would get her out. Nadia didn't look back. I watched the car until it disappeared out of sight.

I will never give up. Never.

Epilogue

Returning from Yemen in November 1992, after seeing Nadia, her health deteriorating, her morale annihilated, her entrapment obvious, Miriam remained resolute in her pursuit of liberty for Nadia and her children: to procure the safe and justified return of Nadia to her rightful place; to right a wrong.

Taking legal advice and in sheer desperation she offered a quid pro quo deal to the Yemeni government. In return for Nadia and her children, she offered to drop all charges against Gowad Abdul Majid, Nadia's owner. Not only did she offer an olive branch of peace, she also invited the Yemeni government to take all the praise for their 'co-operation'.

They accepted and the charges were dropped as a goodwill gesture. Despite the government's verbal commitment of good intent, it was all to no avail. The Yemen reneged.

Nadia needs all available assistance so that she is not lost to this life of torture, repression and waste, along with others in this unholy predicament.

This is not just a 'story' for Miriam – it has been her life for nearly thirty years. Where it will end is in the lap of the gods. Miriam would like it to end with the return of her daughter, Nadia and her children. Simple? As you will have seen, it most certainly isn't.

Imagine, if you will, that this is your life, that this has happened to your own flesh and blood. Imagine a strange man touching her, beating her, raping her, impregnating her then laughing smugly in her face as she suffers. Imagine your flesh and blood enduring these degrading, incalculable atrocities. A slave.

What would you do? Give up? Forget it?

With the perpetrators of these crimes unpunished and free, mocking our complacent British judicial system and our Foreign Office – all at the expense of Miriam's family – this book has been written as Nadia's only chance of freedom.

For God's sake, she deserves that. There has been enough suffering, enough damage done as she endures a fate that her own father arranged for her – despite having fled Yemen in 1956 to escape such a fate himself.

Let her come home with her children and shake off the shackles of repression. Then she can prove to the world that she *is* free.

'Please don't forget me. Don't leave me here too long. Please.'
Nadia Muhsen, Taiz, Yemen. February 1992

Sold

Zana Muhsen with Andrew Crofts

For fifteen-year-old Zana Muhsen and her younger
sister Nadia, born and raised in Birmingham, a
six-week holiday with relatives in North Yemen
sounded like the trip of a lifetime.

It turned into a living nightmare. On their arrival
Zana and her sister discovered that their father had
literally sold them into marriage and that they were
helpless prisoners. The girls had to adapt to a
completely alien way of life, living in primitive stone
houses with dung-plastered walls and no running
water. They suffered rape, frequent beatings and
the terrifying ordeal of childbirth on bare mud
floors with only old women in attendance.

After eight years of misery and humiliation,
Zana escaped - and her story is as shocking as it
is heart-rending.

An essential companion to *Without Mercy*,
this is Zana's own story.

<u>Out of Iran</u>
One Woman's Escape From The Ayatollahs

Sousan Azadi with Angela Ferrante

Born into the wealthy, westernized élite of the Shah's
Iran, Sousan Azadi grew up in luxury. In her privileged
circles the thunder of approaching revolution was easy
to ignore. Then the Shah fell and in the terrifying new
fundamentalist regime of Ayatollah Khomeini Sousan
and her friends were branded *taghouti*, devil's followers.
They were hunted, their children brainwashed,
their property confiscated.

Alone with her son after the death of her husband,
Sousan became an easy target. She was flung into
jail, where she witnessed terrible suffering inflicted
in the name of 'immodest behaviour' and 'indecency'.
Only when she caught the eye of a Mullah, who
clearly expected sexual favours in return, did she
escape. But real freedom still lay beyond the
snow-capped Zagros mountains, in Turkey - a
hazardous route for a woman and child to take.

Out of Iran grips and involves the reader as it
recounts one woman's courageous struggle for
survival in fanatical, war-torn Iran.